Men in Wonderland

Men in Wonderland:

THE LOST GIRLHOOD OF
THE VICTORIAN GENTLEMAN

Catherine Robson

PRINCETON UNIVERSITY PRESS

PRINCETON AND OXFORD

Library of Congress Cataloging-in-Publication Data

Robson, Catherine, 1962–
Men in wonderland : the lost girlhood of the Victorian gentleman / Catherine Robson.
p.   cm.
Includes bibliographical references (p.) and index.
ISBN 0-691-00422-6
1. English literature—19th century—History and criticism. 2. Girls in literature. 3. English
literature—Male authors—History and criticism. 4. Carroll, Lewis, 1832–1898—Characters—
Girls. 5. Ruskin, John, 1819–1900—Characters—Girls. 6. Innocence (Psychology) in
literature. 7. Gender identity in literature. 8. Children in literature. 9. Sex role in literature.
10. Men in literature. I. Title.
PR468.G5 R63 2001
820.9'352054—dc21   00-048321

This book has been composed in Sabon

www.pup.princeton.edu

Printed in the United States of America

10   9   8   7   6   5   4   3   2   1

For my mother and my father

PATRICIA AND COLIN ROBSON

Contents

Illustrations

Acknowledgments

THIS PROJECT began as a dissertation: it owes a tremendous amount to my exemplary committee. Cathy Gallagher has been, and continues to be, a source of true strength and inspiration. She gives out both a sense of intellectual delight and extremely practical advice: I cannot thank her adequately for these gifts. Tom Laqueur's enthusiasm has also been infectious; I shall always be grateful for his careful reading and warm support. Carol Christ directed the master's thesis on De Quincey that contained the original seed of this longer work: I have benefited greatly from her broad scholarly knowledge of the nineteenth century. I consider myself extremely fortunate to have been part of a marvelous dissertation group from 1992 to 1995, and would like to thank its various members, especially Kate Brown, Bill Cohen, Cheri Larsen Hoeckley, and Laura Green, for their many spirited observations.

I presented an overview of this work to the Fellows' Seminar at the Townsend Center for the Humanities at the University of California, Berkeley: I thank all the participants for their responses, particularly Hayden White and Carol Clover for their enlightening comments. My involvement over the years with the Dickens Project at the University of California, Santa Cruz, has been truly enriching, and provides me with an extraordinary intellectual community of Victorianists. Jim Kincaid has been a generous colleague in many different ways, not least by sending me the bibliography of *Child-Loving* long before the book was published; I am also indebted to Jeffrey Spear for sharing his fine work on Lewis Carroll with me. I should also like to thank James Eli Adams and the anonymous reader for Princeton University Press: their comments on an earlier draft of the manuscript proved invaluable during the revising process. I feel very fortunate to have worked with editor Mary Murrell and her assistant Karen Ancharski, and am extremely grateful to Richard Isomaki for his deft and intelligent copy-editing. Here at the University of California, Davis, I have been the happy recipient of numerous faculty research grants and a faculty development award; the Davis Humanities Institute also honored me with a fellowship that gave me much-needed time to write. I am particularly grateful for support from the Department of English, most notably the guidance of my chair, Linda Morris, and my colleagues in the nineteenth century, David Simpson, Kari Lokke, and Peter Dale. My graduate research assistants have improved the project in very tangible ways. The late and much-missed Jane Hotchkiss's enthusiasm for the topic buoyed me up on many an occasion; Christine Colon was a meticulous bibliographical researcher; Blythe Creamer, who came to the project in its last few crucial months, kept me going with her irrepressible vivacity and astute perceptions.

I have enjoyed rare intellectual and emotional support from other friends: Laura Berry, Sarah Cole, Jane Garrity, Lily Hamrick, Alessa Johns, Annie Karlsson, Karen Jacobs, David Robinson, and Ramie Targoff have all contributed in their own ways. I would also like to thank Alison Bray, Jane Leek, and Ian Little back in England for long-distance good cheer. Most of all, I wish to express my gratitude to my husband, Jamie Jensen, and my parents, Patricia and Colin Robson. All of our lives have been immeasurably changed in the last two years by the wonderful arrival of twins Thomas and Alexander: thus my intellectual preoccupation with imaginary little girls has been well and truly challenged by the presence of two very real little boys. I have only been able to complete this study during such a joyfully chaotic and sleep-deprived period because of the loving labors of my family. My mother and father have flown to our assistance on numerous occasions, and welcomed us all into their home in Yorkshire for long stretches of time so that I could write in relative peace. The lion's share of child-care, however, has fallen to my husband, who has maintained incredible good humor throughout. Indeed, Jamie has provided loving support at every stage of this project: I could not have written it without him.

Portions of chapter 2 appeared in an earlier version of "The Ideal Girl in Industrial England," *Journal of Victorian Culture* 3, no. 2 (1998): 197–233. I am grateful to the publishers, Edinburgh University Press, for permission to use the material here.

Men in Wonderland

Introduction

"A boy phenomenon, perhaps?" suggested Nicholas.
"There is only one phenomenon, sir," replied Mr.
Crummles impressively, "and that's a girl."
(Charles Dickens, "Nicholas Nickleby")

THIS BOOK explores the intimate relationship between middle-class men and little girls in nineteenth-century British culture. *Men in Wonderland* traces the ways in which a number of male authors in this period construct girlhood and analyzes the exact nature of their investment in the figure of the girl. The idealization and idolization of little girls, long acknowledged features of the Victorian era, cannot be thought of without reference to a pervasive fantasy of male development in which men become masculine only after an initial feminine stage. In this light, little girls represent not just the true essence of childhood, but an adult male's best opportunity of reconnecting with his own lost self. The works of the individuals discussed at length in the study ahead—Wordsworth, De Quincey, Dickens, Ruskin, and Carroll—exhibit in various ways this male myth of feminized origin. Juxtaposing these literary texts and art forms with a range of other cultural productions such as philanthropic tracts, conduct books, government reports, fine art, and popular journalism, *Men in Wonderland* demonstrates both the evolution of the idea of the ideal girl in the nineteenth century, and the manifestation of the concept of original girlhood in genres that would seem less driven by personal motivations. Although this fantasy of development by no means holds universal sway, it nevertheless makes its way into general currency because of its appeal to an important and influential strain in nineteenth-century discourse, a strain that is noticeably middle class, religious, paternalist, sentimental, nostalgic, and conservative.

Recognizing the existence of such a historical phenomenon brings numerous benefits to Victorian studies. In particular, this perception fuels the reassessment of the oeuvres of a variety of literary artists, especially inasmuch as it complicates the narratives of pedophilic desire that have habitually been employed to explain the work of the nineteenth century's most infamous girl-lovers (Ruskin and Carroll figuring here as the two most familiar examples of the type). More broadly, the identification of

such a paradigm advances our understanding of such important characteristics of the age as its fraught constructions of masculinity, its obsession
with loss, its rampant sentimentality, and its intense valorization of the
little girl at the expense of mature femininity.

In many ways, to point out that the Victorians thought of early childhood as a feminine era is to state the obvious. After all, here at the beginning of the twenty-first century, the world of infancy and young childhood
is still largely perceived as a female domain: not only does the care of little
children continue to be primarily woman's responsibility, but the terms
with which the early period of childhood is characterized—a time of
"softness" and "vulnerability," requiring "gentleness" and "protection"—remain resolutely feminized. For these reasons, Freud's account
of the process by which human beings come to understand sexual differentiation remains problematic: because of the feminine aura of those early
days, it is hard to swallow his theory that all children initially believe
themselves to be "little men," and that only upon noticing their "lack"
do little girls regretfully give up this fantasy.[1] If childhood is a feminized
world now, it was even more so in the nineteenth century: whereas male
babies today are soon dressed in clearly coded "masculine" apparel and
colors, large numbers of Victorian photographs of scowling boys in short
frocks exist to remind us that brothers and sisters used to be "clothed
alike," as Coleridge wistfully recalls in "Frost at Midnight." Although
the breeching ceremony of the early modern period—the great day when
a six- or seven-year-old boy would shed his girlish dress and don trousers—had more or less fallen into obscurity for the Victorians, it was not
until the twentieth century that boys, in any of the social classes, would
wear obviously gendered clothing before this relatively advanced age.[2]
Perhaps more significantly, for many boys of the middle and upper classes
the age of six or seven signaled the removal from maternal or feminine
care in the home into the masculine world of the school: up until this
point, their lessons would have taken place alongside their sisters in a
female-staffed nursery.[3] Trousers and school thus marked the end of the
first phase of existence for boys; girls of these classes, still wearing petti-
coats and pursuing their education, for the most part, at home, experienced no such division between early and later childhood. Given that the
garments and worlds left behind continued to be female, then, the first
six years of male life in the nineteenth century carried a clear stamp of
femininity, especially when viewed in retrospect. While it may be a critical
commonplace that the Victorians adhered to a rigid system of gender sep-

aration, in this particular instance it seems that young boyhood crossed the line, and actually looked more like girlhood.

It is, however, one thing to notice that the early lives of boys found them wearing versions of female clothing and lodged in the female-controlled zones of the house, and quite another to register the depth of passionate investment in nineteenth-century writings that both insist that perfect childhood is always exemplified by a little girl, and that, despite the logical and biological impossibilities of the stance, lament a man's lost girlhood. To understand the climate that fostered the growth of a fantasy of primary and ideal femininity, it is necessary to examine the beliefs that informed the Victorians' fascination with the idea of the child. The account here begins with a brief summary of the general historiography of childhood in eighteenth- and nineteenth-century studies, and then moves to a consideration of the complicated and contradictory origins of the concept.

Since the publication of Philippe Ariès's *Centuries of Childhood* in 1962, it has generally been accepted that the idea of childhood is a fairly recent invention.[4] According to current explanations, childhood's birth is coincident with the rise of the middle class in late-seventeenth- and eighteenth-century Europe, and its infancy appears to draw strength from the twin sustenances of the Evangelical movement and Romantic thought.[5] Historians document the growth of philanthropic concern for children, which manifests itself in institutions like the Foundling Hospital, the burgeoning Sunday school movement, and early campaigns for the abolition of exploitative labor, while those on the literary trail register the central importance of the child in the writings of Jean-Jacques Rousseau, William Blake, and William Wordsworth.[6] Contemporary scholarship claims that this interest in the child grows ever more particularized as the nineteenth century progresses: by virtue of the rapid pace of industrialization and population expansion, runs the argument, the plight of the laboring and the indigent child becomes hugely obvious and eventually energizes massive legislative reform and the erection of comprehensive educational and social welfare systems for the working-class child.[7] Investigating Victorian domestic ideology's construction of the inviolable middle-class home, feminist critics and historians contend that the life experience of the child of comfortable means came to be shaped with comparable rigor in this period.[8] This is also an era, it is maintained, in which the child and its properties become the subject of specialized legal and medical discourse.[9] Furthermore, the figure of the child evolves into a dominant icon both for elite and popular consumption: six hundred

5

thousand copies of *Cherry Ripe*, an engraving by the Royal Academician John Everett Millais, are not enough to satisfy public demand in 1880, while Charles Dickens's thirty-year career furnishes a veritable kindergarten of child heroes and heroines for the collective mind.[10]

This overview gives a sense of the highly visible centrality of the child in any number of arenas and at all class levels in Victorian life. More difficult to describe is the meaning carried by the idea of the child in this period for the influential middle-class community that constitutes the primary focus of this study. Because the era of childhood was of paramount significance to two powerful, and apparently opposed, systems of thought, one would expect to find deep and irresolvable contradictions embedded at the heart of the nineteenth century's perception of children. On the one hand, to thinkers as various as Locke, Rousseau, and Wordsworth the child represents a pure point of origin, deeply connected to the natural and primitive world, and as yet unmired by the sullying forces of language, sexuality, and society.[11] On the other, the eighteenth-century revival of hard-line Puritan attitudes in some strains of the Evangelical movement brought to the fore the doctrine of the primary corruption of human nature: the child comes into this world as a bearer of original sin, a creature of fundamental depravity. And yet in spite of this radical disagreement, these two different visions of the child turn out to be remarkably amenable to each other in the daily practice of nineteenth-century life and discourse.[12] Up until fairly recently, the secular bent of literary and historical studies has resulted in a disproportionate emphasis upon the prominence of the Romantic idea of the child in the Victorian period: consequently the Evangelical perspective, and its perceived extremism, has been given relatively short shrift. In the past fifteen years or so, however, the importance of acknowledging the deeply religious, if complicated and often conflicted, character of at least the first two-thirds of the nineteenth century has become more widely appreciated. In consequence a more balanced view of the child's combined heritage is now beginning to emerge.[13]

Between the 1730s and 1830s the Evangelical movement galvanized British Christianity, affecting practically all denominations from the established to the Nonconformist sects. While Evangelicals came to be active in every sphere of social reform in the nineteenth century, the primary tenor of this new religious enthusiasm was essentially personal and domestic: adherents were encouraged to scrutinize with unprecedented intensity the states of their own souls and those of others, especially family members, and to conduct with great reverence such home-centered activities as private and family prayers, meditation, and Bible study. Within such a regimen of spiritual examination, attention to the child was particularly marked. This watchfulness, however, took various different and sometimes competing forms. For those Evangelicals, both inside and outside the Church of England, who subscribed to Calvinistic doctrines of original sin, it was imperative to guide and educate children to give them the best opportunity of redeeming themselves, so they might obtain God's grace.

To modern, and even to many contemporary standards of judgment, the strict codes of supervision and punishment levied by zealots endeavoring to save children from their corrupt natures often ran dangerously close to cruelty. Even though this residue of earlier theological thinking insisted on the fundamental wickedness of children, it nevertheless concurred with the otherwise opposed Romantic code in placing tremendous emphasis on the care of the child, and in seeing the world as a continual source of moral danger. Many other Evangelically minded Christians, however, found themselves turning away from theories of original sin toward ideas more overtly compatible with Romanticism's idealization of children: in this frame of mind, Scripture could, for example, be reinterpreted in line with Wordsworth's ideas about the child, and thus "texts urging us to become as little children were now about innocence, rather than, as in Puritan dogma, about obedience."[14] Children, then, were to be closely observed because they offered adults glimpses of an original heavenly purity. Perhaps not surprisingly, those whose secular or religious beliefs promoted such a glorified view of childhood could on occasion be just as exacting as the most doctrinaire Calvinist on the subject of acceptable child behavior.

These different strains of Victorian Christianity, then, found themselves variously in contention and agreement with Romanticism's view of the child as pure and innocent, but ultimately colluded with its insistence upon the central importance of childhood. While such theoretical positions had obvious implications for the ways in which children were perceived, just as significant were the derived effects of Evangelical Christianity's relocation of the sacred from the supernatural and ecclesiastical, to the personal and familial, realm. In this essentially domestic religion, the ideal Christian home and its occupants became "objects of sentimentalization, bordering on worship."[15] The mid-nineteenth-century crisis of belief that famously struck down many middle-class Evangelicals, causing them to turn away from institutional religion and search elsewhere for salvation, strengthened this sense that the family, and most particularly, the child at its heart, offered an alternative access to grace and purity. On a still deeper level, the story of Adam's ejection from Paradise in Genesis, previously important to the perception of childhood because of its explanation of the source of original sin, increasingly offered itself as a myth of personal development to middle-class Victorian individuals, both religious and otherwise. Evangelical Christianity's drive toward self-examination had led the way to making religious narratives much more personally applicable: now, as John Gillis puts it, whether or not orthodox belief was present, the Garden of Eden "ceased to be a place, and became a stage of life," the time of childhood (7). In a move that has huge significance for this particular project, such retrospective imagining of the early years of life as a paradise of innocence and purity not only placed an absolute line of division between childhood and adulthood, but also declared that same adulthood to be a time of postlapsarian guilt and gloom.

Understanding both why this model was so compelling to middle-class men and why those childhood years were most satisfyingly embodied in the figure of a little girl will be a major task in the chapters ahead. For now, we can notice in broad outline a couple of factors touched upon earlier. Men from comfortable backgrounds in this period were far more likely to have experienced a definitive break between those early years in the feminized nursery and their subsequent careers in the wider world than women of their class, whose lives were generally expected to be bounded by the home. Furthermore, this same gendering of the home, and its concurrent transformation into the locus of the sacred, not only had the effect of creating that domestic, and now much vilified, paragon, the Angel in the House, but also her ideal daughter.[16] On those occasions when paradise was imagined as the primary, lost stage in the journey of life, rather than the sanctified home, then the perfect little girl formed its most apt symbol.

While this project plainly situates itself within the historiography of childhood, it simultaneously has relevance and allegiance to a number of other important scholarly arenas. My analysis owes a huge debt to the pioneering labors of academic feminism over the past twenty years, particularly to its careful explication of nineteenth-century constructions of the feminine, and the concomitant emergence and consolidation of domestic ideology.[17] Furthermore, this study finds a home in the burgeoning world of masculinity studies, a field that has recently grown out of the work of these feminist precursors. Like many of the works in this area, the present investigation is part of the movement to complicate our understanding of the complexities and contradictions that both challenged and supported nineteenth-century gender ideology: while earlier historical and critical studies often reproduced the Victorians' division of the "separate spheres," now "the 'private' is being reformulated to take account of men, in the same way that the scope of the 'public' has been progressively enlarged to take account of women."[18] Although my work has benefited from contemporary examinations of the subtle stratifications and shifting patterns within the English class system, and of the anxious constructions of different styles of masculinity, in the nineteenth century, *Men in Wonderland* takes a relatively broad swathe of middle-class male life as its area of investigation. The term *gentleman* is thus included in the book's full title simply to indicate that the principal subjects of this study are of the well-to-do classes.[19]

If this project participates in both childhood and masculinity studies, then it also aims to contribute to the current investigation into the construction of transgressive sexualities in the Victorian period. For the first two-thirds of the twentieth century, nineteenth-century figures who appear to display desires other than those expected within normative conjugality were generally analyzed in the light of a single, and now largely outmoded, theory that invoked the familiar narrative of a repressive Victorian culture. In this hydraulic account, the sexual urge was forced underground by prudish proprieties, only to burst out triumphantly and obscenely in aberrant and unnatural forms.[20] Carroll's and Ruskin's evident fascination with little girls, to be named "paidophilia" in 1906 and catalogued under "Abnormality" by Havelock Ellis in his *Study of the Psychology of Sex*, constitutes one of the various eruptions in this story. Literary critics working in the shadow of this model had few options open to them in their study of Carroll and Ruskin, for they could only support, deny, or ignore (and this last course was the road most taken) the portrait of the artist as pervert. Michel Foucault's challenge to the repression hypothesis, however, excited a wealth of investigation into the constructed nature of sexuality and the historical emergence of different categories of "deviants."[21] Consequently it became possible to examine the case of the Victorian girl-lover from different perspectives, and to consider how his obsessions might be related to those of his society.[22]

Foremost amongst today's investigators is James R. Kincaid, whose *Child-Loving* assimilates Ariès to Foucault.[23] Kincaid concurs with *Centuries of Childhood*'s basic argument about the recent emergence of the concept of the child, but adds his own twist. Given that the apparent absence or presence of sexuality became a key factor in the separation of adult and child, it was inevitable that both the dividing line, and the child itself, should have become heavily eroticized. The very act of creating a pure, asexual, blank child produces sexual desire: the emptiness cries out to be filled. The child, then, was created as the infinitely desirable Other. According to Kincaid, the pedophile becomes an indispensable figure in the drama: he is the imaginary monster that we have created to reassure ourselves that our own desires for the lovely child are proportionate.

Kincaid's argument is compelling, but it is important here not to collapse together two historically distinct moments or to ignore the question of gender (boys and girls appear to be equally fascinating in his account). The beginning of widespread cultural interest in the child and the recognition of the figure of the pedophile are not simultaneous events, but are separated by over a hundred years. The point is not to deny that sexual desire may be present in the gentleman's obsession with the child, but to ask questions about the cultural origins of that desire, to consider what *else* that adult interest might be signifying in the period before the pronouncements of medicalized discourse effectively closed down all explanations other than the diagnosis of individual pathology. Concentrating upon certain male writers' conceptualization of their childhood selves suggests that temporally displaced self-love[24] is a major theme not only in the cultural productions of the Victorian era, but also in its famous programs of social reform. Likewise, insisting on a marked tendency in this period to reimagine the young self as feminine brings gender issues to the fore and highlights the crucial links between attitudes toward children and domestic ideology.

On this latter point, I make a more concerted argument for the primary importance of girls to the Victorian imagination than Carolyn Steedman, who in *Strange Dislocations: Childhood and the Idea of Human Interiority* agrees with Kincaid that in the nineteenth century, children were "distributed across the sex-gender system" in ways that are now impossible to recover. Yet she cannot help noticing that "when the child was watched, written about and wanted, it was usually a feminised set of qualities (if not a female child) whose image was left behind for our analysis."[25] Steedman's admission is hardly surprising: while her project is a wonderfully broad scrutiny of "the social and psychic consequences of embodying what is lost and gone in the shape and form of a child" (viii), she conducts this inquiry through a very particular search for avatars of Goethe's Mignon, who "after all the cultivated androgyny of her presentation, turns out to be a girl in the end" (9). *Men in Wonderland*, most notably in its final chapter, turns up its own share of Mignons, but it is rather Steedman's attention to the wide-ranging effects of the adult's retrospective construction of the state of childhood that makes her book so important: this work, I hope, draws strength from her clear-sighted and often moving exploration of the investments adults place in the child through their beliefs, desires, and fantasies, and their use of "living bodies as expressions of the deepest springs of the self" (170).[26] Ultimately, however, *Strange Dislocations* is interested in recovering the child, and registering the distortions forced upon it by the adult's perspective: *Men in Wonderland* gives precedence to the adult fantasizer and thus tells a significantly different story.

This elucidation of the distinction between Steedman's work and my own preoccupations suggests a number of other important lines of demarcation. Of primary concern here is the male figure who constructs, in one way or another, a fantasy of his feminine childhood. Although ventures into related areas will help substantiate the argument, this emphasis necessarily excludes a range of undoubtedly interesting fields of inquiry. This book by no means attempts a comprehensive overview of the origins and appearances of the idealized girl in nineteenth-century literature and culture. It says very little about how women writers in this period manipulated the figure of the child in their works, autobiographical, fictional, or otherwise. Similarly, although Lewis Carroll's writings are examined, it generally avoids the genre of children's literature.[27] Furthermore, juvenile masculinity, which is obviously the main interest of Claudia Nelson's *Boys Will Be Girls*, gets scant attention in this study. All in all, then, I concentrate on the essential peculiarity of my central finding and trace only the twists and turns of a singular narrative through the nineteenth century.

The narrative told is of the rise and fall of the ideal girl, revealing the concomitant progress of the myth of the gentleman's lost girlhood. While the principle of organization is broadly chronological, and while all sections set examinations of the works of single figures against considerations of wider historical contexts, the exact approach to different types of cultural materials varies from chapter to chapter. Certainly there are strong threads that run throughout the entire project: first, the preceding discussion of the influence of religious belief and practice on the social and individual perception of childhood resumes at junctures in all chapters, most noticeably in the first three. Other connections are formed, second, by the continual invocations of two key literary texts and, third, by the repetitions of an iconic vision of the adult male and the little girl. The nineteenth century learns how to think about the sacred content of childhood and the blasphemy of child labor *through* Wordsworth's *Ode: Intimations of Immortality* and Barrett's "Cry of the Children": lines from these poems recur as touchstones in the public and private discourses of the child examined in chapters 1, 2, and 5. In one way or another, all five chapters present pictures of man and girl together. On some occasions the couple appears in the mainstream of everyday Victorian life—Little Nell and her grandfather walk hand in hand away from the wildly popular *Old Curiosity Shop*; Carroll's Alice stops to listen to the White Knight's song; most ominously, sensational literature of the 1880s depicts the girl and the man in danger in *Dr. Jekyll and Mr. Hyde*, and the girl in danger *from* the man in the scandal sheets of muckraking journalism. More often, however, the image of man and girl is buried in little-read texts or private correspondence—summoned up in De Quincey's tear-stained reconstruction of the night of tenderness he shared with young Kate Wordsworth; excitedly re-created in Ruskin's celebration of his breathless dancing with an Irish schoolgirl; or figured in Carroll's enigmatic photographs of girls even when the adult male is ostensibly absent. All three of these recurrent features, then, unify a project that deliberately adopts a range of methodological techniques.

Chapter 1 places accounts of childhood development in the poetry and prose of William Wordsworth and Thomas De Quincey in relation to one of the numerous trajectories within the history of childhood. A study of the emerging concept of the juvenile delinquent and the provision of specialized care for young offenders provides a representative demonstration of the ways in which ideas about the child evolved between the last quarter of the eighteenth century and the midpoint of the nineteenth. General theories of childhood come to rely on absolute divisions between adult and child, corruption and innocence, masculine and feminine: by 1850 it is a truism that there is nothing so unlike a criminal as a little girl. Wordsworth presents two important images of the child: the vital boyish self of *The Prelude*, and the otherworldly girl, variously depicted as Lucy or his sister Dorothy, whose experience is ruptured in death, or allowed no maturation. De Quincey appropriates solely the latter half of the representation and applies it to his own autobiography, identifying the young self as consistently feminine, and definitively cut off from the adult by the fact of death. This is the paradigm that will provide the Victorians with an increasingly attractive image of the innocent self of childhood, isolated from a progressively threatening world.

Chapter 2 considers the ramifications of this mode of perception by scrutinizing a constellation of texts from the early 1840s. Readings of

Dickens's *Old Curiosity Shop* and Sarah Stickney Ellis's *Daughters of England* show how the model works as both personal and national fantasy, for the young girls in novel and conduct book alike are imagined as memorializing not only the past selves of their older male relatives, but also the rural idyll of a bygone England. Juxtaposing these works with the report by a royal commission in 1842 on children's employment in the mines and Elizabeth Barrett's short poem "The Cry of the Children," I examine the contradictions inherent within Victorian society's views of girlhood. While Little Nell and Ellis's exemplary daughters embody the deathly perfection of the era's idealizing depiction of young femininity, the government report, and Barrett's response to it, construct a radically different picture of the distinctly nonideal existence of a large proportion of the nation's little girls. The horrifying visions of exploited girl-labor brought to the public eye make it abundantly clear that innocent girlhood is not an universal phenomenon, but an economically contingent construction; more particularly, focus upon the active body of the working-class girl reveals it to be disturbingly sexual. Contained within these unresolved conflicts of the 1840s are the elements that will ultimately destroy the conception of the little girl as both repository of purity and moral worth, and fit representative of the Victorian gentleman's lost childhood.

Chapter 3 deals solely with John Ruskin, the first of the two notorious girl-lovers of this project. Here the angle of approach alters significantly: rather than relate Ruskin's literary representations of the self and of juvenile femininity to broad historical movements and public discourses, I present the economic, social, religious, educational, and familial circumstances of his immediate personal background. The following paradox is thereby highlighted: although Ruskin's autobiography *Praeterita* supplies a strong example of the paradigm that has general currency in the Victorian era, his existence is certainly not paradigmatic for his class and gender in this period. I study the self-feminizing tropes of the autobiography and describe the ways in which Ruskin's "school-girl" text of the 1860s, *The Ethics of the Dust*, reproduces the essential elements of the myth of the little girl's antiquity. In Ruskin's schema, young femininity is connected to the unsullied and vital purity of long-lost origins, and placed in opposition to the defiled world of the present day and a miserably compromised and decrepit male maturity. Ruskin's principal mode of representing the little girl within this myth is to view her in terms of the ancient and precious stones of the earth, to depict her as a brilliantly hard gem, jewel, or crystal: an erotics of aesthetic impenetrability appears again and again in his prose. This beautiful unyielding crystalline girl is not only an object of desire, however, but ultimately *Praeterita*'s figure for both the lost self of childhood and the continuing true self.

The study of Lewis Carroll in chapter 4 makes a virtue out of the fact that this particular worshipper of juvenile femininity left behind no autobiographical reconstructions of his own early years. In the absence of a textual narrative setting forth a fantasy of original femininity, I focus on Carroll's passion for the new phenomenon of photography and ask whether the images produced by this Victorian invention offered him an alternative means of substantiating a lost past. The photograph, simply through the mechanics of its technological process, coincides with the nineteenth century's dominant mode of viewing children: Carroll's studies of little girls evince an uncanny ability to confound oppositions, most notably that between adult and child. In stark contrast, tableaux or "photographic moments" from *Through the Looking Glass* and *Sylvie and Bruno* send quite different messages: without photography's inherent ability to combine past and present in a single image, Carroll's textual fancies paint only the most sentimental of portraits of the little girl, her signifying potential radically reduced by the inclusion of adult figures, usually the nostalgic old man, within the scene. Seen from this perspective, Carroll's decision to avoid the genre of autobiography is to be applauded: this is an artist who is much more likely to find a successful form for his fantasies of the little girl when he is able to efface the traces of his own presence.

The fifth and final chapter charts the destruction of the fantasy of the ideal girl. Anxieties about girls and sexual activity begin to move into mainstream discourses in the last quarter of the nineteenth century, finding their high-water mark in the *Pall Mall Gazette* of July 1885. The luridly titled "Maiden Tribute of Modern Babylon," W. T. Stead's sensational exposé of what he claimed was the regular and widespread debauching of virgins in London, led to the raising of the age of consent in the Criminal Law Amendment Act of that year. The furor is a continuation of the unresolved conflicts examined in chapter 2: still at issue is the glaring disparity between the construct of idealized girlhood, and the depiction of girlhood as a lived experience for the working class. The worries aroused by the working-class girl, implicitly sexual in the 1840s, are now explicitly sexual, and the archetypal exploited child is no longer a collier or millworker, but a prostitute. Moral concern, whipped to a frenzy by Stead's tactics, elides the real issue of the economic basis of prostitution and delivers a blanket ruling on sexual activity for all girls under the age of sixteen. To satisfy the desire to establish an all-inclusive realm of protected girlhood, all girlhood, paradoxically, has to be viewed through the lens of sexuality. Cast in this light, girls could no longer play their former role for the Victorian psyche.

The book concludes with a brief glimpse of three prime girl-lovers in the wake of that turbulent summer of 1885. For Ruskin, immersed by turns in madness or idealized reconstructions of the past, there can be no response to the sexualization of his favorite human figure. Carroll, formerly the nineteenth century's closest observer of juvenile femininity, now advises that we all simply turn away. The final glance falls upon Rhymers' Club poet Ernest Dowson, whose brand of little-girl adoration most strikingly demonstrates the change in tenor of the late eighties and nineties. Analysis of his sonnet sequence "Of a Little Girl," reveals that Dowson's child is a potentially sexual receptacle for emotion, rather than the guarantor of the sealed perfection of the man's lost girlhood. Her innocence discussed and legislated out of existence, the little girl tumbles from grace at the end of the nineteenth century, leaving the way clear for a new star to rise. The boy, neglected for almost three generations, returns to embody a new image of childhood for a new age.

Of Prisons and Ungrown Girls: Wordsworth, De Quincey, and Constructions of the Lost Self of Childhood

> 'Twas at an early age, ere I had seen
> Nine summers—when upon the mountain slope
> The frost and breath of frosty wind had snapped
> The last autumnal crocus, 'twas my joy
> To wander half the night among the cliffs
> And the smooth hollows where the woodcocks ran
> Along the open turf. In thought and wish
> That time, my shoulder all with springes hung,
> I was a fell destroyer. On the heights
> Scudding away from snare to snare, I plied
> My anxious visitation, hurrying on,
> Still hurrying, hurrying onward. Moon and stars
> Were shining o'er my head; I was alone,
> And seemed to be a trouble to the peace
> That was among them. Sometimes it befel
> In these night-wanderings, that a strong desire
> O'erpowered my better reason, and the bird
> Which was the captive of another's toils
> Became my prey; and when the deed was done
> I heard among the solitary hills
> Low breathings coming after me, and sounds
> Of undistinguishable motion, steps
> Almost as silent as the turf they trod.
> *("The Prelude," 1805, 1.310–32)*

Instead of merely being a trouble to the peace of the moon and stars, the eight-year-old Wordsworth could legitimately have ended up a trouble to the justice of the peace. While we have all noticed before that young William is transgressing in this passage, our attention had probably been captured by what is really his secondary crime—that when he was out snaring woodcocks, sheer devilment had tempted him to help himself to the birds caught in other poachers' traps.[1] It may not have struck us with sufficient force that the very act of catching game birds was an offense, punishable under the auspices of a statute of 1706, 5 Anne c14:

> [I]f any person or persons, not qualified by the laws of this realm so to do, shall keep or use any greyhounds, setting dogs, hays, lurchers, tunnels, or any other engines, to kill and destroy game, and shall thereof be convicted upon the oath of one or two credible witnesses, by the justice or justices of peace where such offence is committed as aforesaid, the person or persons so convicted shall forfeit the sum of five pounds. . . . for want of such distress, the offenders shall be sent to the house of correction for the space of three months for the first offence, and for every such other offence, four months.[2]

However, the prevalence of woodcock snaring in the region at this period—marked enough to capture Thomas Pennant's interest as he passed through Hawkshead and Graithwaite en route to his *Tour of Scotland* in 1772—suggests that this was an accepted illegality, and in any case, should Wordsworth have been caught red-handed, he would no doubt have been protected by his social class from anything other than a reproach.[3] Nevertheless, according to the strict letter of the law, the behavior described in book 1 of *The Prelude* constituted a criminal act. The fact that the culprit had yet to see nine summers would not, as we shall see, have helped him at all if he had landed up in court.[4] For what we perceive as a boyish prank, an unlucky eight-year-old might have been punished like a man, to the full extent of the law.

This opening focus upon the issue of crime and punishment is simultaneously strategic and arbitrary: this topic, in common with numerous others, offers an opportunity to study attitudes toward childhood in both Wordsworth's poetry and the times in which he lived. *The Prelude*, as a whole, depicts a child whose vivacity is more likely to express itself in legally dubious excitements than in moments of angelic purity, and an adult whose connection with his former self is still strong. In marked contrast stands the *Ode: Intimations of Immortality from Recollections of Early Childhood*, in which "Shades of the prison-house begin to close / Upon the growing Boy."[5] Encapsulated in these lines is a principal—if not the titular—theme of the poem: the innocent liberty of childhood is inexorably replaced by the guilty incarceration of adulthood, an imprisonment that all but severs the man from the child he once was. Wordsworth's oeuvre presents two main ways of understanding childhood and its place in the life-span of the individual, and these different positions find their clearest articulation in *The Prelude* and the *Ode*. A marked contrast also appears in the reception of these poems in the first half of the nineteenth century: the *Ode*, which had been in circulation for over forty years by the time of *The Prelude*'s posthumous appearance, commanded both tremendous popularity and, thanks to its congruence with certain strains of religious thought, a powerful influence on ideas about the nature of the child. The longer poem, although clearly partaking of the newly growing sensibility that rendered childhood a subject for specialized scrutiny, had to wait until the early 1900s and the rise of Freud before it began to gain the preeminence that it holds today.

A context for discussion of Wordsworth's contribution to the evolving discourse of the child is provided by placing his metaphorical prison-house in juxtaposition with the literal jail of the late eighteenth and mid–nineteenth centuries. Throughout the long stretch of the poet's life, numerous currents of change swept over the handling of minors by the forces of law and order: examination of this history, then, allows us to see one of the ways in which the concept of childhood took shape, and became embodied in legislation and institutions during this extremely volatile period. The invention of the juvenile delinquent, the high-water mark of the discourse on children and crime in the 1850s, brings the question of gender into the analysis: the junior criminal, the demonic antithesis of the innocent child of the *Ode*, is invariably male. I return to Wordsworth to examine how gender functions within ideas of childhood in *The Prelude*, on one hand, and in the *Ode* and a number of other especially cherished poems on the other. The final focus in this chapter falls upon Wordsworth's fellow Romantic, Thomas De Quincey, who represents this study's first full example of a worshipper of lost girlhood. Ignoring *The Prelude*'s construct of the vital male child, De Quincey wholeheartedly embraces Wordsworth's other model, in which the child is an idealized, static, feminine presence, definitively cut off from adulthood by the fact of death. Applying this schema to the representation of his own life, De Quincey supplies an early example of a paradigm that will both haunt and solace the Victorian age.

Acts of "stealth and troubled pleasure" appear with some regularity in Wordsworth's depiction of his boyhood in *The Prelude*. Although the poet clearly regards his own rural childhood to be as close to ideal as possible (witness his pity for the "liveried schoolboy" Coleridge, "reared / In the great city, 'mid far other scenes",[6] he makes no attempt to represent this period of his life as a time of moral innocence. Snaring woodcocks, plundering birds' nests, stealing the odd boat from some unwitting shepherd, lying to the "good old innkeeper" and running his poor horses into the ground—naughty activities of this type, more or less on the windy side of the law, pepper Wordsworth's account of his early years.[7] Signs of transgression figure largely and impressively in the landscape: the gibbet-mast, "where in former times / A murderer had been hung in iron chains" (11.288–89), is only the most obvious of the markers of crime and punishment that animate the boy's perception of his Lakeland scenery. Far from being a tranquil idyll, childhood in *The Prelude* is beset with "terrors, . . . early miseries, / Regrets, vexations, lassitudes" (1.356–57). The "severer interventions" of Nature (1.370), which promote disturbing emotions, are celebrated by Wordsworth for their formative powers. Young William and his friends are characterized by the volatility and variety of their passions:

> A race of real children, not too wise,
> Too learned, or too good, but wanton, fresh,
> And bandied up and down by love and hate;
> Fierce, moody, patient, venturous, modest, shy,
> Mad at their sports like withered leaves in winds;
> Though doing wrong and suffering, and full oft
> Bending beneath our life's mysterious weight
> Of pain and fear, yet still in happiness
> Not yielding to the happiest upon earth.
>
> (5.436–44)

If the children of *The Prelude* are no angels, then neither is Wordsworth's presiding adult presence in the poem hedged in by sin and guilt. Shades of the prison-house have not closed around the grown man once and for all time: instead of a hopeless lifer, it is a new emancipist who strides into the poem's opening lines:

> A captive greets thee, coming from a house
> Of bondage, from yon city's walls set free,
> A prison where he hath been long immured.
> Now I am free, enfranchised and at large,
> May fix my habitation where I will.
>
> (1.6–10)

This mood of confident optimism is, however, soon replaced by a crisis of vocation: it would certainly be false to the poem's fluxes and refluxes of feeling to imply that positive emotions are maintained at all consistently

19

throughout its extended length. *The Prelude* nevertheless allows us to believe that all periods of human life can be times of hope, of new beginnings and possibilities: "whether we be young or old,"

> Our destiny, our nature, and our home,
> Is with infinitude—and only there;
> With hope it is, hope that can never die,
> Effort, and expectation, and desire,
> And something evermore about to be.

> (6.537–42)

The passing of the years can bring "change of growth *or* of decay" (2.179; emphasis added), and the adult, no less than the child, is able to experience "faculties still growing, feeling still / That whatsoever point they gain they still / Have something to pursue" (2.338–41). Prison walls do not cast their shadows—instead Wordsworth sits literally "in the open sun" (9.65) amongst the rubble of the demolished Bastille, consigning a stone from the shattered monolith to the darkness of his pocket. The French Revolution, of course, does not turn out to be the birth of freedom that Wordsworth initially envisages, but painfully (and, most would say, extremely conservatively) he does come, within the poem, to construct an alternative model of inward liberty:

> Oh, who is he that hath his whole life long
> Preserved, enlarged, this freedom in himself?—
> For this alone is genuine liberty.

> (13.121–23)

Given that neither childhood nor adulthood has the monopoly on guilt, hope, or liberty, it is clear that Wordsworth has no desire to set up the two states as polar opposites. Not surprising, then, is *The Prelude*'s presentation of a fluid interconnection between the present writing self and the past remembered self.[8] The poem's long and complicated composition history makes it perhaps inevitable that Wordsworth's position on the nature of this connection fluctuates,[9] but at his most ebullient, the poet will declare that he has access to "Unfading recollections—at this hour / The heart is almost mine with which I felt / . . . The kite . . . Pull at its rein" (1.517–21); that even at the advanced age of thirty-four, "yet the morning gladness is not gone / Which then was in my mind" (6.63–64). More significantly, *The Prelude*'s most important conceptual and organizational structure, the theory of "spots of time," bears witness to the poet's belief that the former self can be revisited, in the same way, for instance, that one could revisit the site of a ruined abbey. The principle of the spots is that Wordsworth is able to "fetch / Invigorating thoughts from former years" (1.648–49): the intensity of emotion experienced, most frequently in childhood, when "We have had deepest feeling that the mind / Is lord and master" (11.270–71) is still available to the adult, albeit in reduced form, years after the event:

> So feeling comes in aid
> Of feeling, and diversity of strength
> Attends us, if but once we have been strong.
>
> (11.325–27)

Whether the result of the revisiting is "fructifying," "vivifying," or "renovating,"[10] the crucial feature for our purposes is the demonstrated ability to return to and identify with childhood's states of mind. As a whole, *The Prelude* elects not to postulate a radical break between childhood and adulthood, choosing instead to see life as a continuum rather than two distinct eras.

Would "Nature's Priest" snare woodcocks? The "Mighty Prophet! Seer blest!" of the *Ode* comes to us, famously, "trailing clouds of glory" rather than a brace of game birds. Lofty diction and capitalization may signal the difference of genre between this work and *The Prelude*, but they also alert us to the fact that the child in the *Ode* bears none of the differentiating characteristics that marked the autobiographical representation. Closer to an abstract essence, this "little Child, yet glorious in the might / Of heaven-born freedom" (ll. 122–23) is primarily defined by his proximity to God, and to "that imperial palace whence he came" (l. 84). The celestial haze that shimmers around our infancy serves as a kind of cordon sanitaire; only when the "growing" of the boy becomes indisputable can negative emotions or compromised morality break through—we will "tremble like a guilty Thing surprised" (l. 148) only when we begin to distinguish between the glorious universe of our preexistence and the world of material fact that we actually inhabit. Adulthood is most fully represented as the culmination of boyhood's gradual process of loss. The prison doors are completely closed upon the adult inmate, whose sensory—most notably, visual—deprivation is as profound as in death, for he is "In darkness lost, the darkness of the grave" (l. 118). Cold comfort, it would seem, are the newly acquired strengths that are adulthood's especial province: "the philosophic mind," gained from knowledge of man's suffering and mortality, and the power to give it utterance, are scant recompense for the loss of "the visionary gleam."

21

The epochs of childhood and adulthood, then, are entirely different eras
in this poem: while the continuum of time and its spatial representation in
The Prelude allowed pleasurable and invigorating visits to the earlier self,
no such access is possible here. "The morning gladness" that still illuminated adult years in the longer poem is extinguished for the man in the
Ode, who is subject to a dogmatically successive temporality: "*nothing*
can bring back the hour / Of splendour in the grass" (ll. 178–79; emphasis
added). Although the speaker claims that "The innocent brightness of a
new-born Day/ Is lovely yet" (ll. 195–96), he is clearly in emotional harmony not with the day's beginning, but the day's end, where "The Clouds
that gather round the setting sun / Do take a sober colouring" (ll. 197–
98). Significantly, the narrator in the *Ode* is watching and describing not
his own childhood but an entirely distinct and separate six-year-old
child.[11] The speaker's younger self is there only by inference, as the one
who had the fullness of perception that defines the lack experienced now.

The "positive" reading of *The Prelude*'s fluidities and "negative" ap-
praisal of the absolutes of the *Ode* in the foregoing pages follows a distinctly twentieth-century path. To modern readers, unswayed by the inti-
mation of immortality that the wondrous perception of childhood is meant
to support, the abiding impression left by the *Ode* is one of loss; we are
repelled both by the saintly child and the gloomy adult.[12] With the notable
exception of Coleridge, who fulminated against the poem's "mental bom-
bast,"[13] Wordsworthian readers in the first half of the nineteenth century
were much more appreciative. As Carl Woodring, U. C. Knoepflmacher,
and, most specifically, Barbara Garlitz have argued, this short work was
"held up as 'the finest poem of the greatest poet within our times,' as
'the high-water mark the intellect has reached in this age,' as the 'divinest
utterance of modern poetry.' "[14] Not only did the *Ode* spawn countless
imitations throughout the nineteenth century, but it had far-reaching effects on extraliterary discourses. Garlitz shows us that the *Ode* occupied
a central position in theological debate about the meaning of baptism, and
that its sentiments permeated an increasingly wide range of discussions
about both the nature, and the correct upbringing, of the child. Far from
being nauseated by the angelic child, or dismayed by the depiction of the
shrunken capabilities of adulthood, then, readers of the *Ode* in the last
century, at least until the spread of Darwinism, seized upon the poem's
developmental philosophy as the expression of noble certainties:

> The ideas . . . that the child is fresh from God and still remembers his heav-
> enly home, that the aura that surrounds childhood fades into the common

light of adulthood, that the child has a wisdom that the man loses—these ideas became the most important and the most common ideas about childhood in the nineteenth century. They attained the status of facts.[15]

It would, however, be incorrect to suggest that the *Ode* was breaking wholly new and unfamiliar ground in its readers' minds: on the contrary, the poem was taken so joyfully to the bosom of the Victorians precisely because it partook of an existing religious climate that had been giving the figure of the child increasing prominence since at least the end of the eighteenth century. While certain strains of Protestant Christianity continued to perceive children as the inheritors of original sin, other currents were much more likely to see childhood as the locus of innocence. This point of view, which effectively transformed the Garden of Eden from a place to a stage of life, naturally found itself largely in sympathy with Wordsworth's progressive narrative of the early bliss of childhood and the falling-off of maturity. Despite the fact that a strict reading of the *Ode* uncovers a variety of heterodox opinions, any number of Victorian churchmen and religious writers seemed perfectly happy to quote the poet's lines as if they were so many glosses on beloved New Testament texts about the child. In the words of a columnist in the *Christian Examiner* of 1850, Wordsworth becomes "a legitimate successor of his spiritual master. . . . you see him calling to childhood, and pleading on its behalf: 'Suffer little children, and forbid them not to come unto me.' "[16]

The Prelude experienced a rather different reception. Primarily composed between 1798 and 1804, when the poet was twenty-eight to thirty-four years of age, and extensively revised at different periods until around 1839, the poem was not published until after Wordsworth's death in 1850. Overshadowed by the publication of *In Memoriam* in the same year, *The Prelude*'s long interment caused both Wordsworthians and non-Wordsworthians to approach it somewhat gingerly. "It seems a large fossil relic," said the *Eclectic Review*, "imperfect and magnificent—newly dug up, and with the fresh earth and the old dim subsoil meeting and mingling around it."[17] Unable to supply either a true shock of the new or the comfortable familiarity of the long-cherished favorite, *The Prelude* fell between two stools, and reviewers and readers alike were not keen to allow it to overshadow the works that they had already decided were the laureate's finest. Extemporizing on Wordsworth's declaration that *The Prelude* and *The Recluse* (the latter unwritten except for *The Excursion* and certain fragments) may be considered to be in the relation to each other of a Gothic ante-chapel and chapel, *Tait's Edinburgh Magazine* pronounced that "we entertain, like many other devotees, a decided preference for these little cells and oratories [the minor pieces] . . . and though we now have an opportunity of carefully perusing the ante-chapel, we see no reason to alter our judgement."[18] *Graham's Magazine* struck a similar note:

> It must be admitted, however, that "The Prelude," with all its merits, does not add to the author's great fame, however much it may add to our knowledge of his inner life. As a poem it cannot be placed by the side of The White Doe, or The Excursion, or the Ode on Childhood, or the Ode on the Power of Sound.[19]

All in all, no one seemed ready in 1850, or indeed for half a century more, to give up the conviction that *The Excursion* was Wordsworth's best long poem, and that the *Ode* was his greatest poem of all.

When Mary Carpenter, foundress and passionate advocate of the reformatory school, asks what right we have to call children juvenile delinquents, the influence of the *Ode*, seamlessly conjoined with fervent religious belief, lies heavy about her in her polemic: for Carpenter, these creatures are "young beings but recently come from the hands of their Maker, of whom the Saviour has said, that 'of such is the Kingdom of Heaven.' "[20] The problem of juvenile delinquency was viewed in the mid–nineteenth century as a fairly recent excrescence—"of 70 or 80 years' growth," reckoned a prison inspector when questioned by the Select Committee on Criminal and Destitute Juveniles in 1852.[21] The life span of William Wordsworth, then, provides us with a period that saw immense changes in the public perception of children and crime: by examining the concurrent innovations in philanthropic and governmental policy on the transgressive child, we can cast a sidelight on the emergence and solidification of the concept of childhood over these years. At the same time, this area of investigation is perforce a subsection of the important and wide-reaching discussion, conducted by Foucault, Ignatieff, and others, about the nature and meaning of the profound changes in general penal practices that occurred during this period.[22] A survey may begin in 1769, the year before Wordsworth's birth, when Blackstone, following guidelines that had been prevalent at least since the seventeenth century, codified the rules on the relation between a child's age and its degree of criminal responsibility. The year 1854, which saw the passage of the Youthful Offenders Act, the culmination of around eighty years of increasingly specialized discussion about the problem of refractory children, marks an end point. The account that follows of the developments within these years identifies three principal interwoven strands: first, the attempts of concerned individuals and philanthropic societies to address problems that they felt were neglected by governmental policy, and second and third, the moves in Parliament to change court procedure for child cases, and to provide separate penal institutions for children.

Blackstone's *Commentaries* laid out a general schema: from birth to seven years of age, an infant was thought to be "under the age of discretion, [and] ought not to be punished by any criminal prosecution whatever," while over the age of fourteen, a minor was "equally liable to suffer, as a person of the full age of twenty-one," capitally as otherwise.[23] Between the ages of seven and fourteen, matters were less clear-cut. For this age range, Blackstone explains, "by the law, as it now stands, and has stood at least ever since the time of Edward the Third, the capacity of doing ill, or contracting guilt, is not so much measured by years and days as by the strength of the delinquent's understanding and judgment" (IV, 2, sec. 23). Thus a court and jury had to decide whether a child in this age span were "*doli capax* (capable of distinguishing good from evil)" (IV, 2, sec. 23). If they believed that the child could discern the difference, if the child, for instance, "manifested a consciousness of guilt," then in these cases "our maxim is, that '*malitia supplet ætatem*' (malice is held equivalent to age)" (IV, 2, sec. 23). It was, then, entirely possible that children, even in the lower range of the seven-to-fourteen band, would suffer the severest punishments:

> [T]here was an instance in the last century where a boy of eight years old was tried at Abingdon for firing two barns; and, it appearing that he had malice, revenge and cunning, he was found guilty, condemned and hanged accordingly. Thus, also, in very modern times, a boy of ten years old was convicted on his own confession of murdering his bedfellow, there appearing in his whole behaviour plain tokens of a mischievous discretion; and, as the sparing this boy merely on account of his tender years might be of dangerous consequence to the public, by propagating a notion that children might commit such atrocious crimes with impunity, it was unanimously agreed by all the judges that he was a proper subject of capital punishment. (IV, 2, sec. 23)

In practice, however, relatively few children were hanged in the late eighteenth and early nineteenth centuries, but they were not necessarily saved by compassion for their tender years: in the face of England's notorious "Bloody Code," many judges commuted capital sentences for children and adults alike to transportation.[24] With reference to less serious of-

25

fenses, it is interesting to note that although children theoretically had no special legal privileges, the number of minors actually appearing before court was very low in comparison to nineteenth- or twentieth-century rates. J. M. Beattie has shown that in the late 1700s, "less than seven per cent of those charged before the Surrey and Sussex assizes were under eighteen," which leads him to speculate that "it is likely that young children caught stealing would have been frequently dealt with informally— cuffed and whipped on the spot perhaps rather than being sent to trial."[25] Although we can therefore hypothesize that in an unofficial fashion, distinctions were made between the young and the mature offender, the fact remains that the letter of the law did not sanction this, and if children ended up being transported or sent to prison, there was no thought to provide separately for them during this period.

The problem of unsegregated incarceration of children and adults was thrown up almost incidentally by the work of John Howard, who published his important investigation, *State of the Prisons of England and Wales*, in 1777, following four years of prison visiting. While Howard principally concerned himself with the dire results of the prisons' unhygienic conditions, he did not forebear to comment on the moral contagion that was rife in the indiscriminate mingling of prisoners: "[I]f it were the aim and wish of magistrates to effect the destruction present and future, of young delinquents, they could not devise a more effectual method than to confine them so long in our prisons, those seats and seminaries, as they have been properly called, of idleness and vice."[26] Howard's remarks were not entirely without precedent. Sir John Fielding, the renowned blind magistrate of Bow Street and brother of the novelist, was noticeably reluctant to commit young offenders to prison because of their inevitable exposure to hardened criminals inside. Rather than attempt a cure of the prison system, Fielding had turned his attention to the prevention of delinquency amongst the young, and his efforts to send boys at risk to sea eventually led to a full-scale program run by the Marine Society, which dispatched over ten thousand juveniles to the regular and merchant navies between 1756 and 1862.[27] This early instance of a desire to focus upon the specific problem of crime and the young was followed in 1788 by the inauguration of the Royal Philanthropic Society, which sought to provide residential care in Hackney for potentially refractory children.[28]

While preventative measures like these addressed themselves expressly to the child before any indictable crime had been committed, it was to be some time before the convicted child met with special treatment. The burgeoning of enthusiasm for general penal reform did, however, work to expose and create the separate problem of the juvenile prisoner. Ironically enough, the increase of concern about the child ran parallel with the expansion of child conviction rates. The belief that juveniles were responsible for a great deal of crime seems to have intensified in the early decades of the nineteenth century, particularly when the level of prosecutions rose sharply in the years of peace after 1815.[29] Numerous forces were at work: massive population growth and urbanization no doubt led the way, but the creation of new criminal offenses, the institution of a regular police force, and the extension of the powers of justices of the peace also played important roles. The increasing availability of criminal statistics and the corresponding growth in the scientific study of crime helped to create an atmosphere of panic, inducing a flurry of philanthropic and governmental activity.[30] The formation in 1815 of the Society for Investigating the Causes of the Alarming Increase of Juvenile Delinquency in the Metropolis reveals the specificity of contemporary fears, while its transformation into the Society for the Improvement of Prison Discipline and for the Reformation of Juvenile Offenders three years later clearly shows the trajectory of the reformers' attention. Although 1816 heard the first recommendation for a separate juvenile penal system from the Parliamentary Committee on the Police in the Metropolis, the call was ignored, and the provision of institutions for refractory youths continued to be a private endeavor, focusing on reform rather than deterrence. Farm colonies at Stretton in Warwickshire opened in 1818; on occasion the Crown would pardon convicted juveniles if they agreed to go to homes of this type.[31] As the century progressed, this rural model of the reformatory, "the Warwickshire plan," in common with De Metz's *colonie agricole* at Mettrai in France, influenced the establishment of other institutions like the Philanthropic Society's farm school at Redhill (1849) and Mary Carpenter's Kingswood (1852).

In the meantime, members of Parliament had been attempting to alter court procedure for young offenders, pressing in particular for summary powers of conviction for local justices dealing with petty offenses, so that children would not be committed to prison to await trial. Bills to this end, however, failed in 1821 and 1829, and although a Select Committee on the Police in 1834 drew unambiguous attention to the difficulties created by the current state of affairs, it was not until 1847 that changes were introduced. The Summary Jurisdiction Act of this year gave justices power to try children under fourteen summarily for petty larceny, and was then extended to children under sixteen in 1850. The introduction of distinct penal institutions for all juveniles took a little longer. Admittedly there were a number of experiments with separate punishment systems for children: the prison hulks *Bellerophon* and *Euryalus* were expressly set aside for boys in 1823 and 1825, but they produced extremely discouraging results, in that eight out of ten inmates were reconvicted.[32] Within the structure of the penal colonies in Australia, a separate enclave named Point Puer was created in Van Diemen's Land in 1834, expressly to receive "little depraved felons," as Sir George Arthur, the island's lieutenant-governor, described them.[33] Point Puer became an integral part of a new program initiated by the opening of Parkhurst prison on the Isle of Wight in 1838. The first prison specifically built for juveniles in England, Parkhurst was intended to provide two to three years imprisonment for boys before they were transported to Australia, to work for private masters if they were tractable, or to Point Puer if their conduct was poor. Dogged by the criticisms of reformatory school adherents like Carpenter, and given no clear organizational policy in its founding act, Parkhurst never gained the support of public confidence. Although it limped along until 1864, the prison lost much of its sense of mission (and, apparently, any optimism in its inmates' minds) when transportation came to an end in 1852.[34] In any case, there had been no certainty in these years that a juvenile offender would automatically end up in Parkhurst, as the following exchange reveals. A dialogue in 1847 between an examiner on the Select Committee on the Execution of the Criminal Law and the governor of the House of Correction at Tothill Fields gives a brief glimpse of a pitiful narrative:

"What has been the youngest Offenders [*sic*] you have had?"
"Under Six Years; Five and Three Quarters."
"Did you see that Boy?"
"Frequently."
"What was his Appearance?"
"He was an Object of Wretchedness and Misery."
"What did his Age appear to be?"
"I thought him Six Years of Age; but I conversed with him, with a view of ascertaining the Fact, and satisfied myself that he was not Six."
"The Magistrate who committed him is very short-sighted, is he not?"
"Yes."
"And deaf also?"
"I think he labours under such an Infirmity."[35]

Only in 1854, with the passage of the Youthful Offenders Act, did treatment of convicted children become standardized: courts were empowered to give children younger than sixteen a hybrid sentence consisting of an initial fourteen or more days in prison, and then a period of two to five years in a reformatory school. Run by voluntary societies, but certified by the Home Secretary, these schools were supported, wherever possible, by financial contributions from the inmates' parents. The compromise between prison punishment, with its accent on retribution, and the reformatory principle of the special school, naturally displeased the most ardent reformers. Even so, Matthew Davenport Hill, longtime supporter of the Warwickshire plan and Mary Carpenter's fellow campaigner, was jubilant, believing that the act would "be considered in future times to form a great epoch in the jurisprudence of this country."[36] Within four years of the act, over fifty certified reformatory institutions came into existence, and the concept of specialized treatment for the child criminal was firmly established.

Whig versions of history provide one way of understanding the process of change outlined above: we move from the dark ages of the eighteenth century, where there is no thought of differentiation, to the moral enlightenment of nineteenth-century reform, with its emphasis on the particular, and its deployment of legislation to institutionalize its classifications.[37] Other interpretations are, of course, possible. Susan Magarey, for instance, argues persuasively that Peel's reform of the penal code helped to "legislate into existence" the problem of the child criminal:

> His stated aim was merely "to look at all the offences which are now punishable by death, [and] to select those . . . which can be safely visited with a mitigated Punishment." He cannot be described as the deliberate inventor of juvenile delinquency. But his statutes did extend to certain previously only casually or domestically regulated behaviour of the young, all the means of state coercion provided by the criminal justice system.[38]

Wishing to give this kind of explanation its due, I am more especially interested in asking how factors like the legislative or the demographic are aided and abetted in their creation of the juvenile delinquent by the newly forming consciousness of what childhood should be. Mary Carpenter's oft-repeated statement to the Select Committee on Criminal and Destitute Juveniles in 1852 that "children should not be dealt with as men but as children" would have had little or no meaning before 1770, for without communal agreement about the meaning of the concept of "children," the utterance founders in tautology.[39] Within the span of Wordsworth's life, however, the idea of childhood gains recognizable form, drawing its strength and its meanings from a variety of sources. Foremost amongst these meanings, I argue, are the sentiments of the *Ode*, particularly when they are perceived as alternative expressions of Holy Writ. Abstracted from the poem, the belief that the child has but recently come to us from the hand of God carries an inescapable double edge: it both promotes the reformers' zeal, for surely there is a sacred and moral imperative to preserve the heaven that lies around all human beings in their infancy, and it gives rise to a punishingly high expectation of children's behavior.[40]

The latter effect creates a powerful paradox that resounds in the discourse of juvenile delinquency in the mid-nineteenth century: children who do not behave as children should behave are not children. "Can these be children?" is the Reverend Micah Hill's repeated question in his prize-winning essay on juvenile delinquency, while Mary Carpenter maintains that only by abstracting young offenders from their habitual environments might they be "gradually restored to the true position of childhood."[41] Matthew Davenport Hill's description of the typical junior criminal lays stress upon his precocious unnaturalness:

> [He] is a little stunted man already—he knows much and a great deal too much of what is called life—he can take care of his own immediate interests. He is self-reliant, he has so long directed or mis-directed his own actions and has so little trust in those about him, that he submits to no control and asks for no protection. He has consequently much to unlearn—he has to be turned again into a child.[42]

The child criminal is a freak of nature, a toddling anomaly: for a commentator in 1851, he is a "hideous antithesis, an infant in age, a man in shrewdness and vice, [bearing] the face of a child with no trace of childish goodness."[43] Evidently there is no room for shades of gray, for degrees of naughtiness along an incremental scale, in this highly prescriptive conception of child behavior. The absolute division of adult and child, achieved not only in penology but in a range of practices and discourses, results in no less rigidity within the new category of the child, which can only countenance the true child of innocence and purity, and the "not-child," the juvenile delinquent. The construction of the ideal inevitably spawns its demonized opposite. It is not difficult to assign class labels to the two positions; Davenport Hill's implicit horror of the self-reliant lad in the quotation above shows how intrinsic to his conception of childhood is the dependency of the protected upper- or middle-class child. Nor, and more importantly for my continuing argument, is it hard to see how the poles can be hopelessly gendered. In the reformers' polemics, as indeed these brief examples have already shown, the child criminal is almost always male, the "little man," the Artful Dodger of popular renown. While the number of girls committed to prison during this period was far smaller than the number of boys, the young female offender did nevertheless exist. The paucity of information about the condition and behavior of imprisoned girls, however, is only exceeded by the infrequency of their appearance in the discourse of juvenile delinquency.[44] To all intents and purposes, then, the transgressive child is male. Does it inevitably follow that the ideal child is always a girl?

This brief investigation of the history of the juvenile criminal demonstrates how general ideas about the nature of childhood were evolving in the period between 1770 and 1850 and reveals how strongly these concepts relied on divisions between adult and child, corruption and innocence, and, ultimately, male and female. This particular historical trajectory may now be left behind to look at the role played by gender in the evocations of the child, first within Wordsworth's poetry, and ultimately in De Quincey's prose. There can be little doubt that the poet represents his younger self in *The Prelude* as the little boy he actually had been: there, in all the clarity of bright sunlight, making "one long bathing of a summer's day" stands a "five years' child, / A naked boy" (1.294, 291–92). The gender identity of childhood in the *Ode* comes not in utter nakedness, but veiled in those trailing clouds. True, our attention is continually drawn to the masculine, from the "happy Shepherd-boy" to "the Babe [who] leaps up on his Mother's arm" and "the Child among his new-born blisses" (ll. 35, 49, 86), while we look in vain for girls in this poem. Their exclusion, however, is not accidental. Wordsworth focuses upon the sex whose life's journey supports his thesis: it is man's gradually increasing consciousness of the progressive deterioration of his powers that gives the sole proof that things were not always thus. The Child may well be Father of the Man, as the *Ode*'s epigraph from "My Heart Leaps Up" would have it, but an awful lot of patrimony goes missing along the way. The masculine life span, the passage from babe to child, to boy, to youth, to man, illustrates the incremental process of loss. Heaven-scented infancy, the concept that enraptured the Victorian reader, is pitifully brief for the male: Wordsworth shows us that the "six years' Darling of a pigmy size" playing with "some little plan or chart," improvising some public ritual, "A wedding or a festival / A mourning or a funeral," is already beginning to "provoke / The years to bring the inevitable yoke" (ll. 87, 91, 94–95, 124–25). "Dialogues of business, love, or strife" (l. 99) follow in strict succession, widening the social sphere that will paradoxically cage the grown boy in the prison of his own adulthood.

Would examination of the course of a feminine life have served Wordsworth's purpose in the same fashion? Reference to the poet's most celebrated works on the girl suggests not: the tendency for the feminine to represent arrested, or at the least, lagged development in Wordsworth's oeuvre means that girls' relationship to the glory of childhood is not seen through the diminishing lens of loss.[45] On the contrary, Wordsworth's girls stay much closer to the source of heavenly light than his boys, and consequently they more easily embody the spirit of childhood innocence propagated by poems like the *Ode*. This privileged position has its drawbacks: given that childhood is constructed as a completely separate period, imbued with celestial radiance, it shows unmistakable similarities to Christian images of death. Unlike the conception of childhood in *The Prelude* that breathes vitality and potentiality, the glorious stasis of infancy in this alternative construction has literally nowhere to grow and thus finds its most complete representation in the little girl who dies young. Figures like the Winander boy, the Danish boy, and the little lad in book 7 of *The Prelude*, whom Wordsworth wished to see embalmed in his immaculate infancy, remind us that the poet is not operating under the dictates of any dogmatic system of gender attribution, but girls are repeatedly shown to have a special relationship with the essentially nostalgic conception of childhood perfection celebrated by the *Ode*. Lucy Gray cuts an emblematic figure: reaching the center of the wooden bridge, and no further, she is literally frozen in time, forever "a living Child" tripping upon the lonesome Wild. Although mortality is dispiritingly present in Wordsworth's source story for this poem ("The body however was found in the canal"), "Lucy Gray" replaces the child's death with her eternal existence in the state of childhood.[46] It is a sleight of hand that would raise no worries in the mind of another of Wordsworth's famous girls, the intransigent little maid of "We Are Seven." Girls in Wordsworth's work defy the ordinary mechanics of temporal succession, existing in an ideal childhood worlds away from the prison-house gloom.

Wordsworth's sister Dorothy demands attention in any analysis of the poet's depiction of girlhood. A mere twenty months younger than her brother, Dorothy nevertheless is drafted into service as the representative of an earlier state of Wordsworth's life. Consequently, in "Lines Written above Tintern Abbey," when the poet's attention finally turns to his hitherto unacknowledged companion on the riverbank, it is to celebrate his sister's existence as some kind of time-delayed doppelgänger:

. . . in thy voice I catch
The language of my former heart, and read

My former pleasures in the shooting lights
Of thy wild eyes. Oh! yet a little while
May I behold in thee what I was once,
My dear, dear Sister!

(ll. 116–21)

Although Wordsworth does not preclude the possibility of further development for Dorothy ("in after years . . . these wild ecstasies shall be matured / Into a sober pleasure" [ll. 137–39]), it is implied that she will always be a few steps behind her brother's progress. In *The Prelude*, the tendency to identify Dorothy with images of beginning creates the impression that she enjoys an extended residence in the earlier phases of life, in the time of childhood; she is "a kind of gentler spring" (13.245), "another morn / Risen on mid-noon" (6.212–13). Even in this poem, where, as we have seen, the poet has ample congress with the boy he once was, the presence of Dorothy as a living embodiment of the spirit of childhood plays a crucial part in maintaining what Wordsworth describes as "a saving intercourse / With my true self" (10.914–15).

If Dorothy's appearances are thus infused with a sense of her lagged development, then the idea of her complete arrest was responsible, at least in Coleridge's mind, for the creation of another important female figure, Lucy. When he read "A Slumber Did My Spirit Seal," one of the four or five poems now known as the Lucy poems, his explanation of the genesis of this "most sublime Epitaph" was that "most probably, in some gloomier moment [Wordsworth] had fancied the moment in which his Sister might die."[47] Whether or not we give credence to this theory, this collection of lyrics offers another perspective on gender and childhood in Wordsworth's work. It is hard to be precise about the age that Lucy reaches before she is so unkindly cut off—"Three years she grew in sun and shower" would seem to insist that she gains sufficient maturity to be "Nature's Lady," while "Strange Fits of Passion I Have Known" needs her old enough to be the speaker's beloved. Nevertheless, it is clear that both before and after death, Lucy participates in a relationship with nature that closely approximates the undifferentiated unity of self and landscape enjoyed, albeit as a compensation for the loss of earlier glories, by the child of the *Ode*. Commenting to Isabella Fenwick on the lines about "Obstinate questionings / Of sense and outward things" (*Ode*, ll. 142–43), Wordsworth explained that he intended to represent his inability in childhood to draw lines of distinction between inner and outer:

I was often unable to think of external things as having external existence, and I communed with all that I saw as something not apart from, but inherent in, my own immaterial nature. Many times while going to school have I grasped at a wall or tree to recall myself from this abyss of idealism to the reality.[48]

In dispelling the illusion of the continuity between the self and the world, the rough texture of that hastily touched wall is a sure harbinger of those other walls waiting to cast their punitive shadows: stone divides the boy from "that imperial palace whence he came" (*Ode*, l. 85). Lucy's experience is quite otherwise. Alive, she can barely be distinguished from nature's other productions: she is a "Violet by a mossy stone," and hers is "the silence and the calm / Of mute insensate things."[49] The grave brings "difference" to (or, more obviously, *from*) the speaker, but not, it seems, to Lucy, whose contact with uncompromising wood and stone reveals not her separateness from nature, but her unity with it:

> She neither hears nor sees
>   Roll'd round in earth's diurnal course
> With rocks and stones and trees![50]

Throughout Wordsworth's early and best-known work the idea of childhood proposed by the *Ode* finds its most apt embodiment in the figure of the dead girl, for her sealed sweetness ensures the desired insularity and immutability of glorious infancy. By the end of 1812, however, the poet had experienced the death of children in far more devastating form: Catharine, his second daughter, died at the age of three years in June, and barely six months later he lost six-year-old Thomas, his second son. "It is the fact, though not easy to explain," Mary Moorman has commented, "that Wordsworth wrote poems about his two daughters,[51] but not about any of his three sons, not even about the treasured second boy . . . whose death . . . was a well-nigh unbearable blow to him (except the little epitaph, 'Six months to six years added,' which, according to Mary Wordsworth, 'it took him years to produce')."[52]

It would be presumptuous to suggest that Wordsworth's ability to write about Catharine's death reveals any difference in the degree of his pain, nor have we any clue that it mattered more or less to him than his son's death, but certain tendencies of thought are unveiled by the artist's reimagining of autobiographical material. "Maternal Grief" presents us with a fascinating case in point. Describing the work as "in part an overflow from the Solitary's description of his own and his wife's feelings upon the decease of their children" (*Excursion*, 3.636–79), Wordsworth added "*for private notice only*" that "it faithfully set forth my wife's feeling and habits after the loss of our two children within half a year of each other" (4:477n). Despite this explicit biographical referent, the poem recasts the three-year-old and the six-year-old as twin sister and brother, and then allots death only to the "lovely Girl." "Maternal Grief" conveys a resigned sense of the inevitability of the loss, for the *Ode*-like evocation of the child's residence on earth cannot help but focus our minds on the similarities between the residue of preexistence and the afterlife:

> The Child she mourned had overstepped the pale
> Of Infancy, but still did breathe the air
> That sanctifies its confines, and partook
> Reflected beams of that celestial light
> To all the Little-ones on sinful earth
> Not unvouchsafed.

(ll. 14–19)

The closing lines of Wordsworth's more famous—and considerably more powerful—effusion on Catharine's death, the sonnet "Surprised by Joy," tell us that "neither present time, nor years unborn / Could to my sight that heavenly face restore" (ll. 13–14). Once again, the girl is seen as heavenly while she is still alive, and although her passing is the "most grievous loss," "the worst pang that sorrow ever bore" (ll. 9, 10), we are struck by the possibility that her death causes not the rupture, but the continuation, of the childish sweetness of her life.

The death of Catharine Wordsworth is commemorated not only in her father's poetry, but also in the writings of Thomas De Quincey.[53] Fifteen years the poet's junior, De Quincey first wrote to Wordsworth in 1803, declaring himself to be a passionate devotee of his poetry, and then came to take up a tentative place in the Lakeland literary circle some four years later. De Quincey's perception of childhood forms a bridge between Wordsworthian and Victorian conceptions and helps us to understand more fully the far-reaching implications of the *Ode*'s celebrity, and the installation of the ideal feminized child in popular consciousness. The intellectual debt that De Quincey owed to Wordsworth, particularly on the subject of the relation of childhood to man's subsequent development, is enormous, but the prose writer's points of departure from the poet are of considerable significance. As we have seen, Wordsworth's oeuvre sets forth two important constructions of childhood, the "boyish" model of the long-suppressed *Prelude*, and the *Ode*'s conception of an idealized innocence, which finds embodiment in little girls of otherworldly purity.

Although Dorothy has claims to represent an aspect of the poet's younger self, Wordsworth primarily depicts himself in childhood as the boy he actually was. The poet, then, uses little girls to epitomize certain ideas about childhood that are not necessarily autobiographical. De Quincey takes a different course, becoming in the process an early advocate of a developmental myth that reaches far into the Victorian psyche. Making wholesale appropriation of the *Ode*'s account of heavenly infancy and all its feminized accretions, the younger writer applies this model to his own life, even though the move necessarily entails a gender crossing. It is in this context that we must place his seemingly extravagant reaction to Catharine ("Kate") Wordsworth's death: at the age of twenty-six, De Quincey not only experiences the loss of a beloved child and a representative of the transient loveliness of infancy, but feels himself thrown headlong into a reenactment of the loss of his own childhood.[54]

Two days after De Quincey had received the news of Kate's death from Dorothy Wordsworth, he wrote his second letter of condolence to her, dwelling with embarrassing fervor on the special relationship that had existed between him and this three-year-old girl:

> My greatest consolation is that she must have lived a most happy life. . . .
> Oh what a thought of comfort it is also that I was one of those who added to her happiness. What tender what happy hours we passed together! Many a time, when we were alone, she would put her sweet arms about my neck and kiss me with a transport that was even then quite affecting to me. Nobody can judge from her manner to me before others what love she shewed to me when we were playing or talking together alone. On the night when she slept with me in the winter, we lay awake all the middle of the night—and talked oh how tenderly together: When we fell asleep, she was lying in my arms; once or twice I awoke from the pressure of her dear body; but I could not find in my heart to disturb her. Many times on that night— when she was murmuring out tender sounds of endearment, she would lock her little arms with such passionateness round my neck—as if she had known that it was to be the last night we were to pass together. Ah pretty pretty love, would God I might have seen thy face and kissed thy dear lips again![55]

To the Wordsworths and their circle, De Quincey's uncontrolled arrogation of the privilege of chief mourner was distasteful and inappropriate. "Mr De Quincey burst into tears on seeing Wordsworth and seemed to be more affected than the father," noted Henry Crabb Robinson, who met the two men on the day that the news had broken. Wordsworth's expressions of grief, Robinson felt, "became a man both of feeling and strength of mind"; the younger man's "sensibility," on the other hand, although he had "no doubt" about its genuineness, seemed to him "in danger of being mistaken for a puling and womanly weakness."[56]

De Quincey's excessive response to Kate's death was fueled by a variety of emotions: certainly he had lost his greatest and only uncritical ally in his uneasy relationship with the prickly Wordsworth clan, a connection that always meant far more to him than it did to them. This explanation alone, however, cannot even begin to account for his sustained evocation of that night of passionate tenderness in his letter to Dorothy. Furthermore, whatever understanding we might have of this narrative is complicated by the knowledge that as soon as he was back in the Lake District, De Quincey repeatedly restaged the nocturnal embrace, now with the cold stone of Kate's final resting place:

> I returned hastily to Grasmere; stretched myself every night, for more than two months running, upon her grave; not (as may readily be supposed) in any parade of grief; on the contrary, in that quiet valley of simple shepherds, I was secure enough from observation until morning light began to return; but in mere intensity of sick frantic yearning after neighbourhood to the darling of my heart.[57]

This revelation appears in the last of a series of four essays entitled "Society of the Lakes," which was published in 1840. The reasons that De Quincey gives in the piece for his transport of grief are both inconclusive and mutually unsupportive. On the one hand, he explains that he had always viewed Kate "as an impersonation of the dawn and the spirit of infancy," and that this way of seeing her, combined with the accident of her death occurring at dawn in early summer, "recoiled so violently into a contrast or polar antithesis to the image of death that each exalted and brightened the other" (2:443). His alternative rationale for his behavior provides the essay with a jarringly fanciful conclusion. His fitful classical pedantry coming to the fore, De Quincey claims that he must have been suffering from "the old Pagan superstition of a nympholepsy" (2:445), that is, the heartsickness of a mortal man in hopeless love with a nymph. What De Quincey does not do, however, is comment upon the obvious similarities between the death of Kate Wordsworth and the "tragedy" of his own infancy, the death of his beloved sister Elizabeth.[58] It is through the lens of this earlier event that I wish to scrutinize the intensity of desire for physical contact with the lovely lost girl.

Like Wordsworth's daughter, Elizabeth had a "sweet childish figure," an "angel face," and "heavenly lips," and she died at dawn in early summer.[59] And in the same way that De Quincey spoke to Dorothy Wordsworth of the passionate attachment between Kate and himself only *after* the child had died, he can tell us of the "beauty and power" of his sister only from the vantage point of her loss. We are introduced to Elizabeth in "The Affliction of Childhood," the first chapter of the *Autobiographic Sketches*, learning that she died young before we know anything about her life.[60] Indeed, until we discover that Elizabeth's death is the cause of the "Affliction," we could almost imagine, were it not a logical impossibility, that we are reading of our author's own early death. The chapter's opening paragraph, the very beginning of this version of De Quincey's autobiography, is an announcement of that life's premature conclusion:

> About the close of my sixth year, suddenly the first chapter of my life came to a violent termination; that chapter which, even within the gates of recovered paradise, might merit a remembrance. "*Life is finished!*" was the secret misgiving of my heart; for the heart of infancy is as apprehensive as that of maturest wisdom in relation to any capital wound inflicted on the happiness. "*Life is finished! Finished it is!*" was the hidden meaning that, half unconsciously to myself, lurked within my sighs; and, as bells heard from a distance on a summer evening seem charged at times with an articulate form of words, some monitory message, that rolls round unceasingly, even so for me some noiseless and subterraneous voice seemed to chant continually a secret word, made audible only to my heart—that "now is the blossoming of life withered forever." (1:28)

Our knowledge of this sudden and cruel rupture is thus established immediately and necessarily haunts our subsequent reading of De Quincey's evocation of the anterior historical period of his childhood. As the chapter develops, it becomes apparent that the reader's experience is analogous to that of the young De Quincey: only in the unpleasantness of his post-lapsarian world does the child realize that he previously existed in a state of bliss. Paradisiacal infancy, "such a peace, so unvexed by storms, or the fear of storms" (1:29), is therefore described primarily by contrasting it to the events that ended it, and succeeded it. Little wonder, then, that such enormous emphasis should be placed on the rupture itself, for it both severs and creates, granting definition to an otherwise unrepresentable eventless happiness. The moment of loss turns out to be the most enjoyable moment of finding: De Quincey's express desire in "The Affliction

of Childhood" is not that Elizabeth might live again, but that "the parting
. . . should have lasted for ever" (1:42). Without the decisive break, De
Quincey would have no means of access to his lost paradise: "Were it not
in the bitter corrosion of heart that I was called upon to face, I should
have carried over to the present no connecting link whatever from the
past" (1:55).

Through the frame of his sister's death, De Quincey sets about the retrospective fashioning of his heavenly infancy. The fact that this account is
suffused in biblical language and relies heavily on the Christian myth of
the Fall is hardly surprising, given the deeply religious nature of De
Quincey's upbringing: more notable, perhaps, is the exclusion, to all intents and purposes, of any references to his mother, a stern Evangelical
with distinctly Calvinist leanings.[61] Although De Quincey's faith remained
strong throughout his life, his rejection of his mother's doctrines is implicit in his construction of a childhood utterly untainted by original sin.
As has already been discussed, such a course was by no means unusual in
this period, and neither was De Quincey' s application of key religious
tropes to his own personal history. The exact configuration of these
tropes, however, does demand particular attention, for De Quincey's insistence on the innocent femininity of the Garden of Eden has important
ramifications.

Elizabeth plays the central role in De Quincey's narrative. Nine years
old at the time of her demise, and three years De Quincey's senior, she is
primarily represented for us as the mirror image of her brother, "having
that capacious heart overflowing, even as mine overflowed, with tenderness, and stung, even as mine was stung, by the necessity of being loved"
(1:36).[62] The eldest of the four De Quincey children then living at home,
Elizabeth is made synonymous with "the peace, the rest, the central security which belongs to love that is past all understanding" and that, according to the writer, characterized his early childhood (1:29). Giving
profound thanks to Providence that his "infant feelings were moulded by
the gentlest of sisters, not by horrid pugilistic brothers" (1:32), De
Quincey takes pains to represent his complete emotional and physical
absorption in an essentially feminine realm, which found him "with three
innocent little sisters for playmates, sleeping always amongst them and
shut up forever in a silent garden from all knowledge of poverty, or op-
pression, or outrage" (1:34).[63] When Elizabeth's death is brought into this
garden, De Quincey is forced to recognize the general fact of mortality,
and also finds himself expelled from a feminine Eden of loving connections. For De Quincey, the ending of union with his sister brings about

an understanding of the self as both finite and separate. In the meditation on solitude that follows the description of Elizabeth's funeral, the child's awareness of death is expressed in the same breath as his understanding of division from a nurturing female: "Even a little child has a dread, whispering consciousness, that, if he should be summoned to travel into God's presence, no gentle nurse will be allowed to lead him by the hand, nor mother to carry him in her arms, nor little sister to share his trepidations" (1:48). The era that succeeds this first epoch is defined not by girlish empathy, but by fraternal combat. In the ominously titled "Introduction to the World of Strife," the young De Quincey's peaceful coexistence is ruthlessly replaced by the violent rule of his brother William, the eldest son. William creates a realm of masculine competition, forcing the reluctant young Thomas to join him in his fights with working boys from the mill, and to war against him in the continual conflicts of their two imaginary kingdoms, Gombroon and Tigrosylvania. Even the swiftness of William's taking off (he is sent away to school, where he dies of typhus fever) does not interrupt the inexorable roll of this education of antagonism: "The World of Strife" is immediately succeeded by "The Warfare of a Public School," and a pattern of an unlooked-for and undesired male rivalry is set for life.

De Quincey's autobiographical writings, then, present us with a life with a marked bipartite structure: an initial period of feminine happiness comes to an abrupt and definite end and is succeeded by a harsh and competitive masculine world. While he does not claim explicitly that all men undergo this two-part drama, neither does De Quincey appear to consider his own experience idiosyncratic (at least in this particular respect). Consider the implication of these comments, which are ostensibly about the education of the upper class:

> [A]t nine or ten the masculine energies are beginning to develop themselves; or, if not, no discipline will better aid in their development than the bracing intercourse of a great English classical school . . . the effeminate [are there forced] into conforming to a rule of manliness. (1:151)

Male children, we can then infer, do not become truly masculine until a fairly advanced age (though not, it should be noted, a sufficiently advanced age to make us suspect that De Quincey is talking about puberty). "Effeminacy" is primary, while the masculine character of the later phase is the secondary phenomenon, and so far from innate that it sometimes must be fostered by societal pressure. Proof that De Quincey regards the

40

transition from original femininity to enforced masculinity as violent and absolute appears elsewhere in his writings. Pondering once again the early life experience of boys of his class, De Quincey gravely tells us in "Levana and Our Ladies of Sorrow" that the public school system exacts a terrible toll of human life:

> The rules of Eton require that a boy on the foundation should be there twelve years: he is superannuated at eighteen, consequently he must come at six. Children torn away from their mothers and sisters at that age not unfrequently die. (13:363)

The melodrama of De Quincey's utterance is clearly informed by his belief that one phase of his existence was definitively terminated at the age of six, the year when he was permanently deprived of his reflection in the "familiar eye" of sister Elizabeth.[64] Nevertheless, the quotation also bears witness to De Quincey's conviction that his own experience was neither unusual, nor as extreme as it might have been.

The theoretical ramifications of De Quincey's apparent belief in the existence of a primary feminine phase of infancy in the male life-span place him in both agreement and contradiction with his master, Wordsworth. De Quincey's assertion that "not . . . all which pre-exists in the child finds its development in the man" (1:121) is at one with the *Ode*'s melancholy insistence that adulthood is a contracted version of childhood's plenitude; the same cannot be said, however, of his parallel claim that the mind has absolute access to the richness of infancy. Primarily through the agency of opium and its trances, visions and dreams, De Quincey discovers what he is convinced is a general human truth, that "there is no such thing as *ultimate* forgetting" (3:437), for the mind is the site of the constant and continuous presence of each moment of an individual's life. Here De Quincey is evidently far more in tune with *The Prelude*'s governing philosophy, even though that poem's vital little boy, energetically displaying his moral complexity and potential for growth and action, has no place in the *Autobiographic Sketches*.[65] Wordsworth's ability to reimmerse himself in the feelings of his childhood, we remember, was wholly underwritten by his declarations of a continuum between the boy who experienced and the man who remembers. The gender shift in De Quincey's account, however, renders any such notion of continuity untenable, and the prose writer has recourse instead to a seemingly incoherent amalgam of Wordsworth's models. Insisting both on the "sealed and settled" loveliness of his feminine childhood (3:315), and on his abil-

41

ity to remember and recapture its exact sensations, De Quincey must construct images of his infancy that are simultaneously absolutely lost, and yet fully, and concretely, realized.

One such construction is the lost city of Savannah-La-Mar. While De Quincey is generally fond of employing archaeological metaphors to talk of the history of the self (consider "in these incidents of my early life is found the entire sub-stratum" from the 1856 revision of the *Confessions of an English Opium Eater* [3:233]), this short piece from *Suspiria de Profundis* refutes the assumption of the essential interconnection of historically distinct stages. Instead of digging through the overlaid strata of civilizations to discover the outlines of the primal city, De Quincey portrays himself as one who "in dreams" "cleave[s] the watery veil" of the ocean to visit a lost world, cast down in its entirety by an earthquake to a "submarine asylum sacred from the storms that torment our upper air" (13:360). The import of this short essay, De Quincey would have us believe, is the justification it offers for the necessity of tragedy in the life of a community, and in the life of man: "[U]pon a night of earthquake [God] builds a thousand years of pleasant habitations for man. Upon the sorrow of an infant He raises oftentimes from human intellects glorious vintages that could not else have been" (13:361). I would argue, however, that the image of the submerged crystalline city works toward quite another end. "Savannah-La-Mar" exhibits a hermetically sealed idyll, the site not for a developing psyche, but a place that will never know change or progress or the events of adult life, yet is fully material, and complete in all its details:

> We looked into the belfries, where the pendulous bells were waiting in vain for the summons which should awaken their marriage peals; together we touched the mighty organ keys, that sang no jubilates for the ear of heaven, that sang no requiems for the ear of human sorrow; together we searched the silent nurseries, where the children were all asleep, and had been asleep through five generations. (13:360)

In the context of his oeuvre, "Savannah-La-Mar" is unique, an unusual solution to De Quincey's problem of finding tangible representation for an immaterial concept. With far more frequency do we encounter the most obvious and most satisfying embodiment of his past life: this is the figure of a young girl, who is repeatedly co-opted into the crucially constructive drama of De Quincey's separation from infancy. Scattered throughout his writings are girls whose absence is of far greater moment to De Quincey than their brief presence in his life. A typical history runs as follows: a young girl is thrown into association with our hero, discovers that her tribulations and adversities, not to mention the depth and sincerity of her feelings, exactly match those of her newfound friend, and the two find temporary solace in each other's company. De Quincey's identification with this female counterpart allows him to draw out the pathos of his own situation without appearing unduly self-indulgent, but all too soon, the sister-self is swept away into oblivion, forever beyond his attempted rescue.

Most famously this is the career of Ann, the pathetic sixteen-year-old streetwalker of the *Confessions*. In this instance, however, De Quincey must overcome considerable obstacles to present the friend from his days as a teenaged runaway in the desired form. To be precise, he must erase the traces both of her sexuality and its potential criminality, and of her maternal care. Evidently keen to show off his open-mindedness by talking frankly of the friendships he contracted with members of "that unhappy class who subsist on the wages of prostitution" when he too was a "walker of the streets," De Quincey nevertheless gives no direct representation of the overtly sexual nature of Ann's trade and repeatedly talks of her as a brutalized, rather than a soiled, figure (3:359, 360). Moreover, far from seeing her as a possible defendant up on a charge of solicitation, De Quincey takes pains to explain that Ann is the victim of a "ruffian who had plundered her little property," one who should by rights "lay her complaint before a magistrate" (3:361). Similarly, although he places a fair amount of emphasis upon the fact that she nurtures him to the point of restoring his life when he faints from hunger, De Quincey has no wish to expatiate on Ann's maternal qualities. Quick to acknowledge that to her "bounty and compassion . . . I owe it that I am at this time alive," De Quincey avoids the concept of Ann as a mother and instead re-creates her as a sibling: "[S]etting aside gratitude, which in any case must have made me her debtor for life, I loved her as affectionately as if she had been my sister" (3:360, 367). In this way De Quincey divests Ann of any characteristics that would interfere with his compulsion to present her as his mirror image, and is thus able to re-create the central security of the home of infancy on the callous streets of London.

This state of affairs, however, exists for a very short time: De Quincey leaves the city on a brief trip to gain security for a loan and on his return seeks in vain to find the friend who had been "overcome by sorrow" at their supposedly temporary farewell (3:367). Just as the desired state of union with sister Elizabeth was figured in the wish that "the parting [might] last for ever," so De Quincey's representation of his relationship with Ann celebrates not their time together, but the experience of severance (1:42). Laboriously detailing the endless inquiries and investigations, the glances at "many myriads of female faces, in the hope" of finding her, De Quincey imagines his connection to the girl to be a continuous near-miss (3:375). The young prostitute is consigned to a perpetual place of nonmeeting, where she is neither dead nor present, but forever being lost: "If she had lived, doubtless we must have been sometimes in search of each other, at the very same moment, through the mighty labyrinths of London, perhaps even within a few feet of each other—a barrier no wider in a London street, often amounting in the end to a separation for eternity!" (3:375).

De Quincey's writings furnish many other examples of the beloved lost girl who is intimately implicated in his self-representation. In the *Confessions* alone we find not only Ann but also the author's self-proclaimed "partner in wretchedness," the miserable little waif in the lawyer's house (3:359). (This "poor, friendless child" was to reappear, it would seem, as the Marchioness in Dickens's *Old Curiosity Shop*, but never, like the prostitute, in real life, despite equally exhaustive searches [3:354].) Furthermore, this repeated doubling of De Quincey and his feminine alter ego accounts for the preponderance of twin sisters in essays and stories that bear less obvious autobiographical motivations. The girl who dreams of the "sweet twin-born sister with whom from infant days hand in hand she had wandered" in "The Daughter of Lebanon" invokes for De Quincey the imaginary configuration of his own childhood, as does the suffering young woman of "Memorial Suspiria," pining for "her dear, loving twin-sister, that for eighteen years read and wrote, thought and sang, slept and breathed, with the dividing-door open for ever between their bed-rooms, and never once a separation between their hearts" (3:454, 13:354). Profoundly absent, yet with the coherent outline of a human (although hardly an individualized) being, all of these girls represent the lost sister, herself the representative of De Quincey's lost and perfect feminine past. The young man's reaction to the death of little Kate Wordsworth can best be understood in relation to the complex and contradictory desires that inform this cherished fantasy of development. Some four or five days after Kate's irrevocable demise, the "memory" of the "pressure" of her "dear body," the embrace of those "sweet arms," the touch of those "dear lips," is given form in the letter to Dorothy. The histrionics on her grave, the "sick frantic yearning after neighbourhood to the darling of my heart," repeat in macabre fashion this retrospective desire for the child's material presence. De Quincey's own girlhood must be both lost to eternity and solid in its embodiment: once she has gone, Kate's physical being is unbearably precious.

When De Quincey wrote "The Affliction of Childhood," he was nearly sixty, living in a small cottage seven miles outside Edinburgh under the care of his three daughters, two of whom were to be with him at his death in 1859. The last fourteen years of his life, spent chiefly in the cottage or in lodgings in the city, were probably the most stable period of De Quincey's tempestuous existence, which had been rocked by the violent tides of life-long opium addiction and no less chronic insolvency. In comparison to "the peace, the rest, the central security" of his idealized childhood, De Quincey's adulthood had been figuratively, and on one occasion, literally, a time of imprisonment. Completely unable to manage his finances and stalked by importunate creditors since his early thirties, De Quincey finally landed in the Canongate Tolbooth, Scott's Heart of Mid-Lothian, in 1832. Although his stay was brief, thanks to a "sick bill" that excused him on the grounds of ill health, the rest of this decade was punctuated by similar crises, and, according to the peculiarities of Scottish law, De Quincey was "put to the horn," and thus liable to imprisonment, on eight further occasions.[66] To evade penal incarceration, De Quincey spent much of his time in hiding or in the debtors' sanctuary at the Palace of Holy-roodhouse. Here his contact with the outside world was limited to Holy-rood's authorized Sunday sallies, and to the clandestine intermediary missions of his children, who were employed in delivering manuscripts and fetching money for the hapless head of the family. "My Father always liked best to have his girls about him," recalled his second eldest daughter Florence. "On me fell the main burden and I know the north and south-backs of the Canongate, George the Fourth Bridge, the cross causeway & c as hideous dreams, my heart rushing into my mouth with the natural terrors of footsteps approaching and rushing down again into my shoes when left to quiet and the ghosts."[67] Ludicrously ill-equipped to handle the responsibilities of his own adulthood, let alone the needs of his large and remarkably long-suffering family, De Quincey retreated in his memoirs to the evocation of a time of paradisiacal calm. Seemingly unaware of the nightmare existence of his own little daughter ("I am sure I never told him what I suffered"),[68] De Quincey focused upon what was for him the absolute obverse of his beleaguered maturity, the figure of the girl, arrested for all time in her childish loveliness.

The Ideal Girl in Industrial England

WILLIAM POWELL FRITH'S PAINTING *Many Happy Returns of the Day* (fig. 1) invites us into the home of a prosperous middle-class family to celebrate the birthday of a daughter of the house.[1] The little girl—five years old?—is decked with ribbons and flowers and placed dead center in the scene, encircled by an overlarge, halolike wreath. Despite the child's centrality, the eyes of her family are not upon her, and she herself looks somewhat apprehensively over to her left. Seven family members, primarily the other children, are busy eating or drinking, or helping others to drinks, presumably in preparation for a toast. The paterfamilias at the head of the table raises his glass, supported by the close attention of the four women—his mother, his wife, a sister or grown-up daughter, and a servant—on the other side of the room. Ignoring their rapt observation, the father looks away from the festivities of the table to his own father, who sits at a remove, oblivious both of the newspaper on his lap and the party to his right.

When John Ruskin wrote about this painting, he focused exclusively upon its literal center, praising the brushwork on the leaves of the garland for signs of "advancing Pre-Raphaelitism," and worrying that the "fair little child" had "too many and too kind friends" and thus was in "great danger of being toasted, toyed, and wreathed into selfishness and misery."[2] The play of glances (not least the child's own side-swept eyes) that can be so readily discerned in this picture, however, argues for quite a different kind of analysis. While the little girl's birthday is the occasion for the celebration, the women's adoring and reverential regard shifts the attention to the individual whose efforts have created the party's necessary underpinnings. The atmosphere of plenitude in this well-insulated nest of domestic comfort both conceals and confirms the activities of the working world outside: the mark of the father's success in the marketplace is that there is no trace of the marketplace in the family circle. No acknowledgment of this wave of feminine homage is made in the father's eyes, however: the object of his loving scrutiny is the grandfather. If the head of the family has temporarily absented himself from his day-to-day commercial activities to preside over this family anniversary, the older man, it seems, has left the world of the present altogether. The daily news is as nothing

FIGURE 1. William Powell Frith, *Many Happy Returns of the Day* (1856). (Harrogate Museums and Art Gallery, North Yorkshire, UK/Bridgeman Art Library.)

to him; the circumstance of his granddaughter's birthday does not cause the old man to focus upon the girl, but takes his gaze to a place that has no apparent location in the picture before us. Unheeding of the present moment and perhaps not far from death, the grandfather, we conclude, is cast back upon his own long-lost past: the "many happy returns" of the title figure less as a hope of future felicity for the girl at the painting's heart than as a description of the old man's ability to recapture the days of his own early life. The little girl, then, seemingly the center of the painting's meaning, is actually playing a facilitating role for the two men in the picture. Snug in bourgeois opulence, she defines the protected and secure home that is the measure of her father's achievements in the public sphere. She also epitomizes a place of safety for her grandfather, but in this instance, the haven exists at a temporal, rather than a spatial, remove from present concerns: the celebration of her youth triggers his ability to re-imagine his own distant childhood. The little girl is the key to male security in both the contemporary and the retrospective moment.

47

Displayed at the Royal Academy's exhibition in 1856, *Many Happy Returns of the Day* was by no means the only picture there that placed little girls at the center of things. John Everett Millais alone exhibited three important paintings that focused upon the figures of girls: *L'Enfant du Regiment*, *The Blind Girl*, and *Autumn Leaves* (fig. 2).[3] This last-named work, which depicts four young girls in a twilit rural scene, forms an interesting complement to Frith's picture. The two paintings undoubtedly operate in different registers: in *Many Happy Returns* we are doubly confined within a cluttered domestic space and the exclusive preserve of the middle class. Millais's open-air grouping presents us with two well-to-do girls, solidly respectable in their dresses of dark green linsey-woolsey, and two children from the working class, the older girl in rough brown cotton, and the younger in a coarse and bulky gown. Although only the two middle-class girls (actually the sisters of the artist's wife Effie, the erstwhile Mrs. Ruskin) meet our gaze, all of the children are united in a mood of solemn and dreamy contemplation, and the work of raking, gathering, and burning fallen leaves seems to be shared without distinction by the three older girls. Clearly it is not part of Millais's project in this picture to ally the figure of the girl with the comfort and leisure of the privileged domestic sphere. Furthermore, while Frith faithfully reproduces all the furnishings and fashions of a bourgeois urban household in the mid-1850s, *Autumn Leaves* eschews historical specificity, achieving instead a sense of timelessness in its evocation of the countryside and seasonal change. If Frith saw his middle-class little girl as the center of the ideal home, Millais appears to connect *all* girls with the beauties of a tranquil bucolic landscape, harmonizing the colors of the children's hair, skin, and clothes with the tones in the fallen leaves and the evening sky. It is, however, the Pre-Raphaelite's decision to place his young girls (all under thirteen years of age, Effie Millais tells us)[4] in relation to a scene so intensely redolent of death and decay that alerts us to the similarities between the two pictures. Frith offers a secular, familial narrative that establishes an intimate link between the elderly grandfather and the little girl: Millais's vision also celebrates an alliance between age and youth, even though his rendition is far more diffuse and saturated with religious connotation—it is, for instance, clearly significant that the youngest girl holds an apple, the emblem of that other Fall, in her hand.[5] The relation between the glowing beauty of the girls' youth and the melancholy of the dying day, the ebbing season, the shriveled leaves, and the drifting smoke is simultaneously one of poignant contrast and mellifluous unity. Arrested for all time in their loveliness, the girls are placed in a context that inevitably promotes our meditation upon the passage of time.

These two paintings of 1856 give an idea of the complex web of symbolic associations that the high Victorian era was weaving around the figure of the little girl. The task in this chapter will be to return to the preceding decade to unravel and analyze three principal strands of this web, and to identify the stresses that both constitute and constrain their fabric. Chapter 1 described the origin of a paradigm of personal development, and showed that Thomas De Quincey chose in retrospect to view his own childhood as a feminine era. Here the focus is upon the paradigm's progress in the early Victorian period, demonstrating that its symbolic congruence to two connected, if less personally motivated, tendencies of the times ensured its dissemination and popularized its appeal. The personal paradigm was readily subsumed both to the collective myth of an idyllic preindustrial England, and, perhaps more significantly, the emergent bastion of domestic ideology. All three ways of thinking strove to construct absolute and immutable places of safety, respectively the perfect childhood, the rural past, and the protected and stable home. All three havens, furthermore, found their ideal embodiment in the figure of the girl. How these combined fantasies affected the representation and public perception of fictional and real little girls during this period forms an important element of this inquiry.

Given her prominence in contemporary ideology, it is unsurprising that the literature of this era should have produced the example par excellence of the ideal girl. From 1840 to 1841 Dickens captured the attention of a mass audience in Great Britain and America by chronicling the pathetic progress of Little Nell in *The Old Curiosity Shop*.[6] Nell is forced to carry the full weight of the threefold symbolic burden just described, despite a narrative that thrusts her onto the miserable streets of a chaotic industrial England. Pushing the ideal girl into the position of the abused child of the working class, the novelist inevitably puts tremendous strain upon the symbolic network that surrounds the child, creating in particular a dangerous—and seemingly inappropriate—eroticism around the figure of Nell. The peculiar trials of the heroine of *The Old Curiosity Shop* can best be understood in the context of a range of other discursive constructions of girlhood from the early 1840s. As we might expect, the hermetic sphere of contemporary conduct literature sets forth the necessary attributes of the perfect girl with admirable clarity. More startling, perhaps, is the specter of innocent girlhood that haunts the complicated world of government reports on child labor.

Like *The Old Curiosity Shop*, the Children's Employment Commission of 1842–43 placed the figure of a girl before readers of its reports, but whereas Nell inspired general devotion, the little working girl excited pub-

FIGURE 2. John Everett Millais, *Autumn Leaves* (1856). (© Manchester City Art Galleries.)

lic outrage. The abused girl constituted—and still constitutes—the central horror of the reports for both contemporary and modern audiences largely because she is depicted as the absolute inverse of the ideal little girl. Instead of enjoying a happy childhood, secure in a protected home in the green heart of the shires of yore, this unfortunate drudge endures a blighted infancy amidst the threatening welter of the workplace in the grimy industrial city of the present. Such a presentation was guaranteed to produce national indignation and a widespread zeal for reform. The strategy, conscious or unconscious, of the commissioners was nevertheless ideologically risky: dwelling on the difference between the abused working girl and the ideal child and concentrating on the details of that abuse, these writers inevitably brought into play a range of evidence and associations that exceeded the requirements of the comparative task and jeopardized the sacrosanct image of the little girl. The horrifying visions of exploited girl-labor threatened to demote innocent girlhood from the status of an universal phenomenon to an economically contingent construction; more particularly, focus upon the active body of the working-class girl revealed it to be disturbingly sexual. Attention to both the official documents, published a couple of years after *The Old Curiosity Shop*, and to some of their reviews and literary responses—most prominently Elizabeth Barrett's poem "The Cry of the Children"—clarifies what exactly is at stake when Dickens presents a heroine with dangerously unfixed class-moorings. Examination of the rifts that appear even as the ideal little girl's popularity begins to build will stand us in good stead when we contemplate the ruins of the concept in the 1880s: for now, the exploited working-class girl is in a Yorkshire coal mine, not a London brothel, but the stresses produced by her image initiate the process that will weaken the ideal girl's ability to represent the sanctity of home and the safety of Olde England, and destroy her claim to stand for the tenderest place of all, the man's remembered childhood.

Sarah Stickney Ellis's *Daughters of England* (1843), one of three sequels to her highly successful *Women of England* (1839), provides a paradigmatic example of the conduct book's definition of the ideal girl.[7] All four volumes, remarkably similar in tone and more than a little repetitious in subject matter, have come to comprise a familiar locus for the dissection of the emergent domestic ideology of the early Victorian period.[8] *Daughters of England*, one might assume, would be the most differentiated of the sister texts: after all, the maternal function, the essential key to the feminine character in this realm of thought, has yet to be demonstrated, at least

51

biologically, in the lives of young unmarried girls. It is certainly apparent that the daughter cannot exude a power of influence equal in degree to that which emanates from the presiding angel of the house, but her relative powerlessness in some ways makes the girl more "feminine" than the grown woman. This distinction operates in other areas too: because they are not literally mothers, having never been sexually active, girls are better suited to represent the self-sacrificing ideal, unperturbed by currents of desire.[9] Altogether dependent, altogether confined within the home, the girl is the diametric opposite of her male relatives and thus forms an essential coordinate in the celebrated doctrine of separate spheres.

Daughters of England clearly demonstrates that the daughter has it within herself to be the ideal embodiment of the perfect home, but also shows us a great deal more. First of all, the myth of original girlhood reappears in Ellis's work as a variation of the dominant ideological theme. Whereas the retrospective construction of childhood as a feminine period figured as an intensely personal consolation in De Quincey's self-fashioning, this author has no autobiographical stake in the paradigm and draws upon its general features for very different purposes. For Ellis, the schema's inherent temporal separation of the man's public present-day persona and his private feminized past provides another version of the spatial division between male and female spheres: in both instances, her narratives imply, the man finds respite from the daily grind by returning to the gentle feminine representative of his childhood and his home. In the second place, by associating the young girl with the countryside, Ellis connects this figure not only with the lost years of individual males, but with a communal, preindustrial past, the golden age of England. To bear the freight of symbolic representation that Ellis heaps upon her, the girl cannot be imagined as a self-willed, vital, energetic being: instead she is necessarily constructed as essentially passive, existing in blissful stasis. Indeed, as we shall see, the stillness required of her would be most perfectly achieved by a girl who was actually dead.

An ethic of self-abnegation pervades all of Ellis's advice to her sisters, but in *Daughters of England* the message is laid on particularly thickly. If girls are not busy asking what they can do for their male relatives, then they should be thinking how best to assist female relatives in their attempts to ease the male burden. Ellis of course presents the ethic as a spontaneous impulse, remarking that "the daughters of a family, from the oldest to the very infant, are all too happy in the exercise of their affections to think of self" (266). Over and above her support of her mother in the multitudinous domestic tasks that ensure the smooth running of a

welcoming household, it is precisely in her role as affective center of the home that the daughter is of greatest service to the men of her family.[10] In these "practical and busy times," the "most laborious occupations both of mind and body" coupled with the "necessity of engaging in those eager pecuniary speculations, and in that fierce conflict of worldly interest" threaten English males with emotional annihilation (133, 11). Their "hearts and minds . . . buried in their bales of goods," the men of business are "compelled to stifle their best feelings," and run the risk of becoming "in reality the characters they at first only assumed" (130, 11). If the daughter is sufficiently affectionate and accommodating, however, "the fire-side pleasures of her own sunny home" (247) will counteract the brutalizing tendencies of the marketplace, and the man's (usually, but not always, the father's) ability to feel will be restored.

While the daughter clearly represents the home as a realm of emotion worlds away from the maelstrom of competitive commerce, her ability to provide a place of solace for the hard-pressed male does not begin and end, so to speak, in the here and now. *Daughters of England* extends and diversifies the girl's role so that she also personifies a temporally distant security. Ellis forges this connection primarily in her discussions of the necessary relation between the feminine and the arts: through their natural affinity for music, painting, and poetry, girls become imbued with art's power of transcending the fleeting moment:

> [T]he object of a daughter is to soothe the weary spirit of a father when he returns home from the office or the counting-house, where he has been toiling for her maintenance. . . . never does a daughter appear to more advantage, than when she cheerfully lays aside a fashionable air, and strums over, for more than the hundredth time, some old ditty which her father loves. To her ear it is possible it may be altogether divested of the slightest charm. But of what importance is that? The old man listens until tears are glistening in his eyes, for he sees again the home of his childhood—he hears his father's voice—he feels his mother's welcome—all things familiar to his heart in early youth come back to him with that long-remembered strain; and, happiest thought of all! they are revived by the playful fingers of his own beloved child. (104–5)

By turning from her own desire ("of what importance is that?") and the charms of the "fashionable air" of the present, the daughter is able to transport her father back to the emotional richness of his childhood, to a sensuously realized past that stands in sharp distinction to the longueur of the working day. Moreover, although the "old ditty" is originally the

connection between the young girl and the man's remembered childhood, the final and the "happiest" thought discards that intermediate link and directly invests the daughter's material presence, those "playful fingers," with the power to revive.[11]

Although this passage provides the most detailed evocation of the young girl's relationship with the man's retrospectively imagined childhood, *Daughters of England* furnishes a wealth of other examples. Still in the realm of music, the girl pianist "can make the past come back unshadowed" for her prodigal brother by playing "the evening hymn they used to sing together in childhood, when they had been all day gathering flowers": "His manly voice is raised. Once more it mingles with the strain. Once more the parents and children, the sister and the brother, are united as in days gone by" (105). Drawing, too, has seemingly occult powers when the pencil is wielded by a young girl intent on serving her male relatives. Ellis encourages her protégées to work on "sketches of scenery, [for] however defective as works of art, [they] are amongst the precious memorials of which time, the great destroyer, is unable to deprive us" (117). In the next sentence, the author moves from her feminine audience, the prospective producers of landscape art, to an unidentified male whose contemplation of the sketches casts him back to his former self:

> In them the traveller lives again, through all the joys and sorrows of his distant wanderings. He breathes again the atmosphere of that far world which his eye will never more behold. He treads again the mountain path where his step was never weary. He sees the sunshine on the snowy peaks which rise no more to him. He hears again the shout of joyous exultation, when it bursts from hearts as young and buoyant as his own; and he remembers how it was for him in those bygone-days, when, for the moment, he was lifted up above the grovelling cares of everyday existence. (117–18)

The memorializing function of the girl, then, is clearly not limited to her ability to create "a well-painted likeness of a departed friend" for the general comfort of the family (122); instead, in the enactment of the arts to which she instinctively inclines, or even in her mere physical presence, she carries the potential to resurrect "those bygone-days" of joy and exultation, sunshine and natural splendor. Hers is the "magic skill which has such power over the past, as to call up buried images, and clothe them again in beauty and youth" (118).

According to Ellis, then, the young girl's execution of the musical and visual arts serves a specific end in the context of the larger project of providing comfort for the male. *Daughters of England* treats poetry in a

slightly different fashion. In this instance, the feminine and the poetic ideal are so similarly constructed as to be practically indistinguishable from each other. A girl's love of poetry is "the fairest rose in her wreath of youthful beauty. A woman without poetry, is like a landscape without sunshine. . . . The idea is a paradox; for what single subject has ever been found to be so fraught with poetical associations as woman herself?" (127). The essence both of poetry and the feminine is to be found in their "inexhaustible sympathies," their expression of the "best feelings" that, we remember, the men of business were compelled to stifle. Antithetical to "our fathers, husbands, sons and brothers [who] are becoming more and more involved in the necessity of providing for mere animal existence," poetry and girlhood are also set in opposition to the debased life of an urban and industrialized England:

> No wonder, then, that in our teeming cities, poetry should be compelled to hide her diminished head. . . . If poetry should seek the quiet fields, as in the days of their pastoral beauty, even from these her green and flowery haunts, she is scared away by the steaming torrent, the reeking chimney, and the fiery locomotive. (123)

In the face of the teeming, steaming, reeking, fiery world of the present, girls and poetry have a sacred duty to represent within the home "the days of . . . pastoral beauty" to revivify those alienated men by reminding them of the countryside of the past. Locating this message in a text that associates the feminine with flowers, landscapes, and sunshine, that earnestly recommends the study of botany and delicate researches into natural history, Ellis browbeats us into accepting that there is a natural link between the girl and England's lost rural heritage.

The role of the daughters of England is thus to represent three places of solace for their male relatives. Whether they are symbolizing the security of the perfect contemporary home or the imagined immutability of the lost childhood or the rural past, Ellis's girls are dealt a remarkably limited hand. Stasis is elevated to the position of an ideal: unsurprisingly, Ellis urges her charges to fend off maturation, to "endeavour to prolong rather than curtail the season of their simplicity and buoyancy of heart": "[O]ne of the greatest charms which a girl can possess, is that of being contented to be a girl, and nothing more" (329). Furthermore, the girl's ideal nature, as we have seen, is necessarily evacuated of self-will or display of character, lest that stability be jeopardized. Constructed thus as a personally volitionless immobility, and repeatedly associated with a long-lost past, the young girl's condition in *Daughters of England* bears a disturbing resemblance to the state of death. Even if she manages to make the transition to womanhood, Ellis impresses upon her charge, her "whole life, from the cradle to the grave" will display all the liveliness and personal fulfillment of a sacrificial deathbed scene: she will be one whose world "is one of feeling, rather than action; whose highest duty is so often to suffer, and be still; whose deepest enjoyments are all relative; who has nothing, and is nothing, of herself; whose experience, if unparticipated, is a total blank" (126).

When Ellis was writing her series of feminine conduct books, a particular group of England's daughters was certainly suffering, and yet was most definitely compelled not to be still. Of course, the author did not intend her words to be applied to all classes: her preface takes care to tell us that the subsequent advice is directed to an audience "expressly limited to the middle ranks of society in Great Britain." The temptation to universalize, however, is not always resisted, as the following passage reveals:

> There is scarcely a more affecting sight presented by the varied scenes of human life, than a motherless or neglected little girl; yet so strong is the feeling her situation inspires that happily few are thus circumstanced, without some one being found to care for, and protect them. It is true, the lot of woman has trials enough peculiar to itself, and the look of premature sedateness and anxiety, which sometimes hangs upon the brow of the little girl, might seem to be the shadowing forth of some vague apprehensions as to the nature of her future destiny. These trials, however, seldom arise out of unkindness or neglect in her childhood. The voice of humanity would be raised against such treatment; for what living creature is so helpless and inoffensive as a little girl? The voice of humanity, therefore, almost universally speaks kindly to her in early life. (246)

The contradictions of Ellis's position here—her simultaneous recognition of the class-specific nature of her prescriptions, and her citation of an all-inclusive ideal—raise an important issue that will be of relevance throughout the forthcoming investigation of middle- and upper-class reactions to working-class deprivation. Ultimately it is impossible to know whether any given member of the privileged classes actually believes that working-class children should experience the same quality of life as more well-to-do children—it is impossible to know whether he or she thinks this to be feasible, or indeed desirable. However, it is quite clear that appeals to an universal standard are made time and again, frequently bolstered by the popular religious texts that hold that we are all God's children, all part of one human family.[12] Whether such appeals are heartfelt, strategic, or both, the ideological power of this concept is readily enlisted to attempt to shame into compliance those in explicit, or tacit, support of an exploitative system.

Appearing at the same time that evidence of the most appalling abuse of some of the nation's children was coming to light, Ellis's complacent pronouncements on the security of English girlhood have a remarkably hollow ring. Fortunately not all contemporary commentators were prepared to let such discrepancies pass without comment. In her three-part review in the *Athenaeum* of the *Report and Appendices of the Children's Employment Commission* (1843),[13] Anna Jameson fulminated about the hypocrisy of a land that embraced the definition of women propagated by writers like Ellis, while simultaneously countenancing a state of affairs that caused a certain class of women to spend their childhoods and their adulthoods laboring in the most degrading and dangerous conditions. Perhaps relishing the distance from those other women writers that is here created by her appropriation of the masculine persona of journalism, Jameson holds forth:

> The press has lately teemed with works of which the condition, the destiny of women is in some form or other the subject,—"Woman's Mission,"—"The Women of England,"—"The Wives of England,"—"The Daughters of England,"—"Woman and her Master,"—"Woman, her Rights and Duties," &c. &c. It is the popular theme of the day. . . . In all the relations between the sexes, [woman] is the refiner and the comforter of man; it is hers to keep alive all those purer, gentler, and more genial sympathies, those refinements in morals, in sentiment, in manners, without which we men, in this rough, working-day world, would degenerate (*do* degenerate, for the case is not hypothetical) into mere brutes. Such is the beautiful theory of the woman's existence, preached to her by moralists, sung to her by poets! Let man, the bread-winner, go abroad—let woman stay *at home*. . . . We really beg pardon of our reader for repeating these truisms—we merely quote them here, to show that, while they are admitted, promulgated, taught as indisputable, the real state of things is utterly at variance with them. Our social system abounds with strange contradictions in law, morals, government, religion. But the greatest, the most absurd, the most cruel of all is the anomalous condition of the women in this Christian land of ours. We call it *anomalous* because it inculcates one thing as the rule of right, and decrees another as the rule of necessity. "Woman's mission," of which people can talk so well and write so prettily, is irreconcileable with woman's position, of which no one dares to think, much less to speak.[14]

The fact that Jameson prefaces the third installment of her discussion of the findings of the Children's Employment Commission with this lengthy diatribe upon "the anomalous condition of . . . *women*" is worthy of investigation. On the one hand, the slippage is justified because the reports revealed that girls were enduring lives that rendered it entirely impossible for them to grow up to be the deft homemakers and loving mothers that domestic ideology claimed were their natural roles. On the other, Jameson is merely reflecting a tendency already within the reports, and the ensuing legislation: despite the titular emphasis upon children, commissioners furnished a great deal of evidence about women's working experiences, and, as we shall see, one of the results of the inquiry was that all females, irrespective of age, were banned from labor in the collieries. This landmark decision, the first absolute prohibition of adult employment, represents a significant shift in the history of labor reform. A brief summary of the parliamentary investigations and statutes that preceded this measure will show that a developing concern for the well-being of working children gradually becomes enmeshed with a specific anxiety about female labor. Standing at the intersection of femininity and childhood, the little girl represents the most sensitive site of all.

Myths of Merrie Englande notwithstanding, child labor, as is frequently pointed out, did not begin with the Industrial Revolution. "Hardly anything above four years old, but its hands are sufficient to itself": Defoe's comments on his tour of the country in the second decade of the eighteenth century are probably a fair representation of lower-class conditions in the entire preindustrial period.[15] Nevertheless, the advent of power-driven machinery and the resultant congregation of large numbers of people in workplace and urban center alike in the late eighteenth and early nineteenth centuries altered the life experiences of many children of the poor. The exact nature of that change has been the subject of considerable debate,[16] but, without courting controversy, we can say that in this era of great population growth, the novel and relatively widespread spectacle of concentrated child labor began to engender concern in a ruling class newly attuned to the idea of childhood's especial claims.

Before attention turned to the burgeoning mills and manufactories of the early nineteenth century, the first indication of interest in the working child's plight appears to have come from Jonas Hanway, whose *Sentimental History of Chimney Sweepers* was published in 1785. Delineating the horrific effects of this dreadful trade upon the unformed boy's (and, very occasionally, girl's) body, Hanway's work prompted the Chimney Sweepers Act of 1788 and ushered in the era of child labor reform. An act of 1802 attempted to curb the exploitation of pauper apprentices,[17] but the more general problem of child labor was not addressed until 1816, when Sir Robert Peel chaired the first major inquiry. This Select Committee on Children, Mills and Factories eventually led to the Factory Act of 1819, but, as had been the case with the earlier legislation, lack of enforcement rendered its provisions meaningless. In comparison with the subsequent important investigations of the early 1830s and 1842–43, Peel's report seems to keep itself at a considerable distance from the working child, even if we allow for the substantial formal differences between select committees and royal commissions. The invited dignitaries—physicians, magistrates, mill proprietors—are asked to speak about the size of rooms, ventilation and temperature, the provision of Sunday Schools, standards of nutrition, and so forth, and there is little direct focus upon or concern about the psychological condition of child employees. Indeed, the witnesses generally concur that "the regularity that is necessary to be kept in cotton works would be a guard to [the children's] morals."[18] It is nevertheless conceded that standards deteriorate—tales of wild ribaldry in the batting room— when the sexes are *isolated* from each other. Apart from this kind of observation, very little attention is given to gender, and the workers' physical characteristics are not subjected to detailed scrutiny: Kinder Wood comments that he is "inclined to think there is a more early arrival to puberty" for girls because of the hothouse effect of the weaving sheds, but the remark appears to excite scientific interest rather than moral anxiety.[19]

Fifteen years later, another select committee on the same topic chaired by Michael Sadler drew considerably closer to the child workers themselves. As casual indicators of the change in mores that was occurring between the reports of 1816 and 1831–32, two pieces of evidence from Glasgow's labor history provide an informative contrast. Figure 3 shows the trade union emblem of the Glasgow Association of Cotton Spinners from around 1820, in this instance painted on a tin tray. At the center of the design stands a well-dressed rosy-cheeked little girl, almost half the size of the burly weaver by her side. Illustrating the motto "UNITED we stand, DIVIDED we fall" that curves above their heads, the two workers are reaching their hands toward each other, acknowledging their profitable and amicable partnership. Far from being a source of anxiety, the diminutive cotton worker is here celebrated as part of "Britains Glory [*sic*]," an essential element of the process that begins with the cotton plant and ends with the merchant ship's voyage to new imperial markets. In the early twenties, then, the child is an unproblematic part of the industry that "Let[s] Glasgow Flourish." By 1832, however, she has become its worst indictment, the preeminent symbol of the suffering caused by the capitalist's rapacious greed. Reporting on a Glasgow public meeting of the Ten Hours Movement in that year, the *British Labourer's Protector* explains that the staging was designed for maximum emotional effect:

> We also had two poor little Factory Girls, whose stunted growth and sickly appearance might well have drawn tears from a heart of flint, placed on the Hustings, near to the Chairman. These two poor Victims of the overworking system, supported a Banner, on one side of which was inscribed— "We pray for the speedy abolition of *ALL* Slavery," and on the other side was written—"The *Christian* Slaves of Britain, beg two hours, off their daily labour."[20]

As this paragraph reveals, the forces behind the movement were well aware that in the fight to reduce working hours for all, the image of the abused child was their most important weapon.[21] In the following year, a parliamentary speech by William Cobbett repeats the Glaswegian stage-dressing in a verbal form: this time there are three hundred thousand little Lancastrian rather than two Scottish girls, but once again they are used as emotive stand-ins for the larger and less clear-cut issues connected to the call for state intervention:

> [A] most surprising discovery has been made, namely, that all our greatness and prosperity, that our superiority over other nations, is owing to 300,000 little girls in Lancashire. We had made the notable discovery, that if these little girls work two hours less in a day than they do now, it would occasion the ruin of the country; that it would enable other nations to compete with us, and thus make an end to our boasted wealth, and bring us to beggary![22]

Before the Factories Regulation Bill was debated in the House of Commons, however, Sadler's inquiry in support of the Ten Hours Movement in 1831–32 had already turned the spotlight on the spectacle of weary children. Hugely—and famously—slanted to prove that most of the evils of the factory system could be laid at the door of the overlong working day, the report's tactics are anything but subtle. The testimony of working men and women (its very inclusion a significant departure from the Peel report) claims that "most of that [the children's bad language and immorality] goes on towards night, when they begin to be drowsy; it is a kind of stimulus which they use to keep themselves awake; they say some pert

FIGURE 3. Trade Union emblem of the Glasgow Association of Cotton Spinners, circa 1820. (Glasgow Museums: The People's Palace.)

thing or another to keep themselves from drowsiness, and it generally happens to be some obscene language."[23] In addition to this extremely pointed line of inquiry, the report also considers more general issues of child exploitation in the workplace. One question was, "Is not conduct grossly indecent often practised by those who have the control over these children in factories?" to which the answer was, "Very frequently."[24] As one might expect, this kind of questioning inevitably introduces gender differentiation into the discussion. In contradistinction to the Peel report, the *mingling* of the sexes in factory life is depicted as dangerous, particularly for young girls:

"Do you find that the children, the females especially, are very early demoralised in them?"

"They are."

"Is their language indecent?"

"Very indecent; and both sexes take great familiarities with each other in the mills, without at all being ashamed of their conduct."[25]

61

Discredited because of its massive bias, this inquiry nevertheless brought moral and sexual issues to the forefront of attention and paved the way for the next decade's intense scrutiny of individual children. The Factory Commission of 1833, instituted in reaction to the manifestly problematic Sadler report, marks the first significant point of successful intervention, leading as it did to the Factories Regulation Act of 1833. This legislation established a minimum age of nine for all workers in textile mills (except silk) powered by steam or water, and also set a maximum forty-eight-hour working week for children between the ages of nine and twelve, and a sixty-nine-hour week for thirteen- to seventeen-year-olds and women. In addition it was laid down that children between nine and twelve were required to attend school and could not work more than nine hours a day, and that the older group and women could not work more than twelve hours a day.[26]

The six reports of the royal commission of 1842–43 took as their area of inquiry "the mines and collieries of the United Kingdom and all trades and manufactures whatever in which children work together in numbers, not included in the Factories Regulation Act."[27] Unlike the London-based select committees, the work of the commission was conducted in the field by individual commissioners, each responsible for a set geographical area. Dismay and disbelief greeted the appearance of the documents when, according to a measure introduced in 1835, they were made generally available, but this public reaction had been preempted within the papers themselves. Because no attempt was made to exclude the commissioners' personal opinions about the conditions and individuals they surveyed, the report already contains the moral response of the ruling-class observer. Thus, when the *Quarterly Review* commented that the documents "disclosed . . . modes of existence . . . as strange and new as the wildest dreams of fiction," or the *Spectator* stated that the "scenes of suffering and infamy . . . will come upon many well-informed people like the fictions or tales of distant lands," they were in effect replicating the sense of incredulity that permeated the complete text.[28] Confronted with the figure of a nine-year-old girl as she emerged from a Huddersfield pit after thrusting corves for twelve hours, Commissioner Scriven writes:

I could not have believed that I should have found human nature so degraded. There is nothing that I can conceive amidst all the misery and wretchedness in the worst of factories equal to this. Mr. Holroyd, solicitor, and Mr. Brook, surgeon, practising in Stainland, were present, who confessed that, although living within a few miles, they could not have believed that such a system of unchristian cruelty could have existed.[29]

The preconceptions of the "well-informed people" who stepped into these "dens of darkness" may well have proved wholly inadequate to the appalling conditions they found there, but preexisting ideas undoubtedly influenced the ways in which the commissioners conducted their questioning and presented their material. To illustrate this point, I focus on the case of one particular subcommissioner, whose report displays certain beliefs and expectations exceptionally clearly, thus helping to identify tendencies that appear, albeit less markedly, throughout the entire document.

Richard Henry (later "Hengist")[30] Horne merits attention not only in his own right, but also because of the happenstance of his friendship with the poet Elizabeth Barrett. Like a considerable number of the other commissioners, Horne had no conventional qualifications for the post.[31] After a dramatic early career in the Americas, in which he participated in the siege of Vera Cruz as a midshipman in the Mexican navy, survived a shark attack and a bout of yellow fever, visited Indian encampments in the United States, and then experienced shipwreck, a ship fire, and a shipboard mutiny, the twenty-five-year-old Horne had returned to England in 1828 to commence a literary life. Described as "a talented, energetic and versatile writer" by the *Dictionary of National Biography*, Horne was the author of a variety of poems, literary essays, and two tragedies.[32] After coming to the attention of Barrett in 1839, he enjoyed a lively correspondence with her for the next seven years. Inevitably enough, Horne's participation in the royal commission formed a topic for their conversation and led Barrett to compose one of her most celebrated "protest" poems, "The Cry of the Children." Barrett's poem is written entirely in the spirit of the government report and thus can legitimately be considered as a kind of literary appendix to the document proper. Examination of Horne's contribution to the report, then, will be augmented by a discussion of the poetic creation that sprang directly out of that work.

Even though the area of Horne's inquiry—"the Iron Trades and other Manufactures of South Staffordshire and the neighbouring parts of Worcestershire and Shropshire"—does not yield as shocking and sensational evidence as the Yorkshire coalfields, his account of "these grimy regions" paints a drab and distressing picture. Methodical and responsible in his reporting of the vile environmental conditions of the district— the cramped dimensions of dwellings, the nonexistence of sewerage, the decrepit and hazardous machine-shops and so forth—Horne reserves his most vehement condemnation for the systematic demoralization of the populace that he discovers at every turn. As in the Glaswegian public meeting or in Cobbett's speech, Horne places the little girl at center stage, using the evidence of her plight as an encapsulation of all that is wrong in industrial society. This is the heart of Horne's criticism: "You will find poor girls who had never sang or danced; never seen a dance; never read a book that made them laugh; never seen a violet, or a primrose, and other flowers; and others whose only idea of a green field was derived from having been stung by a nettle."[33] Although we have no reason to suspect the man's sympathy and sincerity, the bias of Horne's approach may seem strange to a modern audience.[34] This passage occurs in the opening report that summarizes the material Horne has collected in the field: the transcripts of the interviews that yielded this information display his special concerns even more clearly. In common with all evidence sections of the report, the commissioner's questions are not directly represented, and we infer their substance only from the printed testimony of the witnesses.

Picture the scene, then, when a dirty, bedraggled, and undersized girl appears before the urbane and literate Horne. An employee at Mr. Hemingsley's tip and nail factory, she has been working on the manufacture of screws since she was ten. Her statement, here distanced to the third person, is as follows:[35] "[She] does not know what a country dance is, was never at a dance in her life; never saw a dance; never heard of Harlequin and Columbine; has no idea what they are like."[36] What can Horne mean by quizzing barely educated industrial drudges on the conventions of the old English pantomime?[37] This example and the many others identical in type that punctuate Horne's evidence reveal how the subcommissioner is operating under a very particular sense of what girlhood *should* be like. It is hard to determine whether he adopts this strategy as a conscious tactic the better to capture the attention of his ruling-class audience, or whether his compulsion to juxtapose the cherished ideal and the dispiriting reality is a genuine and personal response. What can be said with some certainty is that over the bleak pages of the report hovers the idea of the ideal upper- or middle-class girl, secure and protected in her loving home and her happy childhood, far from the grime and toil of the industrial city. R. H. Franks, the commissioner investigating the collieries of East Lothian, poignantly observes that if only little Mary Neilson, a ten-year-old "coal-putter," were "well-dressed," she "would vie with any child in Scotland in point of beauty."[38] When Horne wishes to put in perspective the demands and dangers facing the child operative working on unfenced machinery, Mrs. Ellis's child pianist is immediately at hand:

> That the accidents which are so continually occurring at Hemingsley's are attributable to "carelessness" is, no doubt, for the most part very true; but let us look at the offence comparatively. A child of the upper or middle classes is practising on the piano-forte: this child does not go over the fingering of the same unvarying passage, from hour to hour, from day to day, from year to year; but has an interesting variety in its practice. Yet the most apt scholar and the most assiduous practiser will now and then miss its distances, and be a little out of its time. It is precisely for this offence that one of these poor children, working in support of itself, and perhaps of its infirm mother, loses a finger or has its hand smashed; and for the carelessness of one second of time is mutilated during the remainder of its life.[39]

Both in explicit and implicit maneuvers, then, Horne brings the ideal child, and more particularly, the ideal girl, into relation with her pitifully abused counterpart. On the simplest level, the presence of that protected child gives the ruling-class audience a way of measuring exactly how far from ideal the conditions in the industrial regions have become. Deeper down, however, the comparative urge seems to be underwritten by a belief, parallel to the Christian tenet that we are all God's children, that all little girls should be sharing certain very specific kinds of life-experiences: whether they be rich or poor, girls should be enjoying their natural birthright of joyful "carelessness," familiarity with green fields and primroses, and a knowledge of the steps of old country dances. Horne's conception of the content of perfect girlhood is thus remarkably similar to that held by Mrs. Ellis.[40] Unable to respond to deliberately incomprehensible sets of questions or placed in diametric opposition to middle-class children, the working girls are thus constructed as the absolute antitypes of the ideal image.

"[M]y 'Cry of the Children,' " Barrett wrote to Horne in August 1843, "owes its utterance to your exciting causations."[41] Barrett's poem shares and extends Horne's assumption that the working girl has been unnaturally severed from the pleasures of childhood and countryside that should be her due, even repeating the subcommissioner's tactics to make its point. Once again, children respond to questions that either have no relevance to the conditions of their existence, or must be translated to their degraded level of experience in order to be comprehended. For instance, when Barrett has her children ask their interlocutor, "Are your cowslips of the meadows / Like our weeds anear the mine?" (ll. 62–

63), she is drawing directly from her friend's transcript, a point made transparently clear by the line's prosaic footnote: "A commissioner mentions the fact of weeds being thus confounded with the idea of flowers."[42] Horne, predictably enough, thought the poem a triumph, and although a certain amount of caviling ensued (it was all too evident, grumbled the *League*, that "Barrett has never visited a spinning mill"),[43] "The Cry of the Children" created a popular sensation and was held to be instrumental in preparing the climate of opinion for the passage of the Factory Act of 1844.

Working within a literary form, Barrett makes creative use of opportunities unavailable to Horne in his role as subcommissioner. Whereas it would be inappropriate for Horne's report to construct a sustained and concrete picture of what ideal girlhood should look like, Barrett is able to achieve this end by drawing on the reader's knowledge of her poem's literary heritage. To a Victorian audience, the poem that, above all others, told the "truth" about the state of childhood was Wordsworth's *Ode* (see chap. 1). By presenting her poem as the modern-day version of the beloved *Ode*, Barrett insists that contemporary industrial life's exploitation of children is a perversion of the natural and sacred order, and that it is her class's responsibility to restore that lost relationship between the child, God and Nature.

Like the *Ode*, "The Cry of the Children" begins in the spring, a time when all young creation celebrates its existence:

> The young lambs are bleating in the meadows,
>> The young birds are chirping in the nest,
> The young fawns are playing with the shadows,
>> The young flowers are blowing towards the west.

(ll. 5–9)

All young creation, that is, apart from the "young, young children" of industrial England, who, entirely contrary to Wordsworth's concept of our gradual movement from childhood's joy to the suffering of adulthood, are *already* weeping "Ere the sorrow comes with years" (l. 2). In the poem's penultimate stanza, Barrett makes her most deliberate allusions to the *Ode*:

> And well may the children weep before you!
>> They are weary ere they run.
> They have never seen the sunshine, nor the glory,
>> Which is brighter than the sun.

They know the grief of man, without his wisdom;
    They sink in man's despair, without its calm;
Are slaves, without the liberty in Christdom,
    Are martyrs, by the pang without the palm,—
Are worn, as if with age, yet unretrievingly
    The harvest of its memories cannot reap,—
Are orphans of the earthly love and heavenly.
    Let them weep! Let them weep!

(ll. 138–49)

Prematurely deprived of the "visionary gleam," the "radiance" and "glory" that should rightly illuminate their early years, these children are even more benighted than the adults in Wordsworth's schema, for they lack the compensations of "the philosophic mind," the "palms" won in the "race" of man's mortality. The only happy child in Barrett's poem is a dead child, a little girl named Alice. In an implicit parody of "We Are Seven," the unlucky survivors fantasize about their sister's grave as a rejuvenating place of rest:

If you listen by that grave, in sun and shower,[44]
    With your ear down, little Alice never cries.
Could we see her face, be sure we should not know her,
    For the smile has time for growing in her eyes.
And merry go her moments, lulled and stilled in
    The shroud by the kirk-chime!

(ll. 45–51)

Those young ones who are denied the comfort of death must labor on as living paradoxes: "[T]he man's hoary anguish draws and presses / Down the cheeks of infancy" (ll. 27–28).

This perversion of the Wordsworthian order causes misery for child, adult, and nation alike. In Frith's painting or Ellis's piano scene, the *protected* girl provided a comforting image of early happiness for her older male relatives; here in Barrett's poem the connection between age and youth is forged *within* the actual bodies and experiences of the children themselves. Consequently age itself can be offered no solace: "The old man may weep for his to-morrow / Which is lost in Long Ago" (l.15). Furthermore, England's ability to conceptualize its rural heritage through the innocence of its children is imperiled: not only are these children wholly ignorant about cowslips, but they have no energy and thus no desire to repair the bond between childhood and nature. Exhorted to "Go out . . . from the mine and from the city" into the delights of the country-side, they declare themselves unfit to return to their "natural" element:

> Leave us quiet in the dark of the coal-shadows,
>   From your pleasures fair and fine!
>
> .   .   .   .
>
> If we cared for any meadows, it were merely
>   To drop down in them and sleep
>
> .   .   .   .
>
> And, underneath our heavy eyelids drooping,
>   The reddest flower would look as pale as snow.
>
> (ll. 64–65, 68–69, 72–73)

The sufferings of Barrett's "children," then, not only indict the country's present and threaten its future, but cut off all access to the richness of the past—"the harvest of its memories cannot [be] reap[ed]" (l. 147) on either the personal or the collective level. And if the precious ideas of childhood and the rural past are trampled in the dust in "The Cry of the Children," so too are the concepts of family and home. Those same male relatives who in Ellis's fantasy derived their sense of security from the presence of the ideal girl are here chastised by Barrett for both the religious and secular betrayal of their familial roles. By causing or ignoring the children's plight, these fathers and brothers blaspheme their sacred duty to represent God the Father on earth and thus plunge their young charges into apostasy: "For God's possible is taught by his world's loving, / And the children doubt of each" (ll. 136–37). Similarly, the men's refusal to remove children from the workplace into the safety of the home has demoralized and degraded the mothers of England. Until the "cruel nation" of Barrett's "brothers" removes its "mailed heel" from the "child's heart," women are powerless to protect or even comfort their offspring: "They are leaning their young heads against their mothers, / And *that* cannot stop their tears" (ll. 3–4). Because the family is in disarray, the home finds no representation in this poem: the sole secure space we see a child inhabit is the "close clay" of Alice's grave; otherwise children are depicted only in "the coal-dark, underground" and in the shadow of "the iron wheels" of the factory.

Following Horne's lead, Barrett incites the zeal for reform by presenting her subjects as pathetic negations of her audience's most cherished notions about children in general, and little girls in particular. Because the poet must tread a fine line between arousing and alienating sympathy, she is, however, constrained to create curiously hybrid children. Realistic depiction of the speech of a brutalized, uneducated child would not serve Barrett's purpose: her little workers therefore speak to us in the poetic periphrases and genteel cadences of an idealized middle-class child.[45] But these voices issue forth from bodies that are designed to show the acceptable side of their difference from the rosy-cheeked and bright-eyed girl of privilege. Barrett's children are metonymically represented by prudently selected signs of exhaustion and misery: the depiction of pale and sunken faces, tear-stained cheeks, weak feet, palpitating hearts, trembling knees, heavy eyelids, and burning pulses allows us to see the working child only as an abused version of the ideal, not as a physical presence in her own right.

Poetic license may allow the girl's body in "The Cry of the Children" to be a simple antithesis of the ideal: an equivalent clarity is not achieved in the government report. Time and again, in all sections of the report, the commissioners' ability to construct a polemical comparison between what *should be* and what *is* founders in their recoil from the sight of the girl's body at work.[46] To the fascinated dismay of the gentlemanly observers, the laboring body, continually on the move, proclaims not only its ill-treatment and weariness, but all too tangible evidence of its gender. Lifting up his eyes from the shop floor of a Black Country metalworks, Horne sees not so much an exile from the flowery meadows as an example of female anatomy:

> [H]ow should the girls be expected to retain personal delicacy or decency . . . where the ladders and stairs are so high and so nearly perpendicular that girls ascending and descending are exposed to all who are in the room beneath? If they are carrying any weight which extends the arms, the exposure is quite unavoidable.[47]

The direction of Horne's gaze is not idiosyncratic: all of the commissioners, while completely oblivious to boys' sexual characteristics, return insistently to girls' bodies, noting how they are revealed by scanty, ragged, or missing clothing, displayed in working postures, or glimpsed in the public performance of the "offices of nature." The spectacle of the female body causes the most disquiet in the grimy and sweaty atmosphere of the Yorkshire mines. Nothing, we might imagine, could cause greater consternation than the bare description of the kind of work performed underground by young girls and boys. Here, for instance, is a relatively neutral explanation of one of their occupations:

> "Hurriers" are children who draw loaded corves or waggons, weighing from two to five hundred weight, mounted upon four cast-iron wheels, of

five inches diameter without rails from the headings to the main gates. In the thin seams this is done upon their hands and feet, having frequently no greater height from the floor to the ragged roof than 16, 18 and 20 inches. To accomplish their labour the more easily they buckle around their naked persons a broad leather strap, to which is attached in front a ring and about four feet of chain terminating in a hook.[48]

Outrage at the general obscenity of this sort of abuse of human beings, however, is surpassed by a much more specific anxiety about sexuality. Of prime concern to the dressed adult males who step out of their habitual milieu into the "dark and ill-governed recesses of the mine" is the proximity of exposed young female bodies both to male glances and undressed adult males. To Commissioner Scriven, the physical privations of mine work pale in comparison to the lurking sexual danger: "[I]t is . . . in their moral condition that these persons suffer the most. The evils that exist in that respect arise much from the sexes indiscriminately working together, many of the adult males being in a perfect state of nudity, and the females near approaching it."[49] It seems highly unlikely that the miners themselves would share this opinion: certainly the following tableau presented in Commissioner Symons's report suggests a radical difference of perspective between the perceiving "I" and the community of workers, who appear to be enjoying both a moment of rest and the evident discomfiture of their visitor:

> On descending Messrs. Hopwood's pit, at Barnsley, I found assembled round the fire a group of men, boys and girls, some of whom were of the age of puberty, the girls as well as the boys stark naked to the waist, their hair bound up with a tight cap, and trousers supported by their hips. Their sex was recognizable only by their breasts, and some little difficulty occasionally arose in pointing out to me which were girls, and which were boys, and which caused a great deal of laughing and joking.[50]

Commissioners were also quick to spot danger in other areas that probably occasioned little worry to the workers themselves. To take one example, nervousness was aroused by working practices that, though not physically injurious, brought male and female bodies into actual contact with each other: "cross-lapping," a technique of bringing two intertwined workers up the shaft in a harness, was particularly worrisome, especially when the children were inadequately clothed. Scriven records his reaction to a scene at the pithead: "[T]he girl . . . across the lap of a boy . . . was extremely tender and delicate. I was perfectly shocked at her style of dress;

she was without stockings or shoes, her legs and thighs, which were exposed, being black and filthy."[51] This steady focus upon a revealed female body, continually under threat from male glances, or worse, is maintained in both report and evidence sections; once again, the commissioners' concerns are ventriloquized through the witnesses' responses. Consider some of the following testimonies:

> If I want to relieve myself I go into any part of the pit; sometimes the boys see me when they go by. (Susan Pitchforth, aged eleven)

> The girls' breeches are torn as often as ours; they are torn many a time, and when they are going along we can see them all between the legs naked; I have often; and that girl, Mary Holmes, was so to-day; she denies it, but it is true for all that. (Ebenezer Healey, aged thirteen)

> The getters that I work for are naked except their caps; they pull off all their clothes. I see them at work when I go up. (Patience Kershaw, aged seventeen)[52]

The emphasis on naked breasts, thighs, and genitals, on seeing and being seen, permeates both the direct and mediated evidence produced by the commissioners, with the result that the problem of sex in the workplace threatens to displace the problem of children in the workplace.

In case its audience might be a little slow in getting this message, the *Westminster Review*, which reprinted all of the most salacious sections, saw fit to clarify the issue by tampering with the visual evidence it borrowed from the official document.[53] Page 74 of Scriven's original report, which brought together excerpts from the testimonies of seven girls aged from nine to fourteen, is illustrated by a drawing of a young female (fig. 4). With her hands jammed in her trouser pockets, an averted gaze and a slightly bemused expression, this coal-dust-covered figure is hard to read, but appears to be a solid and self-reliant lass, sufficiently proud of herself to be wearing a necklace with her grimy work clothes. Redrawn for the pages of the *Westminster* (fig. 5), the girl has been transformed into a smirking houri, attracting attention to her semiexposed snowy white breast by cupping it with her hand, and directly soliciting the reader with come-hither eyes. Very occasionally, the report itself is as transparent as this illustration: although Symons predictably frames his response in terms of revulsion rather than attraction, his language in the following observation makes it clear that he is looking at a pair of thirteen-year-olds as if they were prostitutes, not hurriers: "[T]he chain, passing high up between the legs of two of these girls, had worn large holes in their

71

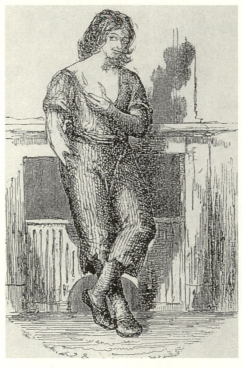

FIGURE 4. Child laborer, from Royal Commission on Children's Employment (1842–43).

FIGURE 5. Child laborer, from "Protection of Children in Mines," *Westminster Review* 38 (July 1842).

trousers, and any sight more disgustingly indecent or revolting can scarcely be imagined than these girls at work. No brothel can beat it." "You . . . have before you, in the coal-pits where females are employed," Symons continues, "the picture of a nursery for juvenile vice which you will go far and wide above ground to equal."[54]

Repulsion may threaten to overcome compassion at such moments as these, but on the whole it is readily apparent that the men who worked on this commission were truly appalled by the human misery they unearthed, and that their presentation of these findings is underwritten by a genuine desire to hasten reform. Offering much of its evidence as a series of brief case histories, their document brings a new, novelistic intimacy to the official form, giving unprecedented attention to individual children, and laying a new stress both on their interior state and their physical appearance. Furthermore, whereas earlier reports had displayed relatively little gender differentiation, generally treating children as a single category, these officials were drawn so markedly to the female plight that as objects of concern, grown women tend to rank higher than young boys, though not quite as high as female children. Horne and his fellow commissioners make rhetorical use of their culture's growing idealization of the figure of the little girl, choosing to indict the industrial system on the grounds that it severs girls from their true and natural relationships with the joys of childhood and countryside and the protection of home. This intensity of focus upon the girl, however, has mixed results. Although Elizabeth Barrett, in the cleaner and more controllable world of propagandistic literature, is able to create an industrial child whose differences from her ideal sister could easily be removed by the compassionate intervention of her audience, the commissioners' unremitting concentration upon the working girl turns up material evidence that is ultimately unassimilable.

In the final estimation, this infamous display of the all-too-explicitly gendered body of the working girl to the early Victorian ruling-class audience posed a double threat to the figure of the ideal girl. To keep hold of her symbolic power, the ideality of the little girl must be universal; it cannot be contingent upon accidents of class and fortune. The evident sexuality of the laboring body in motion, worlds away from the inert stillness of the ideal figure, demands two mutually contradictory responses that nevertheless point toward the same result: either the working-class girl is an entirely different being from her ideal sister, in which case the ideal girl loses her claim to universality and thus loses her power; or the working-class girl, sexualized body and all, is the same as her ideal sister, in which case the ideal girl loses the innocent blankness that allowed her to fulfill the complicated terms of her symbolic contract, and thus loses her power. The fact that images of idealized girlhood continued to proliferate and be venerated for the next forty years or so shows the tremendous resilience of the concept in the face of attack. Nevertheless the angle of the affront here offered in the early 1840s serves both to indicate from what direction the final fatal blow will issue, and to explain why a mounting sexual tension will accompany the little girl's ever-rising popularity in the intervening period.

After the royal commission of 1842–43 published its findings, Lord Ashley introduced a factory reform bill. When the bill finally made it through both houses of Parliament, however, its original provisions relating to mine work had been significantly weakened. Despite murmurs of dissent in the Lords, girls and women were totally excluded from colliery labor, but the proposed prohibition of boys under thirteen was soundly defeated. The Commons knocked the age down to ten, with the proviso that those between the ages of ten and thirteen should only work alternate days, while the Lords kept the age at ten, but threw out the limitation, also refusing to pass a ban on apprenticeship or to support the stipulation that only men between the ages of twenty-one and fifty should have charge of lift machinery.[55] Nevertheless, Horne, giving an account of these proceedings in a biographical essay on Lord Ashley, dwelt upon the act's achievements and represented the crusading peer uttering a divine fiat that delivered femininity from the taint of physicality: "[T]o the female children and women, hereto confined [in the mines and collieries], he has said—'You are free, and shall do the work of beasts in the attitude of beasts ... no more.' "[56] Joining the existing collection of measures designed to prevent the exploitation of child workers, the total ban within this piece of legislation insisted that females must also be guarded by the severest forms of government intervention: receiving double protection on account of her tender years and her gender, the little girl now sat somewhat uneasily in the very center of the picture.[57]

Horne's portrait of Ashley appeared in 1844 in his *New Spirit of the Age*, a two-volume collection of essays on the day's living luminaries, both literary and scientific, secular and divine.[58] The chapter on the philanthropic lord, which also describes Dr. Southwood Smith's and Horne's own endeavors in the field of child labor reform, was immediately preceded by an encomium upon the talents of the young Charles Dickens, commenting on his oeuvre from *The Pickwick Papers* to *A Christmas Carol*. While the chapter, both the first and the longest in the work, abounds in praise, nothing captures Horne's attention quite so thoroughly as the "tragic power, the pathos and the tenderness" of the novelist, and it is Dickens's handling of the death of Little Nell that stands out above all.[59] Stands out quite literally, in fact, for Horne's admiration of the burial scene is so great that he is compelled to lay out the entire passage in his own text as if it were poetry, "blank verse of irregular metre and rhythms."[60] To Horne, the depiction of "the closing of this early grave" is "of deep pathetic beauty," and "worthy of the best passages of Wordsworth."[61] From prolonged concentration on the continually moving bodies of the girl workers of Wolverhampton and the incessant action of the little Yorkshire hurriers, we now turn to what should be the stillest form of all, the dead body of Little Nell.

The Old Curiosity Shop is a story of a perfect girl who is denied the home that is her rightful sphere and cast into the frenetic territory of the dispossessed. By means of this radical displacement, Dickens gives himself the opportunity to challenge the notion that ideal girls cannot exist outside the privileges of bourgeois domesticity. Preserving all her saintly sweetness despite her distressing family situation and her dispiriting movement through the working world, his heroine exudes a virtue that is self-evidently essential rather than relative. Nevertheless, as we have seen in the government documents, bringing the ideal into conjunction with the abused is a measure fraught with danger for the concept of the ideal: it is precisely Little Nell's removal into the bustle of life and labor that prompts a general fascination with her physicality and imbues the text with its peculiar erotic charge.

The symbolic burden placed on Nell Trent's famously frail shoulders is perhaps the heaviest carried by any girl in literature.[62] From the first she must act as the ideal representative of the three precious havens of a safe home, a happy childhood, and an idyllic rural past, though her personal experience of them is scanty, to say the least, and largely confined to the novel's prehistory.[63] For most of the novel denied her appropriate setting of home and hearth, Nell is, paradoxically, domestic ideology's ambassador-at-large, knowing and acting upon a single desire: she exists to bring light and comfort into her family circle, which in this case is represented only by her feeble and aged grandfather. Only thirteen and, as we are continually reminded, "small for her age" (103), Nell is from the first the fully formed exemplar of feminine self-sacrifice—a perfect lady, even though her grandfather's fall from respectability denies her any secure positioning within the middle class, Kit Nubbles's devoted servitude notwithstanding. Having neither personal desires nor deficiencies, Nell undergoes no change of character in the novel's course. Her long trudge from London through the industrial wasteland of the West Midlands, to Shropshire, is in no sense a quest for self-development, but rather a search for a home where she and her grandfather can recapture the happiness that they supposedly once enjoyed before the novel's action began.

If Nell's identification with the ideal female of domestic ideology is so absolute as to render illustration well nigh redundant, her embodiment of the lost childhood of adult males does demand closer attention. *The Old Curiosity Shop* is filled with the alliances of old men and children. The work from which it sprang, Dickens's ill-fated magazine *Master Humphrey's Clock*, was itself predicated on the idea of an aged cripple gaining solace for himself and three similarly decrepit friends by telling

75

tales "which extract the essence of perpetual youth from dust and ashes."[64] Feminine youth appears to be distinctly preferable: when Master Humphrey weaves stories about the echoes that haunt him in his old house, he notes that "it is pleasanter to imagine in them the rustling of silk brocade, and the light step of some lovely girl, than to recognise in their altered note the failing tread of an old man."[65] The novel's opening chapter nicely juxtaposes the "light step" and the "failing tread" by staging the encounter of Nell and Master Humphrey on the London streets, and then repeats the configuration in even more striking form after the old man has escorted the little girl back to the Curiosity Shop. Musing upon Nell's placement in the midst of the ramshackle bric-a-brac that constitutes the shop's unsalable stock, Master Humphrey presents the conjunction as the paradoxical association of youth and age:

> I had her image, without any effort of imagination, surrounded and beset by everything that was foreign to its own nature, and furthest removed from the sympathies of her sex and age. . . . the only pure, fresh, youthful object in the throng . . . I had ever before me the old dark murky rooms— the gaunt suits of mail with their ghostly silent air—the dust and rust, and worm that lives in wood—and alone in the midst of all this lumber and decay, and ugly age, the beautiful child in her gentle slumber, smiling through her light and sunny dreams. (56)

However, because it is precisely the work of the novel to return Nell to an exact replica of this scene—if anything, her "vaulted chamber" in the ruined monastery at the end is even more redolent of extreme age—we can certainly question whether the alliance is indeed paradoxical in the symbolic economy of *The Old Curiosity Shop*. Commenting upon the "mockery" that names the grandfather's senility "childishness," the narrator makes it clear that it is the young girl, not the old man, who has the claim on antiquity. "Send forth the child and childish man together," he declares, "and blush for the pride that labels *our own old happy state*, and gives its title to an ugly and distorted image" (46; emphasis added). Throughout the novel childhood is indeed the "old" state because it is important not in and for itself, nor for those who are currently experiencing it, but for those who are remembering it from afar. Little Nell, then, the novel's principal representative of childhood, bears her condition entirely as a service for others—or more precisely, for male others. That Nell's gender is a prerequisite for, rather than an obstacle to, this role is borne out by the single gentleman's description of the essential femininity of a transgenerational essence of youth. This man, soon to be revealed as Nell's great-uncle, casually subverts a standard image of aristocratic lineage by substituting the figure of the girl for the patriarch:

> If you have ever seen the picture-gallery of any one old family, you will remember how the same face and figure—often the fairest and slightest of them all—come upon you in different generations; and how you trace the same sweet girl through a long line of portraits—never growing old or changing—the Good Angel of the race. (637)[66]

In her current incarnation, the good angel Nell appears able to embody the childhood of seemingly any and every male—she is the youth of the old schoolmaster's beloved dead lad, of the homeless, nameless man who shelters in the Birmingham foundry[67]—but of course her most important responsibility is to her own family, which is to say, to her grandfather. Her obvious relationship to her aged relative is a simple inversion of their actual bond: time and again, Nell plays parent to her old baby.[68]

Elsewhere, however, the narrator insists that there is a more complex dependency at work. Although the grandfather has only had Nell's company for thirteen short years, a small section of the span of his life, it is claimed that her true significance to him reaches much further back into his sense of self. As we shall eventually see in our examination of the old man's expressed motivations and his behavior toward Nell, this mode of thinking ultimately seems more important to the narrator than to the grandfather himself, but notice what happens in the following passage:

> And yet, to the old man's vision, Nell was still the same. . . . there was his young companion with the same smile for him, the same earnest words, the same merry laugh, the same love and care that sinking deep into his soul seemed to have been present to him through his whole life. (119)

Just as it is intimated that the schoolmaster and his pupil have enjoyed a lengthy relationship with each other ("The two old friends and companions—for such they were, though they were man and child" [261]), the grandfather is said to view his alliance with Nell in a way that transcends literal chronology. By denying that there is a fixed relationship between Nell's importance and the duration of her life, this passage further nullifies the girl's selfhood, suggesting that she exists only as the embodiment of her grandfather's lost childhood.

It is surely significant that at the very moment that Nell is dying, the grandfather's long-lost brother arrives to provide a content for that old man's childhood, insisting that what has actually been lost, and what is now being restored, is the emotional bond between siblings. The bachelor tries to prepare the ground for the reconciliation:

> Say, that you could carry back your thoughts to very distant days—to the time of your early life—when, unlike this fair flower, you did not pass your youth alone. Say, that you could remember, long ago, another child who loved you dearly, you being but a child yourself. Say, that you had a brother, long forgotten, long unseen, long separated from you, who now, at last, in your utmost need came back to comfort and console you. (651)

Now the single gentleman himself speaks up, promising that childhood's close and loving union can be re-created in old age:

> Our love and fellowship began in childhood, when life was all before us, and will be resumed when we have proved it, and are but children at the last. As many restless spirits, who have hunted fortune, fame, or pleasure through the world, retire in their decline to where they first drew breath, vainly seeking to be children once again before they die, so we, less fortunate than they in early life, but happier in its closing scenes, will set up our rest again among our boyish haunts, and going home with no hope realised, that had its growth in manhood—carrying back nothing that we have brought away, but our old yearnings to each other—saving no fragment from the wreck of life, but that which first endeared it—may be indeed but children as at first. (652)

Despite an almost comical overinsistence—this scene is packed full with pairs of reunited old men—this last-ditch attempt to sustain the grandfather by providing him with a different form of relationship with his childhood is a dismal failure; once Nell is gone, he has no desire to keep living, and soon follows her to the grave. In another place, we might imagine that the reappearance of the beloved brother would facilitate the recapture of childhood's plenitude. In *The Old Curiosity Shop*, however, all the energies combine to insist that the true representative of an old man's past is a little girl: she allows that past to be simultaneously absolutely present and absolutely lost, for although her living being gives full embodiment to that time of imagined richness, the fact of her different gender makes it clear that there can be no return.

Nell's relationship with England's rural past is symbolically congruent to her alliance with the childhood of old men. Although she has lived in the city all her life, Nell's instinctive reaction to the collapse of her grandfather's fortunes is to insist that they set out for "some distant country place remote from towns or even other villages," "a green and fresh world," "where we may live in peace" (124, 423). Nell is not alone in feeling that a journey "into the deep green shade" is the natural thing to do: a desire for the countryside, according to the narrator, lurks within most of "those whose life is in a crowd or who live solitarily in great cities as in the bucket of a human well" (173). In some, the longing for green fields is barely recognized as such—"old clerks who pass [birds in cages in Covent Garden Market] on their road to business" are so alienated from their rural heritage that they "wonder what has filled their breasts with visions of the country" (44)—while others are sufficiently aware of their expulsion from the garden to listen "disconsolately to milkmen who spoke of country fairs, and told of waggons in the mews, with awnings and all things complete and gallant swains to boot" (171).

As Nell gets closer to the little village in Shropshire that is to be her final resting place, it becomes increasingly apparent that her journey into the heart of rural England is also a movement back in time: if Dickens slips from references to the contemporary "Her Majesty" to the earlier "His Majesty" in the course of his writing, this is only one indication of a return to a historically anterior period.[69] The geographical transition from the machine-shops and foundries of the Black Country to Shropshire's rolling hills is represented as a temporal regression to a preindustrial age: once Nell gets "clear of the smoke and furnaces" (437), Dickens marks the landscape with more and more signs of antiquity, a process that reaches its zenith in the ancestral village of Tong.[70] Practically every feature of the rural hamlet proclaims its relationship to a long-distant past—"even change was old in that old place" (480). At her first view of her last home, Nell

> admired everything—the old grey porch, the mullioned windows, the venerable grave stones dotting the green churchyard, the ancient tower, the very weathercock; peeping from among the trees; the stream that rippled by the distant watermill; the blue Welch mountains far away. It was for such a spot the child had wearied in the dense, dark miserable haunts of labour. Upon her bed of ashes, and amidst the squalid horrors through which they had forced their way, visions of such scenes—beautiful indeed, but not more beautiful than this sweet reality—had been always present to her mind. (438)

As this passage reveals, Nell intuitively recognizes her new/old home, even to the extent of knowing precisely which antiquated dwelling-place will be her own. It is made transparently clear to the reader that Nell and the old country village are in total symbolic and emotional harmony with each other: if the hamlet is the fitting setting for the girl because of its sweet, old-fashioned quaintness, then she too is the best representative of this ancient rural idyll.

Before she is allowed to reach this sanctuary, however, Nell has been forced to traverse those "dense, dark, miserable haunts of labour." Deprived of her home, compromised and inadequate though it was, as the result of the old man's compulsive gambling and Quilp's machinations, the girl is brought into relation with labor in two significant ways. In the first place, she must seek paid work to finance the necessities of life, and in the second, she must walk through an appalling industrial landscape on her journey to ultimate peace.[71] Nell's jobs, such as they are—mending the clothes of the Punch-and-Judy men's puppets, selling posies at the races, showing visitors around Mrs. Jarley's waxworks, and, finally, acting as the curator of the village church—are as close to genteel as Dickens can manage, but the simple fact of Nell's presence in the labor market is enough to compromise her already worryingly unfixed class status. The novelist, of course, relishes this opportunity to show that Nell's virtue transcends whatever economic and social position she occupies at any given time: the ideal girl is still ideal even when she has neither the financial security nor the respectability of a middle-class home.

This move on Dickens's part is by no means as radical as it could have been—espousing the ideality of a girl who happens to be in a working-class position is not, after all, the same thing as making an out-and-out working-class girl your ideal. Nevertheless, the novelist takes pains to differentiate his position from those versions of domestic ideology that attempt to ally the sanctity of femininity with the sanctity of class divisions. Dickens lays bare the lineaments of such thinking in a delicious encounter between Nell and the archsnob Miss Monflathers. Proprietor of a Boarding and Day Establishment for Young Ladies, Monflathers reproaches Nell for working for Mrs. Jarley:

> "Don't you know," said Miss Monflathers, "that it's very naughty and unfeminine, and a perversion of the properties wisely and benignantly transmitted to us, with expansive powers to be roused from their dormant state through the medium of cultivation?" (308)

Lest we assume that she includes Nell in the privileged company of those who should be governed by Mrs. Ellis's rules for feminine conduct, the schoolmistress delivers her second thrust:

"Don't you feel how naughty it is of you," resumed Miss Monflathers, "to be a wax-work child, when you might have the proud consciousness of assisting, to the extent of your infant powers, the manufactures of your country; of improving your mind by the constant contemplation of the steam engine; and of earning a comfortable and independent subsistence of from two-and-ninepence to three shillings per week? Don't you know that the harder you are at work, the happier you are?" (308)

The ludicrous result of this modification of domestic ideology's language of service to fit working-class children shows that the theory's adherence to any transcendent notion of universal femininity is a sham.[72] The ideologue's concluding remarks make it clear that there is one rule for the rich, and one for the poor:

"The little busy bee," said Miss Monflathers, drawing herself up, "is applicable only to genteel children.

"In books, or work, or healthful play"

is quite right as far as they are concerned; and the work means painting on velvet, fancy needle-work, or embroidery. In such cases as these," pointing to Nell, with her parasol, "and in the case of all poor people's children, we should read it thus:

"In work, work, work. In work alway
    Let my first years be past,
That I may give for ev'ry day
    Some good account at last."

(309)[73]

While Nell's brushes with employment never bring her anywhere close to "the manufactures of [her] country" or "the constant contemplation of the steam-engine," her literal path across the nation leads her into the very thick of industrial England. After she and her grandfather have been dropped by the canal barge in the "centre of some great manufacturing town" (412), we follow their slow progress over the three nights and two days it takes them to cross the vast and terrifying conurbation. Although no proper names are provided, ample internal evidence makes it easy to work out that the travelers are moving through the urban sprawl that stretches from Birmingham to Wolverhampton.[74] Occupying only two of the seventy-three chapters of this work, the descriptions of the industrial netherworld and its brutalized denizens nevertheless make a tremendous claim on our attention, for the unrelieved ferocity of Dickens's writing here has no parallel elsewhere in the novel. The following paragraph gives some indication of the complete picture:

Advancing more and more into the shadow of this mournful place, its dark depressing influence stole upon their spirits, and filled them with a dismal gloom. On every side, and far as the eye could see into the heavy distance, tall chimneys, crowding on each other, and presenting that endless repetition of the same dull, ugly form, which is the horror of oppressive dreams, poured out their plague of smoke, obscured the light, and made foul the melancholy air. On mounds of ashes by the wayside, sheltered only by a few rough boards, or rotten pent-house roofs, strange engines spun and writhed like tortured creatures; clanking their iron chains, shrieking in their rapid whirl from time to time as though in torment unendurable, and making the ground tremble with their agonies. Dismantled houses here and there appeared, tottering to the earth, propped up by fragments of others that had fallen down, unroofed, windowless, blackened, desolate, but yet inhabited. Men, women, children, wan in their looks and ragged in attire, tended the engines, fed their tributary fires, begged upon the road, or scowled half-naked from the doorless houses. Then came more of the wrathful monsters, whose like they almost seemed to be in their wildness and their untamed air, screeching and turning round and round again; and still, before, behind, and to the right and left, was the same interminable perspective of brick towers, never ceasing in their black vomit, blasting all things living or inanimate, shutting out the face of day, and closing in on all these horrors with a dense dark cloud. (423–24)

Dickens's representation of this district (exactly the area that will be investigated by R. H. Horne) bears scant relation to his allegorical depiction of the northern industrial town in *Hard Times* (1854).[75] Coketown's machinery may be likened to "melancholy-mad elephants," but they are not writhing, "tortured creatures"; rather we are impressed by their giant and stately monotony, the "measured motion" of their impassive efficiency.[76] Similarly the automaton-like workers of the later novel have little in common with the savage industrial populace of *The Old Curiosity Shop*.[77] Largely unfamiliar with the North until the mid-1850s, Dickens constructs the new industrial England in his earlier novel not as a world of solid and oppressive uniformity, but as an inherently unstable land of nightmare. This contemporary Hades, instinct with noise, fire, and frenetic, unpredictable motion, is thus all the more differentiated from the quiet stability that invests both Nell and the rural past she represents.

Consequently, it is disturbing that at this stage of her journey, Nell resembles the unfortunate inhabitants of this hellhole inasmuch as she too is begging on the road, "wan" in her looks, and if not "ragged in attire" thanks to her skill with the needle, certainly inadequately shod. The ideal girl and the industrial poor are equally helpless to ease each other's plight, as this instance reveals:

> [Nell] approached one of the wretched hovels by the wayside, and knocked with her hand upon the door.
> "What would you have here?" said a gaunt miserable man, opening it.
> "Charity. A morsel of bread."
> "Do you see that?" returned the man hoarsely, pointing to a kind of bundle on the ground. "That's a dead child. I and five hundred other men were thrown out of work three months ago. That is my third dead child, and last. Do you think I have charity to bestow, or a morsel of bread to spare?"
> The child recoiled from the door, and it closed upon her. (427)

This is the one point in the novel where Nell is unable to display her spiritual superiority, to compensate for her material poverty by providing inexhaustible supplies of sympathy or domestic assistance. The ideal girl cannot begin to palliate the problems of an industrial inferno that appears to make children its especial targets for destruction.

As we shall see later, perceptions of Nell are seriously affected by her close encounters with work, workplaces, and workers. Nevertheless, the girl's relationship to the working class always remains one of proximity, never one of identity. Dickens's late introduction of a *true* working-class girl into *The Old Curiosity Shop* fully underscores this fact. Another thirteen-year-old female, nameless until Dick Swiveller dubs her "the Marchioness" to add a little class to a tawdry game of cribbage in the kitchen, appears almost exactly at the midpoint of the novel. The two girls never meet, and the only narrative connection between them is formed by Dick, who at the beginning of the novel is a prospective suitor for Nell's hand, and at the end is married to the Marchioness.[78] Nell and the Marchioness are not only physically separated—Nell has long left London to roam the country by the time we glimpse the other child, whose life of domestic slavery amounts to a sentence of house arrest in Sampson Brass's law offices—but they also inhabit different genres, receiving markedly distinct treatment from Dickens's pen.[79] When the Marchioness is finally able to leave the house, she moves directly into the realm of fairy tale,[80] but up until this point, her miserable existence is realistically represented, without recourse either to the idealism or sentimentality that dog Nell's every step.

Thomas Hood commented in his review of the novel halfway through publication that the depiction of "this diminutive maid-of-all-work . . . seems intended . . . to warn us that the most ill-used children are not to be found in factories."[81] Certainly the Marchioness is the embodiment not only of the quintessential abused working-class child, but of the quintessential abused *working* child. "There never was such an old fashioned child in her looks and manner," claims the narrator. "She must have been at work from her cradle" (332). The Marchioness endures an underground existence equal in its inhumanity to the working lives of the children of the Yorkshire mines:

> One circumstance troubled Mr Swiveller's mind very much, and that was that the small servant always remained somewhere in the bowels of the earth under Bevis Marks, and never came to the surface unless the single gentleman rang his bell, when she would answer it and immediately disappear again. She never went out, or came into the office, or had a clean face, or took off the coarse apron, or looked out of any one of the windows, or stood at the street-door for a breath of air, or had any rest or enjoyment whatever. Nobody ever came to see her, nobody spoke of her, nobody cared about her. Mr Brass had said once, that he believed she was "a love-child," (which means anything but a child of love,) and that was all the information Richard Swiveller could obtain. (349)[82]

This girl's plight is perhaps even worse than that of a hurrier, for she not only suffers from overwork, but from neglect and malicious cruelty as well: Mr. Brass's sister Sally both starves her servant and subjects her to habitual bullying. Dick watches as the woman, who is also his employer, is impelled

> without the smallest present cause, to rap the child with the blade of the knife, now on her hand, now on her head, and now on her back, as if she found it quite impossible to stand so close to her without administering a few slight knocks. . . . Mr Swiveller was not a little surprised to see his fellow-clerk, after walking slowly backwards towards the door, as if she were trying to withdraw herself from the room but could not accomplish it, dart suddenly forward, and falling on the small servant give her some hard blows with her clenched hand. The victim cried, but in a subdued manner as if she feared to raise her voice. (353)

Thus when the Marchioness begs Dick, "Don't you ever tell upon me, or I shall be beat to death" (532), her words employ no casual hyperbole; her only friend's subsequent expostulation, "This poor little Marchioness has been wearing herself to death!" (585), also has the potential to be literally true.

We all know too well, however, that in this novel death comes to the ideal girl, not to the chronically malnourished, repeatedly abused, persistently deprived child of the working class: this latter girl, improbably enough, winds up with *The Old Curiosity Shop*'s happiest ending. Nell and the Marchioness may not be bound together by plotlines, but as this swapping of ultimate fates reveals, they are constructed as mutually complementary characters. The most significant feature of this doubling is the reallocation of class-specific traits that it licenses: from evidence already cited, we can see how the static, home-centered life of the ideal girl is here ironically attached to the lower-class waif (who, to complicate the situation further, bears that implausible upper-class moniker). More interesting for our immediate concerns is the related fact that in *The Old Curiosity Shop*, the working-class girl's body is shrouded from our view, while the physicality of the ideal girl is the object of intense narrative interest. The description that accompanies the Marchioness's first entrance in the novel tells us all we ever learn about the child's appearance: "Dick leant over the table, and descried a small slipshod girl in a dirty coarse apron and bib, which left nothing of her visible but her face and feet. She might as well have been dressed in a violin case" (332). Thus Dickens confines the domestic servant as much within her clothes as within the house, and, despite the fact that she works continually, never shows us her body in the revealing act of labor. The case is entirely different with Nell: her movement in and through the world of work results in an astonishing degree of attention upon her physical presence.

Given that Dickens places his heroine in both metaphorical and literal circulation, it is perhaps not surprising that his narrative focuses so frequently upon the parts of Nell's body most intimately connected with movement—which is to say, her feet. While another character, as we shall see, tends to direct his glance somewhat higher up, the narrator and others keep us in constant contact with the state of Nell's lowest extremities. Nell sets the style herself in the early part of the novel: "Let us wander barefoot through the world," she says to her ruined grandfather, "rather than linger here" (148). From the very first day of walking, when we are told that "one of her little feet was blistered and sore" (179), to the end of their ramblings, we hear progressively more dire reports about the condition of Nell's shoes, are asked to imagine the print of "her tiny footsteps in the moss" (247), and listen to concerned bystanders tell her that the roads of the industrial conurbation were "never made for little feet like yours" (421). As Nell lies dying in the next room, her grandfather eulogizes his darling's ruined shoes:

> See here—these shoes—how worn they are—she kept them to remind her of our last long journey. You see where the little feet were bare upon the ground. They told me afterwards, that the stones had cut and bruised them. She never told me that. No, no, God bless her! and, I have remembered since, she walked behind me, sir, that I might not see how lame she was—but yet she had my hand in hers, and seemed to lead me still. (649)

In comparison with the outrageous behavior and pronouncements of Quilp, Nell's infamous predator, such concern with these relatively uncontroversial portions of the girl's body may seem decorous and unobjectionable.[83] We should notice, however, that this emphasis nevertheless gives us the opportunity to think directly about Nell's bare flesh and the tortures it endures.[84] It is certainly worth asking whether we should be more unnerved by Dickens's implicit desire to supply us with such a concrete way of imagining Nell's bodily suffering than we are by Quilp's explicit voyeurism. Admittedly this vibrantly malevolent dwarf's apparent admiration for the girl is not limited to an appreciation of her feet. When he decides to sleep in her (vacated) bed, or invites her to sit upon his knee, to become the second Mrs. Quilp, or to give him a kiss, it is Quilp's delight to itemize Nell's body parts, allocating each segment an appropriate adjective. "Chubby, rosy, cosy, little Nell," in Quilp's words, would make him a "little cherry-cheeked, red-lipped wife" (125, 93); this "fresh, blooming, modest little bud" is to him "so small, so compact, so beautifully modelled, so fair, with such blue veins and such a transparent skin, and such little feet, and such winning ways" (125).

Passages like these have inspired much twentieth-century comment on Dickens's prescient construction of the pedophile,[85] but it seems to me that Quilp's eroticization of the prepubescent girl is both too blatant and too studied to be truly disturbing. After all, the last-quoted sentence is delivered, Dickens tells us outright, by a man who is "speaking very slowly, and *feigning* to be quite absorbed in the subject" (125; emphasis added). Quilp cannot really upset us because he is calculating, not compulsive, and displays absolutely no signs of being overmastered by obsession. Although he is positioned as the ne plus ultra of girl-threatening monstrosity, the dwarf's lasciviousness is actually a red herring, serving to deflect our recognition of an infinitely more worrying general tendency of the novel. Loosened from the glue of respectability, Nell's symbolic relationships take on altogether different dimensions: it is her alliance with old men, most notably with her grandfather, that is ultimately the most disquieting aspect of *The Old Curiosity Shop*.

Our nervousness begins as the novel opens. Nell is alone walking the streets, perilously close to Covent Garden, London's traditional red-light district, when she "solicits" Master Humphrey. Forced by her grandfather's reckless gambling to cross the city on money-borrowing missions, Nell has already said good-bye to the ideal girl's domestic role, and thus compromised her sacrosanct status. (That Dickens was aware of the dangerous game he was playing with his heroine is revealed by an alteration to the manuscript version of the child's first conversation with Master Humphrey. When the old man asks her what she has been doing so far afield, Nell had originally replied "Selling diamonds," but the novelist eventually dropped this unsettling and potentially equivocal response.)[86] Although Humphrey does lead the child home, his behavior is not above suspicion: when Nell asks for directions, he responds, perplexingly enough, "Suppose I should tell you wrong?" He deliberately avoids "the most frequented ways" in his route to her door, so that the girl cannot recognize her whereabouts and run off (45, 46). Back in his own house, the old man settles himself into the ample cushions of his easy chair and proceeds to fantasize about "the child in her bed" (55), an imagined scene of stillness very different from the streetwalking he has actually experienced with the girl. The pattern established here in the opening chapter is repeated throughout the novel: although Nell is continually dropped into situations where her movement cannot seem other than socially and sexually ambiguous to the eyes of watching men, Dickens always attempts to erase the ambiguities by maintaining that the child's body is invested with an essential stillness that no motion can disturb. For the moment I will leave unanswered the question of whether or not this tactic is ultimately successful (and, indeed, whether Dickens really wants it to be), examining instead the most obvious ways in that the novelist insists upon his heroine's inertia.

Nell may spend the bulk of her time in the novel walking the 150-some miles from London to Shropshire, but our abiding impression is of her supine figure. I have already commented that her journey cannot promote any character development because she is fully formed from the start; even more noteworthy is the lack of change in Nell's physical position from the beginning to the end of *The Old Curiosity Shop*. Master Humphrey's vision of the child sleeping in the midst of the shop's musty relics and the novel's closing tableau of Nell's deathbed in the ruined monastery are, to all intents and purposes, the same scene. Even though different artists illustrated these chapters, there are no significant variations in their renditions because Dickens's two descriptions are practically identical (figs. 6 and 7).[87]

Narrating her journey toward the bed of death from the equally still bed of sleep, Dickens employs numerous strategies to convince us that Nell's apparent movement is an illusion. One device is set in place very early on: through the medium of Master Humphrey's fancy, the novelist overtly signals that the complete story of the novel is prefigured in the static moment that closes chapter 1. Seeing the conjunction of Nell and the heaps of unbuyable objects around her as "a kind of allegory," the old man muses, "It would be a curious speculation . . . to imagine her in her future life, holding her solitary way among a crowd of wild grotesque companions" (56). Thus, although it may appear that Nell is dangerously available as she wanders through the market, this scene asserts that she is not, and never has been, for sale. Similarly, although the bustle of her multifarious encounters suggests a welter of movement, reference back to this original tableau demands that circulation be subjugated to stasis. Nell's existence as a paradox of moving stillness is perhaps captured most succinctly when she lands employment with Mrs. Jarley and becomes the "wax-work child." As the narrator of the histories of the dead people represented by the waxworks in this traveling show, the child is both removed from, and participating in, the world of motion. The girl's final job—as narrator of the histories of the dead people buried in the old church—is of course much more to her taste, for the troublesome active element is at last expunged. Through her contact with churches, or more precisely, with their graveyards, Nell reaffirms her predisposition for stasis at every stage of her journey. Constitutionally unable to pass a cemetery without lingering around its graves or engaging the sexton in morbid conversation,[88] the girl displays a fascination with mortality that of course prefigures her own impending demise. It would, however, be wrong to assume that death will bring any great change to Nell. As we have seen, Nell's symbolic relationship with both the historic past and the childhoods of old men has from the first denied her any kind of autonomous existence. Nell's ultimate death simply makes literal what has been metaphorically true throughout *The Old Curiosity Shop*; having continually

FIGURE 6. "The Child in Her Gentle Slumber," Dickens, *The Old Curiosity Shop*, chap. 1

striven to associate his heroine with stasis, Dickens succumbs to the inevitable when he finally endows her with its most permanent form.

It is nevertheless a debatable point whether this insistence upon Nell's stillness manages to banish the erotic interest in the child's body. The tactic of bringing the ideal girl into relation with the working class does not result in a triumphant affirmation of the universality of the ideal; rather, it opens the door to the possibility that the bodies of both types of girl are equally sexualized. In *The Old Curiosity Shop*, Dickens avoids the obvious danger of the working-class girl's sexuality by evading the issue of the Marchioness's body altogether, but in transferring working-class mobility to Nell, he lays his heroine open to all kinds of threats. As the symbolic, albeit paradoxical, representative of the happy childhood, the stable home, and the idyllic past, Nell should indeed inspire desire—she is, after all, the treasured haven that guarantees the Victorian reader's sense of security—but a desire that is diffuse and unlocated. Dickens, in his zeal to prove that her ideality is independent of class constraints, forces the girl to confront her symbolic antitypes and thus puts her in a position that promotes not a general longing but a highly specific, body-centered

FIGURE 7. "At Rest," Dickens, *The Old Curiosity Shop*, chap. 71

eroticism. As a result, Nell's most precious relationship—her symbolic bond with her grandfather—becomes eerily and disconcertingly sexualized.[89] Furthermore, her alliance with stasis and death, itself supposed to counteract the arousing associations of movement, is suffused with sexual desire.[90]

The curious quality of the grandfather's relation with his grandchild is perhaps best shown by juxtaposing the old man with Quilp, the spurious archlecher. Let us return to the scene where the dwarf was behaving at his worst. Quilp and the old man sit together in the shop, the former apparently torturing the latter by devising ever more excessive compliments about Nell:

> "She's so," said Quilp, speaking very slowly, and feigning to be quite absorbed in the subject, "so small, so compact, so beautifully modelled, so fair, with such blue veins and such a transparent skin, and such little feet, and such winning ways—but bless me, you're nervous. Why neighbour, what's the matter? I swear to you," continued the dwarf, dismounting from the chair and sitting down in it, with a careful slowness of gesture very different from the rapidity with which he had sprung up unheard, "I swear

to you that I had no idea that old blood ran so fast or kept so warm. I thought it was sluggish in its course, and cool, quite cool. I am pretty sure it ought to be. Yours must be out of order, neighbour."

"I believe it is," groaned the old man, clasping his head with both hands. "There's a burning fever here, and something now and then to which I fear to give a name." (125)

As both the reader and Quilp know, the grandfather's hectic pulse is ostensibly caused by his gambling mania, and at this moment he is desperately waiting to hear whether the dwarf will supply him with more money to finance his addiction. Put into such close relation with Quilp's commodification of Nell's body, however, the old man's hot blood cannot help but make us uneasy.

Our disquiet is hugely intensified later in the novel, when once again the grandfather's compulsive gambling and Nell's unprotected physical presence are brought together to form a disturbing amalgam. Forced by a raging storm to take shelter in a public house of dubious respectability, Nell is dismayed when her grandfather is effortlessly drawn into a game of cards, and she retires to a rented room to try to rest:

> At last, sleep gradually stole upon her—a broken, fitful sleep, troubled by dreams of falling from high towers, and waking with a start and in great terror. A deeper slumber followed this—and then—What! That figure in the room!
>
> A figure was there. Yes, she had drawn up the blind to admit the light when it should be dawn, and there, between the foot of the bed and the dark casement, it crouched and slunk along, groping its way with noiseless hands, and stealing round the bed. She had no voice to cry for help, no power to move, but lay still, watching it.
>
> On it came—on, silently and stealthily, to the bed's head. The breath so near her pillow, that she shrunk back into it, lest those wandering hands should light upon her face. Back again it stole to the window—then turned its head towards her.
>
> The dark form was a mere blot upon the lighter darkness of the room, but she saw the turning of the head, and felt and knew how the eyes looked and the ears listened. There it remained, motionless as she. At length, still keeping the face towards her, it busied its hands in something, and she heard the chink of money.
>
> Then, on it came again, silent and stealthy as before, and replacing the garments it had taken from the bedside, dropped upon its hands and knees,

91

and crawled away. How slowly it seemed to move, now that she could hear but not see it, creeping along the floor! It reached the door at last, and stood upon its feet. The steps creaked beneath its noiseless tread, and it was gone. (301)

No threat that Quilp supplies can make our flesh creep like this passage. Of course, as Nell soon discovers, the mysterious figure is her grandfather, penetrating her chamber to pick her pocket bare. In the highly charged atmosphere created by the ideal girl's displacement from her rightful sphere, the old man's specific greed for money has an unsettling tendency to resemble other forms of desire.[91] For Nell, this experience is frighteningly similar to one of the "mournful fancies" about her grandfather that oppressed her even when they were living at the shop: what would she do, she wonders, "if one night, he should come home, and kiss and bless her as usual, and after she had gone to bed and had fallen asleep and was perhaps dreaming pleasantly, and smiling in her sleep, he should kill himself and his blood come creeping, creeping, on the ground to her bedroom door" (121).

The creeping menace of the grandfather's hot blood soaks into the symbolic structures of *The Old Curiosity Shop*, contaminating even the sanctified relation between little girls and the childhood of old men. Thus the narrator's vision of the gentle alliance between the grateful male relative and the self-denying young girl is transformed into a frightening scene of domination, in which a voracious man plunders the child of her intrinsic loveliness. As Nell herself puts it, the fantasy has turned into "a dreadful dream. . . . A dreadful horrible dream. It is a dream of grey-haired men like you, in darkened rooms by night, robbing the sleepers of their gold" (405). The vicissitudes of Nell and her grandfather's economic fortunes cast them into a world in which even the stillness of the grave is suspect, and our final vision of the couple does nothing to bring our uneasiness to a final resting place: "They laid him by the side of her whom he had loved so well; and, in the church where they had often prayed, and mused, and lingered hand in hand, the child and the old man slept together" (663).

To return to our starting point: in *Many Happy Returns of the Day* the girl may be casting a rather anxious glance in her grandfather's direction, but we are unlikely to sense any true cause for alarm in this painting. Well-wadded with material goods, Frith's bourgeois family is living the life imagined in Ellis's conduct books and has no need to scrutinize the necessary connection between its birthday girl's ideality and her social position. Conditions are entirely different in the royal commission's reports and *The Old Curiosity Shop:* the government official and the novel-ist alike take their ideal girls out of the home into an industrial world where the divisions of class and prosperity and the problems of sexuality are equally pressing and intimately intertwined. Apart from that flicker of discomfort in Frith's little girl's eyes, the family party registers only self-satisfaction: the fact that the artist found his model for the aged grandfather in the workhouse remains strictly an offstage irony.[92]

The Stones of Childhood:
Ruskin's "Lost Jewels"

> I never get any credit from anybody for my geology, and
> it is the best of me by far.
> (*John Ruskin, letter to Mary Gladstone, 1878*)

Very close to the end of *Praeterita*, his autobiography, John Ruskin tells us of his only "full collision" with D'Israeli, which occurred at an official banquet hosted by Dean Liddell in Oxford for the Princess of Wales.[1] A day or two before this grand event, Ruskin explains, "the Planet Saturn had treated me with his usual adversity in the carrying out of a plot with Alice in Wonderland" (35:505). The complete enjoyment of a clandestine evening with the Liddell girls, of "a bright fireside, and a laugh or two, and some pretty music," had been ruined when bad weather forced their parents to give up a social engagement:

> Well, I think Edith had got the tea made, and Alice was just bringing the muffins to perfection—I don't recollect that Rhoda was there; (I never did, that anybody else was there, if Edith was; but it is all so like a dream now, I'm not sure)—when there was a sudden sense of some stars having been blown out by the wind, round the corner; and then a crushing of the snow outside the house, and a drifting of it inside; and the children all scampered out to see what was wrong, and I followed slowly;—and there were the Dean and Mrs. Liddell standing just in the middle of the hall, and the footmen in consternation, and a silence,—and—
>
> "How sorry you must be to see us, Mr. Ruskin!" began at last Mrs. Liddell.
>
> "I never was more so," I replied. "But what's the matter?"
>
> "Well," said the Dean, "we couldn't even get past the parks; the snow's a fathom deep in the Woodstock Road. But never mind; we'll be very good and quiet, and keep out of the way. Go back to your tea, and we'll have our dinner downstairs." (35:506)

Ruskin is "disconsolate": he has known these "children" "from the nursery," and now that they are in their teens and early twenties, he "never get[s] a sight of them" (35:506).

This tale of thwarted intrigue bubbles up a day or two later to form "a little ripple of brighter converse" in the polite formalities of the royal banquet (35:505), attracting the attention—and apparently the smiles— of princess and politician alike. Later, when "the door from the nurseries" opens and Rhoda Liddell, "as exquisite a little spray of rhododendrom ferrugineum as ever sparkled in Alpine dew" (35:507, 508), joins the company in the drawing room, D'Israeli immediately sees his chance. Advancing toward her, and "[b]owing with kindly reverence," he pronounces this introduction: "*This* is, I understand, the young lady in whose art-education Professor Ruskin is so deeply interested!" (35:508). Collapse of the entire party, we assume, ensues.

A first reaction to this snippet of old "gossip," as Ruskin calls it, is probably one of surprise—surprise to find the nineteenth century's most iconic little girl, the famous lodestone of the Reverend Charles Dodgson's desire, Lewis Carroll's celebrated literary and photographic muse, appearing (albeit in a supporting role) in the autobiography of the nineteenth century's *other* most infamous girl-lover. The happenstance that Alice Liddell is also an object of fascination (though not, we might note, of paramount fascination) to John Ruskin makes the Victorian world seem simultaneously cozily, and disconcertingly, small. The last two chapters have presented the cult of the little girl within the context of large-scale cultural, economic, and social movements. Now we appear to be in danger of seeing the vast and complex canvases of a turbulent and burgeoning age shrink down into charming, or perhaps not so charming, vignettes of deanery life, in which the Reverend Dodgson pops over from his college rooms to propose a game of croquet, or an outing on the river, while Mr. Ruskin, that "old conger eel" of a "Drawling-master," drops by once a week to give a sketching lesson,[2] or, in later years, slips round in the evening for a surreptitious muffin. In this light, Christ Church houses the epicenter of a certain specialized form of Victorian desire: girl loving becomes the predilection of a couple of troubled Oxford dons, stirred to admiration (or more) by the bewitching daughters of Dean Liddell. And yet, as we shall see in this chapter and the next, Charles Dodgson and John Ruskin reach that deanery garden by means of routes that encompass as many divergences as convergences: even cursory attention to the defining circumstances of each man's life reveals that there is no simple or single formula for the production of a Victorian girl-lover. Ultimately the appearance of the same little girl in both men's stories is both fascinating and meaningless: Alice and paradox are not easily parted.

Once we have recovered from this coincidence, we may find another matter for our consideration in this seemingly casual anecdote, a matter that has direct relevance to some of the key questions that have by turns worried and energized Ruskin studies in recent years. Ruskin's story both tells of his desire to be in the presence of young girls, and, with an almost laughable overemphasis, demonstrates a favorable contemporary public reaction to that desire—not only a premier statesman, but also a member of the royal family, is prettily amused. Granted, Ruskin is the teller of this tale, and he may represent the responses of his dining companions in whatever manner he chooses, but if this is indeed a cunningly inserted narrative of self-justification, then it seems to be constructed in a most peculiar and self-defeating fashion: readers of *Praeterita*, then and now, may experience rather different sensations from those of the original audience. In the center of the story, the tense atmosphere created by the dean's unexpected return certainly gives pause: the footmen's consternation, that silence, and Mrs. Liddell's eventual utterance, "How sorry you must be to see us, Mr. Ruskin!" could make one suspect that suspicion of wrongdoing might momentarily have been in the frame. The scent of transgression may seem to evaporate when the drawing-room confab is given the sanction of the paterfamilias—"[N]ever mind," says Dean Liddell, "we'll be very good and quiet, and keep out of the way"—but still a sense of unease lingers that is hardly dissipated by D'Israeli's jovial witticism about the professor's disingenuous enthusiasm for the artistic progress of an "exquisite" female pupil nearly forty years his junior.

In short, unlike those merry dinner-guests of over 120 years ago, we think we know enough to find the appearance of girls in Ruskin's autobiography, as in his life, no laughing matter. Kenneth Clark's gentle appreciation of *Praeterita*'s feminine presences sounds an extremely rare note in twentieth-century Ruskin studies:

> Was there ever an autobiography in which girls are more vividly remembered? Casanova's descriptions of women are often vague and generalized; but every girl Ruskin saw, from childhood onwards, was imprinted on his memory with all her particularities, and set down, after sixty years, as freshly as if she had just entered the room. There is still a tremor as he describes them, his Scottish cousins, the Domecq girls, Miss Wardell, Miss Lockhart, and Miss Tollemache, who, although he didn't succeed in getting within fifty yards of her, was the "light and solace" of a whole winter in Rome.[3]

Even in 1949, when these words were first published in the introduction to the Oxford University Press edition of *Praeterita* (still the only easily available version of the autobiography), Clark's pairing of Ruskin with

Casanova must have seemed singularly disturbing. After all, anybody who knows anything about Ruskin's biography is aware that if he could be called a sexual adventurer, then he certainly did not end up in the "normal" places. If we have a little more information about his life, then we are almost certainly aware that Ruskin's is a story of sexual irregularity—we speculate about exactly which feature of Effie's mature womanliness revolted him on their disastrous wedding night; we shake our heads over his doomed obsession with the nine-year-old Irish girl with the unsettlingly evocative name of Rose La Touche; we roll our eyes at the blindness of the principal of Winnington School, who allowed her prepubescent charges to "romp" unchecked with this middle-aged man. Until relatively recently,[4] elaborating on Clark's perception of the "vivid" descriptions of girls in *Praeterita* has not been a popular course: the assumption seems to be that the reason for their presence is both too obvious, and too embarrassing, to talk about, especially in the midst of readings of a text that, more than any other in this famously difficult and conflicted oeuvre, tends to excite the hagiographic impulse in the breasts of Ruskin scholars.[5] But if we avert our gaze from the girls in the autobiography, do we not run the risk of losing sight of reasons other than the obvious (by which I mean an unexamined notion of the "pedophilic") for their appearance? By following Clark's lead and looking closely at *Praeterita*'s girls, we can properly consider a number of important overarching questions. In the first place, what is the nature of Ruskin's desire for, or admiration of, or obsession with, little girls? And in the second, how is it related to his construction and representation of the self, and to his conception of the erotic?

It is my contention that the autobiographical writings of Ruskin, in common with those of De Quincey, set forth the clearest expression of the developmental fantasy of original femininity that is the especial focus in this study. As close analysis reveals, *Praeterita* tends to represent the self of childhood as a little girl rather than a little boy. Previous chapters juxtaposed versions of this paradigm, as expressed in literary texts, to public discourses that demonstrate, in one way or another, the nineteenth century's developing conceptions about the innate qualities and appropriate content of childhood. This chapter alters the angle of approach and narrows the focus not just to the compass of a single life, but, given the voluminous production of Ruskin's fifty-year literary career and the changing complexities of his views over those years, to a couple of key periods and texts within his history. An important part of this inquiry will be an examination of the particular circumstances—economic, social, religious, educational, and familial—of his life: *Praeterita* offers a strong example of a paradigm that has general, although by no means universal, currency in the Victorian age, but Ruskin's existence is by no stretch of the imagination paradigmatic for his class and gender in this period.

As we shall see, Ruskin's conceptualization of the little girl follows the broad outlines already mapped out in this study. After an initial scrutiny of the imagined early self and the many feminine presences of *Praeterita*, I turn to *The Ethics of the Dust*, a text from the middle of Ruskin's career that is ostensibly both for, and about, girls. Here the formula seen developing in the first two chapters is carefully expounded: young femininity is explicitly connected to antiquity, to the unsullied and vital purity of long-lost origins, and most definitely placed in contradistinction to its exact opposites, the defiled world of the present day and a miserably compromised and decrepit male maturity. Furthermore, the immature feminine body is frequently imagined in a very particular fashion: although one might hypothesize that the girl lover's celebration of his diminutive idol would always be couched in the soft and pliable, would choose to luxuriate in the yielding loveliness of juvenile flesh, Ruskin's rhetorical turns produce not a desirably vulnerable other, but a figure of rocklike impenetrability and adamantine brilliance. The girls of *The Ethics of the Dust* are quite specifically seen in terms of the ancient and precious stones of the earth—as beautiful crystals, gems, or jewels. While this system of representation is not the only form of imagery that Ruskin applies to girlhood, it is nevertheless dominant. Moreover, it offers the clearest way to comprehend the construction of the erotic in Ruskin's writing: viewing the beloved little girl as a gem, as a hard and an aesthetically pleasing object, appears not to be a defense against erotic desire, but a crucial component thereof. With this understanding, the chapter closes by returning to *Praeterita* to demonstrate that Ruskin's fantasized feminized childhood is also, despite its logical untenability, the beautiful unyielding jewel of *The Ethics of the Dust*. Still more poignantly, the crystalline girlish self is not just the lost self of the past, but also the only true self of the present.

At one time Ruskin seemed to suggest that any formal autobiography on his part would be redundant, given that he saw his works as an ongoing life-record, written in decade-by-decade installments: "at twenty, I wrote *Modern Painters*; at thirty, *The Stones of Venice*; at forty, *Unto this Last*; at fifty, the Inaugural Oxford Lectures; and—if *Fors Clavigera* is ever finished as I mean—it will mark the mind I had at sixty; and leave me in my seventh day of life, perhaps to rest" (27:137). As it turned out, that day of rest was not to be: Ruskin denied himself a sabbatical, and at irregular intervals between 1885 and 1889 published twenty-eight parts of a work he called *Praeterita*, a vision of "Past things."[6]

The urge toward autobiography had first manifested itself in the previous decade within the fervid pages of *Fors Clavigera*, Ruskin's impassioned and frequently unhinged series of "Letters to the Workmen and Labourers of Great Britain." Indeed, most of the material in *Praeterita*'s first few chapters had already appeared in *Fors* up to fourteen years earlier. A return to the site of extraction of these passages reveals that Ruskin had felt it necessary at each juncture to justify the inclusion of personal material, making his didactic mission clear with statements like the following: "Have patience with me in this egotism; it is necessary for many reasons that you should know what influences have brought me into the temper in which I write to you" (27:167). Aside from a few vestigial traces of this impulse in the preface, the main text of *Praeterita*, in contrast, contains no such injunctions, and it is not hard to figure out one of the reasons why. To suggest that the details of his life offered the possibility of educating the reader took Ruskin too close to the desire to improve a world he had found increasingly out of joint since the 1860s, and that provoked the "temper" that seemed to be one of the contributory causes of the bouts of insanity that periodically rocked his life from 1878 onwards. Before the serial parts of his autobiography began appearing, Ruskin had already suffered three attacks of mania, and he was to endure two more before he was silenced, to all intents and purposes, by a devastating sixth onslaught in the summer of 1889. *Praeterita* is thus an unfinished work, seized out of the few tranquil moments of the writer's final tempestuous years.

The preface to Ruskin's autobiography makes quite clear his intentions for "these sketches of effort and incident in former years": "I have written them . . . frankly, garrulously, and at ease; speaking of what it gives me joy to remember at any length I like—sometimes very carefully of what I think it may be useful for others to know; and passing in total silence things which I have no pleasure in reviewing" (35:11). The implications of this plan of action are wide-ranging. Most famously, Ruskin omits all mention of his ill-fated marriage to Effie Gray, while the embattled years wrestling with political economy that grew out of *The Stones of Venice* are dismissed with startling brevity (we read, "All that I did at Venice was bye-work" [35:156], for instance, while "1850–60, for the most part [was] wasted in useless work" [35:483]). In essence, Ruskin excludes those elements of his life that had distanced him from his parents, and especially from his father, John James Ruskin, who had been particularly deeply hurt by the transformation of his son from a celebrated and lionized critic of art into a reviled and misunderstood critic of society. Thanks to these exclusions, Ruskin could legitimately close his preface with the following dedication:

> I write these few prefatory words on my father's birthday, in what was once my nursery in his old house,—to which he brought my mother and me, sixty-two years since, I being then four years old. What would otherwise in the following pages have been little more than an old man's recreation in gathering visionary flowers in fields of youth, has taken, as I wrote, the nobler aspect of a dutiful offering at the grave of parents who trained my childhood to all the good it could attain, and whose memory makes declining life cheerful in the hope of being soon again with them. (35:11–12)

That Ruskin should tell us outright exactly where he is sitting as he composes these sentences is not without significance: *Praeterita* is both literally and symbolically written from out of his beloved Herne Hill nursery, from the position of the solitary child of watchful and guiding parents. Indeed, the image of the child in the early chapters of the autobiography is certainly the most distinct representation of the self that we are granted in the entire work. The child Ruskin is characterized primarily as a securely confined yet keenly aware observer: we are shown him sitting like an ornament, as "an Idol in a niche" "in a little recess" in the drawing room, silently and methodically analyzing the patterns in the carpet (35:39), or contentedly sequestered within his South London garden.[7] Here the specific limitations of the writer's childhood experience in his suburban paradise (differentiated from that other Eden by the fact that "in this one, *all* the fruit was forbidden; and there were no companionable beasts" [35:36]) are given credit for their role in shaping Ruskin's intense powers of visual appreciation. "A great part of my acute perception and deep feeling of the beauty of architecture and scenery abroad," he explains, "was owing to the well formed habit of narrowing myself to happiness within the four brick walls of our fifty by one hundred yards of garden; and accepting with resignation the aesthetic external surroundings of a London suburb" (35:165).

Ruskin thus presents a vision of the confined child as the essential nucleus of an adult existence spent gazing upon the splendors of European nature and culture: this is in effect a miniature image of *Praeterita*'s general structure. After the crystalline precision of its early chapters, the autobiography rambles off into the disorder of an inchoate travel-guide. Instead of representations of the self, we are granted only representations of places—allowed to look, as it were, only at a scattered handful of postcards. Francis G. Townsend comments that "the surface arrangement is deceptively chronological, while the real arrangement is that of a portfolio of Turner engravings."[8] Elizabeth Helsinger's essay "The Structure of Ruskin's *Praeterita*" is particularly effective in tracking this "discontinuous mental geography," observing that "Ruskin's constant traveling is never progress: it is the means by which he revisits the territory of a visually extended self."[9] Chronology is replaced by topography: *Praeterita* resolutely rejects the teleological notion of the subject that organizes most nineteenth-century autobiographies, and embraces instead a spatial construction, in which the protected kernel of the observing child is encircled by evocations of beloved landscapes.

Ruskin, then, refuses to allow his autobiography to assume the Romantic tripartite form of paradise, crisis, and reintegration, or even to acknowledge the joining together of moments of being toward an evolving and totalizing narrative of the self.[10] His inability to adopt these models for representing his life story is made quite explicit in a key passage that appears in "Roslyn Chapel," the last chapter of *Praeterita*'s first volume. Here the writer insists that all meaningful development came to an abrupt end for him before maturity was attained. Consequently, the currently writing self looks back over nearly fifty years to the teenage self and sees essentially no difference:

> I had in my little clay pitcher, vialfuls, as it were, of Wordsworth's reverence, Shelley's sensitiveness, Turner's accuracy all in one . . . But so stubborn and chemically inalterable the laws of the prescription were, that now, looking back from 1886 to that brook shore of 1837, whence I could see the whole of my youth, I find myself in nothing whatsoever changed. Some of me is dead, more of me stronger. I have learned a few things, forgotten many; in the total of me, I am but the same youth, disappointed and rheumatic. (35:220)

Claiming that everything that was important in the formation of his character occurred before he was eighteen, Ruskin simultaneously maintains that the young self has persisted into old age ("I am but the same youth"), and that the core of his identity crystallized forever before he stepped across that brook shore into manhood. For the moment, I put aside the first part of this assertion for later discussion and concentrate on the ways in which the autobiography characterizes that young self and its cessation of development.

As already seen, *Praeterita* devotes a considerable amount of its early energies to the depiction of a secure, protected, and enclosed childhood. The passive child at the center of this high-security Eden is, not surprisingly, frequently feminized. Although no special pains are taken to avoid masculine nouns in the references to his younger self, Ruskin draws attention to the fact that his natural sensibilities and his sequestered upbringing made him different from other boys. The difference is apparent both to his own eyes—"I don't know what delight boys take in cricket, or boating, or throwing stones at birds, or learning to shoot them" (35:293)—and to the eyes of his few male associates in childhood, who, "[f]inding me in all respects what boys could only look upon as an innocent, . . . treated me as I suppose they would have treated a girl" (35:83).

This last quotation includes a feature that appears often enough in *Praeterita* to constitute a stylistic tic: the expression *as . . . a girl* and its variant *like a girl* are frequently drafted into service in Ruskin's representations of his child self. The earliest instance occurs in the description of Mr. Northcote's painting of the three-year-old Ruskin, which provides the first, and practically the only, picture we are granted of his physical appearance: "The portrait in question represents a very pretty child with yellow hair, dressed in a white frock like a girl, with a broad light-blue sash and blue shoes to match" (35:21). Given that boys of Ruskin's age and class were habitually dressed in frocks at this period,[11] the simile "like a girl" here is by no means as significant as later rhetorical turns, which find the author comparing himself to girls, and indeed, intensifying the construction by placing himself in the *more* feminine than feminine position. For instance, when the teenaged Ruskin is brought into relation with the entrancing French Catholic daughters of his father's business partner, Juan Pedro Domecq, his unworldly ways are attributed not, as they could have been, to a masculinized monastic existence, but to his being "[v]irtually convent-bred more closely than the maids themselves" (35:179). Similarly, in order to represent his first tentative days of social acclimatization at Oxford, Ruskin makes use of a comparison drawn from the world of debutantes or the pages of a genteel novel and once again renders himself more girlish than the girl described: "[P]oor Clara," we read, "after her first ball, receiving her cousin's compliments in the cloak-room, was less surprised than I by my welcome from my cousins of the long-table" (35:196).

Such rhetorical constructions, intriguing though they are, are perhaps less significant in their contribution to *Praeterita*'s feminization of Ruskin's childhood self than the vividly remembered girls who people the text, as Clark noticed all those years ago. What Clark does not comment upon, however, is the fact that very nearly all of these girls have their lives cut short by early death. The denial of the possibility of maturation that Ruskin insists upon in his "brook shore" assertion is made real in *Praeterita* by a seemingly endless procession of lovely young lasses who fail to make it across the river to adulthood. Dark-eyed little Jessie, Ruskin's vivacious Scottish cousin, is the first to go when she and John are "about eight or nine," and she is soon followed by a host of others. Sometimes the deaths are imagined, rather than literal: the lives of formerly beloved girls who are lost to Ruskin in one way or another are effectively truncated by *Praeterita*'s refusal to grant their adulthood any representation. Thus Ruskin's wife Effie appears only parenthetically as the "little girl" for whose amusement *The King of the Golden River* was written (35:304). In a similar fashion, Adele Domecq, his first love, ceases to have any real existence after the incandescent presence of her fifteen-year-old self had reduced young Ruskin "to a mere heap of white ashes" in his seventeenth year (35:179). On occasion, even when the beloved female does indeed die at a relatively early age, she is remembered and depicted primarily as a much younger being. Here the most important figure is the love of Ruskin's middle age and early old age, Rose La Touche, through the lens of whose loss all the girl-deaths of *Praeterita* are filtered. Although Rose died at twenty-seven of brain fever, she lives in the autobiography primarily as a high-spirited nine-year-old, even commandeering the text with her own precocious expressions and orthographical oddities when Ruskin reproduces her first cherished letter to him in what ended up being *Praeterita*'s penultimate chapter.

Most often, however, death comes to the maiden just as she gives up that maidenhood: we only have to learn that some delicate blossom is to be swept up into an ill-advised marriage, or otherwise oppressed by the demands of adulthood, to know that in a few lines time, she will be gone. Significantly enough, "Roslyn Chapel" provides us with three examples of this phenomenon. The aptly named Miss Withers is "a fragile, fair, freckled, sensitive slip of a girl about sixteen; graceful in an unfinished and small wild-flower sort of a way, extremely intelligent, affectionate, wholly right minded and mild in piety" (35:222). Yet instead of being allowed to bloom in the young Ruskin's presence, Charlotte Withers and the "possibility of meek happiness vanish[ ] forever": her coal-merchant father " 'negotiated' a marriage for her with a well-to-do Newcastle trader, whom she took because she was bid. He treated her pretty much as one of his coal-sacks, and in a year or two she died" (35:222). Nine pages later we encounter Miss Wardell, "an extremely accomplished, intelligent, and faultless maid of seventeen; fragile and delicate . . . a slender brunette, with her father's dark curling hair transfigured into playful grace around the pretty, modest, not unthoughtful, gray-eyed face" (35:231). This time the girl is carried off by overzealous education rather than matrimony, but the outcome, as we learn in this deliberately exhausting sentence, is just the same:

> [A]t Hampstead they went on teaching the tender creature High German, and French of Paris, and Kant's Metaphysics, and Newton's Principia; and then they took her to Paris, and tired her out with seeing everything every day, all day long, besides the dazzle and excitement of such a first outing from Hampstead; and she at last getting too pale and weak, they brought her back to some English seaside place, I forget where: and there she fell into nervous fever and faded away, with the light of death flickering clearer and clearer in her soft eyes, and never skipped in Hampstead garden more. (35:232)

With a brief mention of the "loss of the sweet spirit" of yet another graceful maiden, Miss Sybilla Dowie (35:232), Ruskin concludes the chapter and the volume. The opening of the next volume of *Praeterita* would appear to announce a new era in the writer's existence: the first chapter is entitled "Of Age." Ruskin may literally have attained his majority, but it has already been made clear that his development, as surely as that of the three lost misses, has come to a definite full stop.[12]

Praeterita, then, seems to provide the casebook example of the phenomenon this study describes: Ruskin not only represents his childhood as if it had been a feminine, rather than a masculine, era in his existence, but also, through the repeated invocation of truncated feminine lives, implies that this girl self does not evolve in or into adulthood. As sophisticated readers, we have, of course, no expectations that any autobiography will deliver objective "truths" about a life: all such works, indeed all biographies as well, are necessarily fictions, exercises in mythmaking that allow the writer to construct the history and picture of the individual that he or she desires. While recent studies of *Praeterita* all recognize this fact, they nevertheless have often taken it upon themselves to demonstrate exactly how skewed and partial this life history actually is, particularly in its omissions, as mentioned above, and in Ruskin's largely successful self-censorship of the bitterly conflicted emotions he felt toward both his parents and his mother-substitute and chief-carer in these declining years, his cousin Joan Severn. A desire to pronounce upon the veracity of Ruskin's autobiography is, however, not the only impetus to move back and forth between *Praeterita*'s constructions and other contexts for understanding Ruskin's life. Rather than consider the peculiarities of Ruskin's perspective, I raise the following issue. If *Praeterita* provides a crystallized version of a cultural fantasy of original femininity, does it then follow that the life out of which this autobiography springs is itself particularly representative of Ruskin's class and gender in this historical period?

The answer to this question has to be a resounding no. Nevertheless, it is a rewarding exercise to consider in what points Ruskin's life shares the distinctive features of his age, and in what areas it diverges. Tempting though it may be to imagine that he represents an exaggerated version of the norm—subject to the constraints that afflict the average Victorian gentleman, only more so—such a straightforward diagnosis will not quite fit the case. Ruskin's experience is as often unique, as it is extreme: if *Praeterita*'s expression of the feminized childhood fantasy is paradigmatic, the life is sui generis. In the context of this man's career, such a combination of ideological centrality and personal eccentricity is not without precedent: after all, the man who produced the influential distillation of the doctrine of separate spheres and domestic harmony in the highly popular "Of Queens' Gardens" from *Sesame and Lilies* is the same individual who had no direct experience of the pressures of the working world and whose own marriage was such a notorious failure. In the same way, the fact that a man with such singular life experiences should write an autobiography that encapsulates the key elements of a cherished communal myth seems both inevitable and paradoxical.

A sense of Ruskin's milieu can be gained by considering in turn its economic, social, religious, educational, and familial characteristics. Like his disciple William Morris, another celebrated railer against the twin uglinesses of Victorian capitalism's theory and practice, Ruskin was relieved from the necessity of working for a living by his father's endeavors in the world of trade. John James Ruskin was the product of very mixed and unequal Scottish stock, while the immediate connections of his wife Margaret, his first cousin, were still more humble.[13] Although his intelligence, early education, and desires seemed to point toward a career in law, a number of factors, not least his own father's unstable mental health and poor mercantile abilities, convinced John James to leave Scotland and try his luck in business in London. After ten years working as an employee for shipping firms, John James, with partners Juan Pedro Domecq and Henry Telford, established a sherry-importing company, which eventually, largely thanks to his own diligence and astute management, grew into a healthy financial concern.

Despite this wealth and commercial success, John James and Margaret remained painfully conscious of their origins and never achieved true social ease. In contrast, their aspirations for John, the beloved and phenomenally intelligent only child of their late marriage, knew no bounds. As Ruskin half-humorously and half-seriously delineates in *Praeterita*, John James had a clear idea of exactly how his son should make his mark on the world:

> His ideal of my future,—now entirely formed in conviction of my genius,—was that I should enter at college into the best society, take all the prizes every year, and a double first to finish with; marry Lady Clara Vere de Vere; write poetry as good as Byron's, only pious; preach sermons as good as Bossuet's, only Protestant; be made, at forty, Bishop of Winchester, and at fifty, Primate of all England. (35:185)

Whether or not this is a fair suggestion of his father's ambitious designs, it is evident that John James had no desire for his son to follow him into the sherry business and was happy to be the means of lifting John above the sordid necessity of making money. Although he acted as his son's agent, liaising with the publishing house of Smith, Elder and Company, the financial returns of Ruskin's literary works seem never to have been an issue: indeed, John James chose to underwrite such uneconomic ventures as the inclusion of illustrated plates in *The Stones of Venice*. In all other areas of his life as well, Ruskin fils was handsomely bankrolled by Ruskin père and thus had few restraints on his ability to travel, to purchase paintings and artifacts, even to donate money to friends and favorite causes. Only after both his parents had died and he set up a business to publish and distribute his own works did Ruskin become familiar with the concept of self-earned wealth, but his aims in creating this operation had nothing to do with moneymaking and everything to do with an idealistic desire to end "the fungus growths" of discounts and markups that he felt bedeviled the book-selling trade. To all intents and purposes, then, most of Ruskin's life was marked by a financial dependence on his father that set him apart from the majority of Victorian men: unlike working-class and most middle-class males, he did not earn a weekly wage or a monthly salary, and unlike most upper-class males, he did not come into his own money when he turned twenty-one.

If Ruskin's economic status was unusually compromised, then so was his social position. Despite all the outward trappings of wealth, an Oxford education, and access, gained through his intellectual celebrity, to the highest levels of society, Ruskin's unbroken bond to his parents kept him in close touch with John James's and Margaret's anxious awareness of their own imagined social inadequacy. Furthermore, not only did this nervousness limit the Ruskins' social intercourse with their perceived equals and betters, but it also caused them to slight those who seemed to be below them: Ruskin comments in *Praeterita* that "during the whole of childhood I had the sense that we were, in some way or other, always above our friends and relations,—more or less patronizing everybody, favouring them by our advice, instructing them by our example, and called upon, by what was due both to ourselves, and the constitution of society, to keep them at a certain distance" (35:102). That Ruskin's family money came from trade was not a real or an absolute disability in this mercantile century, but the fact that his family was ashamed of its connections must always have been potentially discomforting.

While invitations to the Ruskins' Herne Hill, and subsequently Denmark Hill, dining and drawing rooms were restricted by these social timidities, they were no less circumscribed by John James's considerable and Margaret's extreme Evangelical sensibilities. The complexities of Ruskin's religious inheritance have been extensively researched by such scholars as Viljoen, Tim Hilton, and Van Akin Burd.[14] Their findings construct a fascinating web of the distinct but interwoven strands of Christian belief that thread themselves through the fabric of everyday life in England and Scotland from the mid–seventeenth century onwards. From Burd's point of view, the connection of both Ruskin's immediate family and its previous couple of generations to a range of denominations, both established and Nonconformist, and including, but not limited to the Churches of Scotland and England, the English Presbyterians, the Episcopalians, and the Congregationalists, is ultimately not as important as their allegiance to the strong waves of Evangelicalism that rocked all of these sects to greater or lesser degrees and at different times in this period.[15] The introduction to this study discusses the ways in which this potent religious movement and its obsession with the problem of original sin simultaneously fights against, and colludes with, the burgeoning tenets of Romanticism to create an ever-growing fascination with the child in the late eighteenth and the nineteenth centuries. This present investigation of the specific characteristics of Ruskin's religious background provides a more nuanced comprehension of the influences of such beliefs on a single life and refines the assessment of just how representative or nonrepresentative this life might be.

If we look primarily to Ruskin's father to estimate his son's economic and social status, it is to Ruskin's mother that we must turn to understand his religious positioning.[16] All surviving records relating to Margaret Ruskin reveal how strongly her faith ruled her life and outlook. Educated in Croydon at an Academy for Young Ladies on "evangelical principles," the then Margaret Cox's removal at the age of twenty to the Edinburgh home of her cousin John James immersed her still further in these pieties, now influenced more strongly by the dominant strain of Calvinism in Scottish Christianity. As Burd explains it, the Ruskin family's religious makeup thus combined mainline Nonconformist beliefs in the sufficiency of the Bible, the depravity of human nature, the atonement of Christ, and justification by faith, with hard-line Calvinistic adherence to the doctrine of predestination, the irresistibility of God's grace, and the final perseverance of the elect. The moral code that devolved from such beliefs was severe and uncompromising: Calvin's insistence that the fallen human condition was a "seed-bed of sin" meant that constant vigilance was required to halt potential backsliding. Visions of hellfire fueled both rigorous spiritual self-examination and the judgment of others and led to a wholesale condemnation of secular laxity and frivolous behavior.

While Calvinistic interpretations of original sin, election, and perseverance inevitably darkened the Ruskins' religious climate, the family's general immersion in the powerful Evangelical currents of the day united it with a relatively broad constituency: certainly Ruskin's accounts of the gloom of his childhood Sundays, both in chapel and at home, find echoes in a wide range of other nineteenth-century texts. What makes his religious experience more unusual is the extent to which it dictated the form of his early education. As we learn from *Praeterita*'s first page, Margaret Ruskin had "it deeply in her heart to make an evangelical clergyman" of her bright and beloved son (35:13). To this end, she made sure that her child was steeped in the key texts of her chosen religious position:

> The sixty-seven *Translations and Paraphrases* from the Bible that came into popular usage in the Scottish churches during the childhood of Ruskin's parents had to be memorized. On Sundays Ruskin found his reading limited to the books that Henry Venn [author of *The Complete Duty of Man*] approved as "written to awaken the conscience." The patience of those nonconformist saints at the stake (described in that Evangelical companion to the Bible, Foxe's *Book of Martyrs*), was ready to edify him. He was also exposed to sententious dialogues, such as that on temptation between Eve

and the serpent in the *Emblems* of Francis Quarles; to the overwhelming sense of guilt in the works of that Particular Calvinist, the Congregationalist and Baptist minister, John Bunyan—the fall and redemption of mankind in his *Holy War*, Christian's toils in the *Pilgrim's Progress* . . . and to the confession of the youthful Bunyan caught in a mill-pit of vice in *Grace Abounding*. (*WL*, 63)

More famously, and more significantly, however, Margaret's "unquestioning evangelical faith in the literal truth of the Bible" led her to subject the young Ruskin to a simple, if demanding, program of study (35:128). *Praeterita* explains it in the following manner:

> As soon as I was able to read with fluency, she began a course of Bible work with me, which never ceased till I went to Oxford. She read alternate verses with me, watching, at first, every intonation of my voice, and correcting the false ones, till she made me understand the verse, if within my reach, rightly and energetically. . . . In this way she began with the first verse of Genesis, and went straight through, to the last verse of the Apocalypse; hard names, numbers, Levitical law, and all; and began again at Genesis the next day. (35:40)

All in all, Ruskin estimates that he and his mother worked their way through the Bible at least six times before he began his university career. While the boy's education was not limited to this syllabus—by the age of seven he was doing daily Latin exercises, and other subjects, eventually taught by visiting masters, were gradually added to the mix—such a profound intimacy with the Scriptures inevitably had a wide-ranging and everlasting effect on Ruskin's life and work. "Every word of them," he tells us in *Praeterita*, was thus rendered "familiar to my ear in habitual music,—yet in that familiarity reverenced, as transcending all thought, and ordaining all conduct" (35:40). As will be seen, Ruskin was eventually to reject his mother's brand of Evangelical piety and the dismal, guilt-laden precepts of her favorite reading matter, but he remained genuinely grateful throughout his life for his daily Bible study, which he regarded as "the most precious, and, on the whole, the one *essential* part of all [his] education" (35:43).

Margaret Ruskin was probably not the sole practitioner of this specific biblical educational program, but the steadfast persistence with which she enforced it must have been quite unusual even in the religiously charged atmosphere of the 1820s and 1830s.[17] So too was the nearly exclusive home-schooling, as we should say today, of a child of Ruskin's sex and relative wealth. Although there are of course famous exceptions (not least John Stuart Mill, who received incredibly demanding and rigorous, and decidedly non-Evangelical, tuition from his father), it is probably fair to say that in nineteenth-century Britain the majority of sons of the middle and upper classes attended some sort of school, either as day or boarding pupils.[18] Education in the home, with or without the provision of a governess, was primarily for well-to-do girls—although again, this was not always the case. In the context of this study, the fact that Ruskin experienced no definitive break from his home environment during his childhood is particularly interesting: as we have seen in our examination of De Quincey, the boy's brutal ejection from the idyllic sororal nursery into the competitive fraternal world of school effectively created the lost feminine self. Not only was Ruskin not sent away to school, either in childhood or his teens, but when he went to university, his mother went too: for the three years that he was in residence at Christ Church, Oxford, Margaret was just over a stone's throw away in lodgings on the High Street, and the standing daily commandment to appear at her tea table was generally, if not always, honored. Kept in London by his business concerns during the week, John James would travel up to Oxford for the weekends. In his education, as in all other aspects of his life, Ruskin remained unusually close to his parents.

If we are tempted to judge John James and Margaret Ruskin harshly for keeping such a relentless grip on their brilliant son, perhaps we should pause to remind ourselves that in a century celebrated for its large families, he was that relatively rare thing—an only child. In this last call on a whistle-stop tour of the informing contexts of Ruskin's life, consider for a moment that this figure, unlike any of the other writers studied here, had no brothers and, more to the point, no sisters.[19] Although *Praeterita* makes some gestures toward an attempt to construct a sister-self out of lively but short-lived cousin Jessie, the truth is that Ruskin saw her only very infrequently on his Scottish summer holidays; her elder sister Mary, who in any case was to Ruskin's eyes rather lumpish and unexciting, joined the South London household fairly late in the day, when she was fourteen and her cousin ten. For Wordsworth, there was Dorothy; for De Quincey, Elizabeth (and Mary and two sisters called Jane).[20] Dickens recalls the blissful days in which he toddled hand in hand with sister Fanny; Letitia and Harriet were to come along a few years later. Dodgson also had a sister Frances, a sister Elizabeth, and a sister Mary, not to mention Caroline, Louisa, Margaret, and Henrietta. Ruskin, however, stands alone: there are no real girls in his garden paradise.

If Ruskin was deprived of juvenile feminine companionship in his early years, he certainly made up for it later on. Having considered *Praeterita*'s self-feminization and a variety of ways in which this writer's experience simultaneously exaggerated and departed from the norms of his place and time, I turn now to a period and a text from the middle of his life, both of which are explicitly concerned with little girls. An analysis of the ways in which girls are depicted in a work *other* than the autobiography both extends our appreciation of their significance to Ruskin and reveals that his modes of representation are in accord with the symbolic meanings that the Victorian age was generally attributing to the figure of the little girl. As we shall see, the girl and the perfect past she represents cannot be properly understood without reference to the oppositional figures of the old man and to the desolate present day.

The period under investigation will be the 1860s, and the text, *The Ethics of the Dust*, published in 1865. While the young Ruskin had no experience of boys' schools, the middle-aged Ruskin was to develop an intense relationship in this era of his life with a much rarer phenomenon, the school for well-to-do girls.[21] The establishment in question was called Winnington Hall, situated near Northwich in Cheshire, and run by a Miss Margaret Bell. Twenty-two miles from Manchester and thirty from Liverpool, the school was nevertheless secluded enough for Ruskin to describe it in the preface to *The Ethics of the Dust* as "far in the country," making it an attractive refuge for him when he lectured in Lancashire and Yorkshire's industrial cities (18:201). Such, indeed, were its charms that he referred to Winnington in the early 1860s as his "second home," visiting on sixteen separate occasions during that decade. Miss Bell, who had initiated the acquaintance, appears to have regarded the frequent presence in her school of the famous author of *Modern Painters* both as a marketable emblem of distinction to impress her pupils' parents and a legitimate educational resource for the girls themselves. Certainly Ruskin threw himself with gusto into all the activities of the school's progressive curriculum, delivering lectures on a wide variety of topics, telling stories at the fireside, supervising outdoor sketching, and even joining in with the dancing and dramatic performances. In his letters to his parents and others, Ruskin represented his sojourns at Winnington as a necessary indulgence: "I get thorough romps and rest here," he told his disapproving father, whereas to Carlyle he described it as a place "where I go sometimes when I want to be—whatever you call it—flattered, or petted, or what not" (*WL*, 287, 392). While individual girls are often singled out for particular praise in his letters, the collective spectacle of lovely girlhood seems to have had an especial fascination. Writing to Margaret Bell after his first visit, Ruskin makes a mock lament that "it is really a hard fate—of which so far as I know—the description is unattempted yet in prose or rhyme— to fall in love with thirty-five young ladies at once" (*WL*, 109).

In truth, the harder fate during the Winnington years was that Ruskin had fallen in love with Rose La Touche, the young Irish girl whom he had first met in 1858, when she was nine and he was thirty-nine. At that time, only four years had passed since the end of Ruskin's disastrous marriage to Effie, and he was still smarting from the humiliating scandal of their very public annulment and her subsequent marriage to John Everett Millais. Although the first meeting with Rose was later to be celebrated as a climactic beginning in *Praeterita*, diary and letter evidence from this period suggests that a couple of years passed before Ruskin saw or thought of her with any regularity.[22] Whatever the intensity of the different phases of Ruskin's interest, however, his fascination was to stretch throughout the following decade, encompassing short-lived periods of optimism and ultimate despair. When Rose turned eighteen in 1866, Ruskin proposed marriage. Rose asked leave to defer her decision for three years, at which point her parents intervened and forbade any further contact. Six years later, as we have already noted, she died of brain fever, having previously struggled with debilitating bouts of a nervous illness throughout her teens and adult life.

Ruskin's emotional life was thus in turmoil during the years in which he visited the school. His religious beliefs were no less disturbed. Once again *Praeterita*, in a celebrated passage, accentuates the dramatic nature of the change. One Sunday in 1858, the same year that Rose walks into his life, Ruskin attends a Protestant service in a Waldensian chapel in Turin and listens to a sermon of distinctly Evangelical hue:

> The assembled congregation numbered in all some three or four and twenty, of whom fifteen or sixteen were grey-haired women. Their solitary and clerkless preacher, a somewhat stunted figure in a plain black coat, with a cracked voice, after leading them through the languid forms of prayer which are all that in truth are possible to people whose present life is dull and its terrestrial future unchangeable, put his utmost zeal into a consolatory discourse on the wickedness of the wide world, more especially of the plain of Piedmont and the city of Turin, and on the exclusive favour with God, enjoyed by the between nineteen and twenty-four elect members of his congregation, in the streets of Admah and Zeboim. (35:495)

Afterwards, Ruskin heads back into Turin, that "condemned city," and "up into the gallery where Paul Veronese's Solomon and the Queen of Sheba glowed in full afternoon light." As his eyes are delighted by the "perfect colour" of the painting, so are his ears entranced by the "floating swells and falls" of music that drift in through the gallery's open windows (35:496). The contrasting poverty of the chapel's world vision and the life-denying ugliness of its adherents are thus devastatingly illuminated: at this moment, *Praeterita* claims, Ruskin leaves behind the narrowness of sectarian belief and embraces an untrammeled enjoyment of divinity, rooted in the faith "that things done delightfully and rightly, were always done by the help and in the Spirit of God." Ruskin quickly qualifies his presentation of "sudden conversion" by admitting in the next paragraph that "that hour's meditation in the gallery of Turin only concluded the courses of thought which had been leading to such an end through many years," but he nevertheless chooses to end the chapter with the words, "[T]hat day my evangelical beliefs were put away, to be debated of no more" (35:496).

Ruskin's admission that his rejection of his mother's religion came about gradually was of course nearer the mark, but even this account of the change implied that his struggles and questionings were effectively resolved by the end of the 1850s. On the contrary, the following decade was for Ruskin a trying and testing time in which, as he put it to a friend in a letter in 1861, he felt himself a prisoner in the Dark Tower of religious doubt.[23] Ruskin's biographers have carefully described the various different lines of attack that had been breaching the defenses of his Evangelical citadel from his Oxford days onwards.[24] Classical empiricism played its part, as did, more famously, the era's geological discoveries and the resultant hypothesizing from authors such as Buckland and Lyell, whose works had led many to question the historical truth of the Mosaic narrative of creation long before the publication of Darwin's *Origin of Species* in 1859. The burgeoning movement of higher criticism, ranging from pioneering German and Dutch scholarship to the writings of Jowett in Oxford and Bishop Colenso in South Africa, intensified the bombardment on Evangelical literalism in its insistence that Scripture could be interpreted like any other book. Other areas of Ruskin's intellectual life no doubt contributed to his questionings: although his impatience with many aspects of John Stuart Mill's thought is well known, Ruskin was nevertheless a careful reader of his rationalist philosophy. Through his friendship with Frederic Harrison, he came to know of Comte's positivism. His im-

113

mersion in the writings of Thomas Carlyle was still more important: the call in *Sartor Resartus* for an universal religion beyond petty denominational squabbling struck a chord and in 1856 had already led Ruskin, in a move that must greatly have distressed his mother, to dub the division between Catholic and Protestant "a stumbling-block of the gravest kind to all thoughtful and far-sighted men" (5:322). All in all, then, the Ruskin of the 1860s was oscillating between rare dark moments in which he fell prey to what Carlyle had called "das Ewige Nein," the possibility that the universe was devoid of a divine presence, and a more consistent, if also troubling, quest for a religious truth unwarped by the constraints of any system of "formal Christianity" (*WL*, 404).

It would be highly convenient if these two currents of upheaval in the man's life could be linked with some definitive causal explanation—if we could say, for instance, that as Ruskin fell away from the stern Evangelicalism of his mother and its resolute insistence on innate human depravity, he replaced a vision of original sin with one of original innocence. In this light, Rose would represent the pure child in the garden, the center of his emotional life, and his new religious vision.[25] Elements of such an argument are compelling, but there are others that militate against it. For one thing, although it must always be acknowledged that we are dealing with Ruskin's *idea* of his wild Irish rose rather than the real person, the individual in question quite resolutely refused to be reduced to an innocent child of Nature. If anything, Rose La Touche was even more of a dogmatic Evangelical than Margaret Ruskin. As she grew into her teens, Rose became more and more infused by a religious fervor that led her not only to compose devotional poetry and other saintly outpourings, but to rebuke Ruskin for his apostasy. "How could one love you, if you were a Pagan?" she wrote in a letter in 1863,[26] irritating her correspondent to the utmost, and no doubt stimulating another of the frequent expostulations against the dangers of extreme piety in girls that appear in much of his writing in this period. Rose and Evangelical religion cannot be simply separated into two different entities, with the former the promise of consolation for the painful problems of discarding the latter.

Given, then, that Ruskin in this era of his life was beset with worries about a girl and worries about his faith, this particular girls' school in Cheshire offered the ideal palliatives. On the latter front, the principal of Winnington School was especially well equipped to listen and talk to a man in a state of religious doubt. Margaret Bell, almost exactly the same age as Ruskin, had weathered a spiritual crisis of her own, and although her early religious training had been exclusively within Wesleyan Methodism, she was well placed to understand the difficulties of this man's efforts to extricate himself from his parents' beliefs. Even though she had witnessed the personal and professional destruction of her minister father in a Wesleyan witch-hunt, Miss Bell had managed to retain her Christian faith and was finding new hope and guidance in the Coleridge-inspired Broad Church movement. (Ruskin himself, despite the fact that he was eventually to enjoy a deep friendship with the Broad Church champion F. D. Maurice, did not find the movement the answer to his quest, but was nevertheless attracted to many aspects of its dogma-free antiauthoritarianism and its desire for social reform.) More important than Miss Bell's newfound religious positioning, however, was her sympathy with the plight of a man who had lost the moorings of his childhood faith, and her tolerant acceptance of his need to question the most sacred orthodoxies. On the former front, the attraction of Winnington is immediately obvious. Ruskin's relationship with Rose never ran smoothly. Even at times when she was not ill and he was relatively confident that they were destined for ultimate happiness, he rarely saw her: Rose was usually in Ireland or traveling with her family on the Continent. In the absence of his chosen girl, Ruskin could find a bountiful and readily available supply of genteel young ladies at Miss Bell's school.

This, then, was the complicated context out of which *The Ethics of the Dust* sprang. The book itself is similarly complex: even in the company of the many genre-defying oddities of Ruskin's oeuvre, this text makes a strong claim to be the most curious work of all. Subtitled "Ten Lectures to Little Housewives on the Elements of Crystallization," *The Ethics of the Dust* was intended, Ruskin maintained, to function as a gloss on the chapter entitled "Compact Crystallines" in the fourth volume of *Modern Painters*. The work, however, is both more and less than a mineralogical treatise. Carlyle, one of the few admirers of the text in its own time or any other, attempted to give an idea of its range by claiming that the author "twisted geology into morality, theology, Egyptian mythology, [and made] fiery cuts at political economy."[27] The form of this work, moreover, is just as strange as its content: *The Ethics of the Dust* is written as a series of quasi-Socratic dialogues between a "Lecturer" (a figure who is never named "Ruskin" in the text but who is self-evidently the author of *Modern Painters* and his other books) and twelve "girls" between the ages of nine and twenty.

Yet if its scope is broad and its form unusual, the central conceit of *The Ethics of the Dust* can be expressed quite simply: girls are crystals and crystals are girls. "My dear children," pronounces the Lecturer, "if you knew it, you are yourselves, at this moment, as you sit in your ranks, nothing, in the eyes of a mineralogist, but a lovely group of rosy sugar-candy, arranged by atomic forces. And even admitting you to be something more, you have certainly been crystallising without knowing it" (18:221).[28] Pinning in their crinolines the better to approximate the form of rose quartz as they dance the Lecturer's "Crystal Quadrille," Ruskin's young ladies, at their best, share the finest qualities of jewels, just as "a well-brought up mineral," in "its pretty ways of behaving" is imagined to emulate the high standards of English girlhood (18:314–15). As Paul Sawyer notes in his excellent chapter on this work, *The Ethics of the Dust* organizes itself around a series of connected antitheses that ultimately reduce to the opposition between active purity and the foulness of decay. As the highest type of active purity in the world of minerals, crystals, formed from the cooperation of innumerable atoms, parallel the potential excellence that is to be aspired to both by individual human beings, formed from particles of dust, and by societies, ideally composed, like the perfect girls' school, of mutually considerate members. For Ruskin, girls and rocks are identical in their purity of energy and the resultant beauty of their form. Maintaining that "[i]t is just as true for us, as for the crystal, that the nobleness of life depends on its consistency,—clearness of purpose,—quiet and ceaseless energy," Ruskin insists that girls are "crystalline in brightness" and "charm infinitely" (18:264, 311).

If his wide-eyed pupils and the crystals of which they are the type stand for pure and active beauty, the Lecturer and the sin-blemished vacillations of his own damaged maturity represent the loss of the principle of straightforward vitality: "[A]ll doubt and repenting, and botching, and retouching, and wondering what it will be best to do next, are vice, as well as misery" (18:264). As it is worked out in the text, this formulation relies heavily on a double conception of age. While *The Ethics of the Dust* takes great pains to point out the difference between the vivacious newness of its twelve young girls and the weary elderliness of the Lecturer, it nevertheless associates the former with antiquity, and the latter with the present day.

Ruskin deliberately widens the gulf between the students and their teacher: although the age distribution of the girls in *The Ethics of the Dust* exactly reflects that of the pupils at Winnington Hall, the Lecturer appears to be freighted with many more years than the writer himself, who was only forty-six at the time of composition. Listed in the "Personae" as "OLD LECTURER (of incalculable age)," the male presence in the text is doubly superannuated. In a letter to his father written from the school two years before he began *The Ethics of the Dust*, Ruskin had commented that his association with these young girls gave him an exaggerated sense of his own elderliness:

> It is curious that I feel older and sadder, very much, in now looking at these young children—it is especially the *young* ones between whom & me I now feel so infinite a distance,—and they are so beautiful and so good, and I am not good, considering the advantages I've had, by any means. The weary longing to begin life over again, and the sense of fate forever forbidding it—here or hereafter—is terrible. I daresay I shall get over it in a day or two, but I was out in the playground with them this afternoon, and the sun was on the grass, and on them—and the sense of loveliness in life, and of overbrooding death, like winter, was too strong. (*WL*, 439–40)

Ruskin's enervated conviction here of the opposition between blighted maturity and the girls' springlike perfection pervades the world of *The Ethics of the Dust*: for the Lecturer, who claims to be perpetually "tired, and cross," the girls in all their morning gaiety are unlikely to be able to comprehend the miseries of old age. The radical difference of perspective is revealed in a conversation ostensibly about an imperfect crystal, described by the Lecturer as "sadly tired." When one of the girls asks what events have led to this pass, the dialogue runs as follows:

> *L.* Trials much like our own. Sickness, and starvation; fevers, and agues, and palsy; oppression; and old age, and the necessity of passing away in their time, like all else. If there's any pity in you, you must come to-morrow, and take some part in these crystal griefs.
> *Dora.* I am sure we shall cry till our eyes are red.
> *L.* Ah, you may laugh, Dora; but I've been made grave, not once, nor twice, to see that even crystals "cannot choose but be old" at last. It may be but a shallow proverb of the Justice's; but it is a shrewdly wide one.
> *Dora (pensive for once).* I suppose it is very dreadful to be old! But then *(brightening again)* what should we do without our dear old friends and our nice old lecturers? (18:324)

"I am not myself afraid of death—but I am afraid—bitterly afraid of old age," wrote Ruskin to a correspondent in 1861 (*WL*, 338). In choosing to endow the Lecturer with the decrepitude he dreads, Ruskin consigns man and girl, the only two categories of human beings *The Ethics of the Dust* really recognizes, to wholly incommensurate universes.

Diagnosis of decay is not limited to the Lecturer's own personal condition in the text. *The Ethics of the Dust* takes considerable pains to show us that the present-day world is a tawdry affair, a sadly diminished version of an earlier splendor. Ruskin evokes a familiar mid-Victorian nostalgia for the bygone idyll of rural England; the meretricious glitter of Crystal Palace, for example, is invidiously compared to the simple neighborhood fairs of the Lecturer's youth. Elsewhere, summoning up the classical, rather than a personal, past, the Lecturer tells the girls that contemporary urban depredations plumb depths that would be almost unimaginable for the ancients: "[T]he vice existing among certain classes, both of the rich and poor, in London, Paris and Vienna, could have been conceived by a Spartan or Roman of the heroic ages only as possible in a Tartarus, where fiends were employed to teach, but not to punish, crime" (18:355). Citing newspaper stories about child murderers like Charlotte Winsor, and "sons like that one who, the other day, in France, beat his mother to death with a stick," the Lecturer seems convinced that in today's world "[t]here is a peculiar horror about the relations between parent and child, which are being now brought about by our variously degraded forms of European white slavery" (18:354). Whichever way we turn in *The Ethics of the Dust*, the immorality of modern life captures our attention.

As the work draws to its close, the Lecturer tries to introduce a more uplifting perspective, claiming that "the great laws which never fail, and to which all change is subordinate, appear such as to accomplish a gradual advance to a lovelier order" (18:357). Altogether too much has been said on the other side, however, for this to ring true. Although a pessimistic opinion from the fourth volume of *Modern Painters* is called up only to be negated, its sentiments, and the Lecturer's explanation of their origin, still seem to express an abiding conviction that the incremental degeneration of the world is readily apparent to the eye:[29]

> *L.* . . . . I said that the earth seemed to have passed through its highest state: and that, after ascending by a series of phases, culminating in its habitation by man, it seems to be now gradually becoming less fit for that habitation. *Mary.* Yes, I remember.
> *L.* I wrote those passages under a very bitter impression of the gradual perishing of beauty from the loveliest scenes which I knew in the physical world; not in any doubtful way, such as I might have attributed to loss of sensation in myself—but by violent and definite physical action. . . . I am still under the same impression respecting the existing phenomena; but I feel more strongly, every day, that no evidence to be collected within historical periods can be accepted as any clue to the great tendencies of geological change. (18:357)

Belief that "the great tendencies of geological change" are actually moving the world toward a higher perfection for the generations yet unborn requires an act of faith: a simple act of observation tells a completely different story. In the book's last pages, when the Lecturer has Mary read aloud seven paragraphs from the fifth volume of *Modern Painters*, he is once again illustrating the difference between "government and co-operation," which are "the laws of life," and "anarchy and competition," which are "the laws of death." This has been the work's organizational antithesis (18:359). At first glance, we imagine that Ruskin is ordering us to perform an experiment, the results of which we ourselves will be able to observe. "Take," we are told, "merely an ounce or two of the blackest slime of a beaten footpath, on a rainy day, near a manufacturing town. That slime we shall find in most cases composed of clay, (or brickdust, which is burnt clay), mixed with soot, a little sand, and water. All these elements are at helpless war with each other, and destroy reciprocally each other's nature and power: competing and fighting for place at every tread of your foot; sand squeezing out clay, and clay squeezing out water, and soot meddling everywhere, and defiling the whole" (18:359). So far we may follow in our imaginary laboratories. But as the passage proceeds, the time frame of observation undergoes infinite expansion:

> Let us suppose that this ounce of mud is left in perfect rest, and that its elements gather together, like to like, so that their atoms may get into the closest relations possible.
>
> Let the clay begin. Ridding itself of all foreign substance, it gradually becomes a white earth, already very beautiful, and fit, with the help of congealing fire, to be made into the finest porcelain, and painted on, and be kept in kings' palaces. But such artificial consistence is not its best. Leave it still quiet, to follow its own instinct of unity, and it becomes, not only white but clear; not only clear, but hard; not only clear and hard, but so set that it can deal with light in a wonderful way, and gather out of it the loveliest blue rays only, refusing the rest. We call it then a sapphire. (18:359)

As the clay turns into a sapphire, so the sand "proceeds to grow clear and hard" and transforms itself into an opal, the soot becomes a diamond, and the water crystallizes into a star of snow. The achievement of such perfection of form may be projected into the future here, but the condemnation of the present moment that has been such a besetting tendency of *The Ethics of the Dust* (and, indeed of all Ruskin's writing from the 1860s onwards) makes it hard to imagine that such beauty can originate in the midst of the contemporary industrial pollution belched forth from that "manufacturing town." The diamonds and sapphires, the flawless crystals that the Lecturer's girls have examined in the preceding nine lectures, have been explicitly presented as the creations of a long-lost past, the distant triumphs of a process of temporal change that has now foundered into decay, corruption, and confusion. The Lecturer may maintain in his final words that "the seeming trouble,—the unquestioned degradation,—of the elements of the physical earth, must passively wait the appointed time of their repose," but the energies of the text as a whole affirm that the time of crystals, the time of "perfect peace," is securely in the past, not the future (18:360).

The Ethics of the Dust, then, a work specifically organized around the encounter of young girls and an old man, not only insists upon an absolute split between these two parties, but also extends the terms of this division to radically opposed conceptions of past and present. The beginnings of time radiate the light and purity of the perfect crystal, while the corruption of the present day can only look back in wonderment to the glory of long ago: sin is not to be found in our origins but in the world's contemporary maturity. Inasmuch as it unequivocally links girls with a perfect lost past, then, this text quite clearly follows the line already traced in this study. And yet the gemmological presentation of this by now familiar formula subtly alters the exact placement of its elements and demands further attention. Although we have most definitely seen girls and stones together in the same frame in the first two chapters—De Quincey, of course, flung himself down nightly on the cold marble of Kate Wordsworth's resting place, the better to luxuriate in the memory of the shared warmth of that bedtime embrace, while Little Nell was continually perching on gravestones until she herself was laid beneath a pavement slab— something different is evidently at work in Ruskin's vision. As the two examples in the previous sentence rather extravagantly demonstrate, the little girl's loveliness is more safely viewed through the lens of death: the burial stones with which she is allied proclaim that her connection with the past is irrevocable. For Ruskin and The Ethics of the Dust, however, the girl is the past and the crystal even as she is physically present. What happens when the lovely young girl is close enough to touch?

Up to now this consideration of Ruskin's girls' school book has evaded any real examination of the erotics of the text. Material for such a discussion is, however, not hard to find: nine-year-old Florrie, eleven-year-old Isabel, and twelve-year-old Lily may be diamonds and sapphires and crystals of quartz, but they are also living, breathing, squirming little girls. Not only teasing exchanges, but stage directions indicating physical con-

120

tact between the girls and the Lecturer punctuate the text with regularity: on the very first page we read that "FLORRIE *reappears, gives L. a kiss*"; fourteen-year-old Kathleen is caught in the act of "stopping his mouth"; Isabel "climbs on his knee" as she utters the words, "Oh you naughty—naughty" (18:292). The girls that Ruskin creates in *The Ethics of the Dust* are completely fascinated by the Lecturer, not only hanging on his every word, but often, in the case of the younger girls, hanging off his person too. Although it is always quite clear who is in control—a desire to supplicate, never to challenge, underlies every advance made by Ruskin's fantasy children—the text presents us with girls who continually initiate moments of touching even as the uncertainty in their half-sentences displays their subjugation. Furthermore, while the Lecturer is largely unviewed himself, we witness him in the act of scrutinizing the girls' physical features: "Nay, if you blush so, Kathleen, how can one help looking?" and "You want to ask something, Florrie, by the look of your eyes" are but two of the many instances in which we see the pupils through the eyes of their male observer (18:222, 223).

The pleasure of looking, and sometimes even of being touched, is also apparent in the letters Ruskin wrote from Winnington. As he tells his father, the girls' dancing is "a beautiful thing to see" (*WL*, 104), while the arrangement of the students at dinner, the sober shades of their dresses contrasting nicely with the white of the tablecloths, puts him in mind of certain beloved works of art: the scene is "like one of the pictures of a 'marriage in Cana' " and "gives the kind of light and shade one sees in the pictures of the Venetians" (*WL*, 104, 105). In letters to his mother, Ruskin conveys considerably more excitement, as the following description of a wild romp in the "new playroom" reveals:

> [T]he little ones had determined to wait for me to have the first game with them in it. So we began with a grand game at cat and mouse—and then at dropping the handkerchief and then we had Irish quadrilles, which end with a wonderful dance in a labyrinth of rings, and as I was to have Lily for a partner, I put my coat on wrong side before, to look like an Irishman; Lily highly approved of this arrangement, and was buttoning it for me as far awry as she could at the back; but Maud and Isabelle wouldn't have it awry, and buttoned it right, as fast as she put it wrong; so Lily at last pulled it off me altogether, and put it on herself over her frock, and tied her hair up in a hard knot, and then we had an Irish quadrille to purpose, till I had no more breath left. (*WL*, 500)

121

At other times, the mood is calmer as he tells her how much he enjoys sketching the girls ("I told her she must not *stir* for ten minutes till I had drawn a curl of hair by chance astray" [*WL*, 518]), or watching them as they listen in rapt attention to Charles Hallé's piano performance of a variation of "Home, Sweet Home": "It was beautiful too to see the girls' faces round, the eyes all wet with feeling and the little coral mouths fixed into little half open gaps with utter intensity of feeling" (*WL*, 527). A few months later, in a work entitled *The Cestus of Aglaia*, he was to write of this vision again:

> The wet eyes, round-open, and the little scarlet upper lips, lifted, and drawn slightly together, in passionate glow of utter wonder, became picture-like,— porcelain-like,—in motionless joy, as the sweet multitude of low notes fell in their timely infinities like summer rain. Only La Robbia himself (nor even he, unless with tenderer use of colour than is usual in his work) could have rendered some image of that listening. (9:78–79)

Ruskin may make frequent gestures in these passages toward aesthetic appreciation (the implied reference to Veronese, the direct one to Della Robbia, even to "coral" and "porcelain"), but the erotic charge of these moments is nevertheless unmistakable. Endless gazing and coquettish conversations; kisses, laps, and wriggling; the breathless excitement of the playroom; little fingers and buttons; most of all, perhaps, the wetness of those eyes and those "little scarlet upper lips," "half-open gaps with utter intensity of feeling"—all of these elements have enormous power to disturb, to alert our already highly attuned sensibilities to the unacceptable presence of the pervert. It is of course an open secret that Ruskin the famous Victorian sage is also Ruskin the infamous Victorian pedophile, but quotations like these make it all too naked.

There is no evidence that Ruskin sexually abused little girls: the exact dynamics of his encounters with real girls—with Rose La Touche, with the pupils at Winnington, with girls in London, France, Italy, Switzerland, the Lake District—remain essentially unknowable. All that we can do at this distance is understand a little more clearly the lineaments of the fantasies that manifest themselves in Ruskin's writings. Such an investigation reveals not only that Ruskin participates in a cultural myth about one sort of relationship between adult men and little girls, but also that the depictions of his desire for girls demonstrate a very particular form of erotic attraction.

The world of soft and flexible moistness summoned up in the last few pages would appear to confirm everybody's worst fears about Ruskin's delight in the loveliness of little girls. Such representations, however, are in the minority in his writing, in fact are hugely outnumbered by evocations of rocklike impenetrability and adamantine brilliance.[30] I make this point not to mount a desperate rearguard defense of the great man's reputation, nor to close down the discussion of desire in Ruskin's writings about girls, but to extend it. As we shall see, this writer's besetting habit of viewing the beloved as both a hard and an aesthetic object is not a defense against the erotic, but a component of it.[31] Reversing the Pygmalion myth, Ruskin transforms the mutable girl into stone.

Though its examples are particularly clear-cut, *The Ethics of the Dust* is by no means the only text in Ruskin's oeuvre that illustrates this tendency: both published works and private writings persistently relate girlish beauty to unyielding stone. Most notable are the depictions that ally the living, breathing form to the snowy marble of classical statuary. As might be expected, the bodies in question are often naked, but the introduction to Rose La Touche's older sister from the third volume of *Praeterita* forms a Ruskinian paean to stony loveliness that falls securely within the realm of well-dressed decorum:

> Emily was a perfectly sweet, serene, delicately-chiselled marble nymph of fourteen, softly dark-eyed, rightly tender and graceful in all she did and said. I never saw such a faculty for the arrangement of things beautifully, in any other human being. If she took up a handful of flowers, they fell out of her hand in wreathed jewellery of colour and form, as if they had been sown, and had blossomed, to live together so, and no otherwise. (35:526)

Here two arresting conjunctions—the sculptor's chisel on white marble and that soft, dark eye; static serenity and graceful movement—set the tone for the subsequent movements between artifice and nature in the celebration of the artless art of Emily's flower arranging: the "wreathed jewellery" she creates (itself a combination of the organic and inorganic) paradoxically displays the blooms at their most natural, inasmuch as they appear to have simply grown into form. Similar combinations are created when Ruskin defines his favorite type of feminine beauty elsewhere in *Praeterita*: "I like oval faces, crystalline blonde, with straightish, at the utmost wavy, (or, in length, wreathed) hair, and the form elastic, and foot firm" (35:231).

Recognizing that these descriptions are characterized by complex interconnections of apparently oppositional terms serves a useful purpose when we turn to more problematic passages from the same pen. Consider, for example, the following words from *The Cestus of Aglaia*, which record a moment from that landmark year of 1858: Ruskin saw a dark-haired Turin girl of around ten years old, "half-naked, bare-limbed to above the knees, and beautifully limbed . . . her little breasts, scarce dimpled yet,—white—marble-like—but, as wasted marble, thin with scorching and rains of Time" (19:83). If one were analyzing this sentence fragment in isolation, it would seem plausible to argue that the relatively late introduction of "marble-like" into the description functions as a defense against the troublingly erotic implications of the sight of naked flesh: the aestheticization of the vision, the transformation of the body into a marble statue, appears to allow Ruskin to move from the dangerous position of a man talking about a particular girl, to the safe haven of an art historian who is musing generally on the relative qualities of sculptors' materials, and on Time. Arousing natural flesh, in this reading, would thus be exchanged for unarousing artistic stone. The fact, however, that the girl's attractiveness elsewhere in Ruskin's writing is so definitively intertwined with her identity with the most beautiful stones of the earth, and that the natural and the artificial are so frequently wreathed together,[32] should make us suspicious of any simple antitheses here. Far from being a defense against arousal, imagining the girl's naked body in rocklike terms is often a necessary condition of the erotic in Ruskin's vision.

One last example, drawn from an unpublished letter, brings together these same components in a markedly different stylistic form. In 1869 fifty-year-old Ruskin is writing from Italy to Joan Agnew, his twenty-two-year-old second cousin:

> Mammy di—the wee girlies must have looked very fit, in Verona in tummer time—me see by itty tat-tatues and me wish ice statues would come ive again—They haven't got anything on ta speak of mammy di—dust a wee Bedgowny tied about waisty with a band of jewels. If me get oo nice band of boo beads, mammy, will oo let me see oo wear oos bedgowny ike at?[33]

Such regressive baby talk, in all its mock-Scottish tweeness, invokes a welter of responses: this is of course private correspondence, never intended for the scrutiny of eyes other than Joan's, but it is startling, to say the least, to know that the author of some of the most challenging and beautiful passages of Victorian prose also wrote these sentences (and indeed many others like it in this period). More germane to the present discussion, however, is the recourse, once again, to "itty tat-tatues" and bands of "jewels." This time the movement is properly Pygmalion-like, from the stone art object to the imagined naked body of the real girl (who, in this case, is actually a young woman), rather than vice versa, but the juxtaposition of elements remains the same. Ruskin's favorite things—girls, precious stones, and frequently precious stones as art objects—are bound up into a single tantalizing form. In Ruskin's particular case, the pedophile and the petrophile are one.

To return to our starting point and Ruskin's final work, *Praeterita*: the lovely girls who drop out of life before maturity also tend to be seen in some relation to the precious crystal. Indeed, when Ruskin first wrote of the tragedy of these extinguished lives in the autobiographical passages of *Fors Clavigera*, he called them so many "Lost Jewels." In the letter bearing this title, Ruskin holds forth in an unsettling amalgam of maudlin self-pity and strained comic bitterness on the problem of "the annual loss of its girl-wealth to the British nation":

> I think the experience of most thoughtful persons will confirm me in saying that extremely good girls, (good children, broadly, but especially girls,) usually die young. The pathos of their deaths is constantly used in poetry and novels; but the power of the fiction rests, I suppose, on the fact that most persons of affectionate temper have lost their own May Queens or little Nells in their time. For my own part of grief, I have known a little Nell die, and a May Queen die, and a queen of May, and of December also, die;—all of them, in economists' language, "as good as gold," and in Christian language, "only a little lower than the angels, and crowned with glory and honour." And I could count the like among my best-loved friends, with a rosary of tears. (29:424–25)

It is Ruskin's habit in *Praeterita* not only to feminize his childhood, but to use the death of young girls to represent the cessation of his development. Given that girls in this man's imagination are frequently associated with jewels and rocks, it comes as no surprise to find that Ruskin's young self is as stony as it is girlish: the lost jewels strung throughout the autobiography symbolize Ruskin's own crystallized identity just as much as they commemorate Jessie, Rose, Charlotte, Sybilla, and all the other Little Nells.

One of the clearest images of the gemlike quality of Ruskin's childhood appears in the description of the Edenic garden already visited: the hard-edged brilliance of this retrospectively constructed childhood idyll finds apt representation in its sparkling fruit. Gooseberries, pears, white currants, and cherries are not tender, succulent consumable foods but rather

125

transfigured jewels, "fresh green, soft amber, and rough-bristled crimson bending the spinous branches; clustered pearl and pendant ruby joyfully discoverable under the large leaves that looked like vine" (35:36). Elsewhere, a "spring of crystal water" (35:19) often accompanies the depiction of the childhood self. It should never be assumed, however, that Ruskin's celebration of rushing waters reveals a fondness for spontaneous motion: as *The Ethics of the Dust* rejoices in what it calls the "active purity" of the perfect jewel, so *Praeterita*'s rivers combine movement and stasis to form a "perpetual treasure of flowing diamond" (35:66). Vital energy always crystallizes into tangible form, and fluidity is frozen into a single moment of beauty.

Nowhere is this more apparent than in Ruskin's description of the improvements he worked upon his Denmark Hill garden, ostensibly for the delight of his cousin Joan and Rose La Touche, then eighteen and seventeen years old respectively. As he explains in the penultimate paragraph of *Praeterita*, a feat of engineering enabled him to bring a sparkling river into his domain:

> I draw back to my own home, twenty years ago, permitted to thank heaven once more for the peace, and hope, and loveliness of it, and the Elysian walks with Joanie, and Paradisiacal with Rosie, under the peach-blossom branches by the little glittering stream which I had paved with crystal for them. I had built behind the highest cluster of laurels a reservoir, from which, on sunny afternoons, I could let a quite rippling film of water run for a couple of hours down behind the hayfield, where the grass in spring still grew fresh and deep. . . . And the little stream had its falls, and pools, and imaginary lakes. Here and there it laid for itself lines of graceful sand; there and here it lost itself under beads of chalcedony. . . . "Eden-land" Rosie calls it sometimes in her letters. Whether its tiny river were of the waters of Abana, or Euphrates, or Thamesis, I know not, but they were sweeter to my thirst than the fountains of Trevi or Branda. (35:560–61)

Ruskin's conception of the vital yet circumscribed childhood he experienced in his other South London garden thus finds representation not only in his crystalline prose, but also in a rippling brook—no natural, uncontrollable torrent this, but a constructed and contained stream, which courses, under his control, over an artificial bed of quartz. In this instance, the child seen in relation to the garden she dubs "Eden-land" is not the young Ruskin, but the young Rose, captured in all the poignant immediacy of the present tense, though she had been dead for many years when these lines were written. Here, as at so many points in the autobiography, the most vital being is a child in a jewel-like setting, a young girl who is present and lost at the same time.

If we cast our minds back to another key image of waters in *Praeterita*, to that "brook shore of 1837" at the close of volume 1, we remember that Ruskin not only insisted that all significant development ceased before he attained maturity, but that the crystallized identity of childhood persisted as the true self throughout his life and into old age. Just as the perfect maidens who failed to live beyond their teens stand as so many examples of Ruskin's essential, end-stopped being, so too does the continuing existence of this self find representation in a young girl. Once the childhood years are past, *Praeterita* would much rather scrutinize a beloved landscape than the man who is perceiving it. However, on the very few occasions that the autobiography does allow brief sights of an adult Ruskin who is in a rare state of happiness or contentedness, *Praeterita* once again makes use of the "feminine simile" it employed in its depiction of the child self. When the forty-one-year-old man becomes the owner of a fourteenth-century missal, "no girl of seven years old with a new doll is prouder or happier" (35:491). Perhaps the most fascinating of these moments occurs when Ruskin represents his own creative process:

> My own literary work . . . was always done as quietly and methodically as a piece of tapestry. I knew exactly what I had got to say, put the words firmly in their places like so many stitches, hemmed the edges of chapters round with what seemed to me graceful flourishes, touched them finally with my cunningest points of colour, and read the work to papa and mamma at breakfast the next morning, as a girl shows her sampler. (35:367–68)

Here, on the sole occasion in *Praeterita* when the author presents himself *as* an author, the adult writing self is not only depicted as a child, but very specifically as a little girl, the competent and compliant daughter.

Of the writers considered in this study, Ruskin makes the most thoroughgoing, and the most heartbreaking, investment in the myth of original girlhood. Although any dalliance with the paradigm obviously involves a willful disregard for objective, logical "truth," Ruskin, in the last years of his writing life, attempts to hold together a truly impossible vision that refuses to countenance the unbridgeable distances between self and other, the living and the dead, and the bodies of the mature male and the immature female. The structure of *The Ethics of the Dust* at least allowed the writer to keep a safe distance between the constituent parts of his identity, but *Praeterita*'s attempt to conjoin the little girl and the old man, the past and the present, into a single figure is ultimately unbearable. In the final estimation, Ruskin's extension of the Victorian fantasy of the gentleman's lost girlhood into a fantasy of the essential girlishness of the true self proves not to be a source of sentimental solace, but a torment.

Lewis Carroll and the Little Girl:
The Art of Self-Effacement

> What do you suppose is the use of a child without any
> meaning?
> *(Lewis Carroll, "Through the Looking Glass")*

WHEN I first read Lewis Carroll's late and unloved work *Sylvie and Bruno*, I was searching for material that might help to bring the Oxford don's two main forms of creative expression, fiction and photography, into relation with his favorite subject in each genre, the little girl. Carroll studies have generally employed one particular girl to do this work for them: Alice Liddell, Carroll's most inspirational muse in both media, is used as a kind of revolving doorway, allowing critics to move effortlessly from one art form to the other.[1] The following passage appears, at first sight, to offer an alternative and less-trodden route to my desired nexus:

> There are some things one *says* in life—as well as things one *does*—which come automatically, by *reflex action*, as the physiologists say (meaning, no doubt, action *without* reflection, just as *lucus* is said to be derived "*a non lucendo*"). Closing one's eyelids, when something seems to be flying into the eye, is one of those actions, and saying "May I carry the little girl up the stairs?" was another. It wasn't that any thought of offering help occurred to me, and that *then* I spoke: the first intimation I had, of being likely to make that offer, was the sound of my own voice, and the discovery that the offer had been made. (398)

The narrator of *Sylvie and Bruno*, a weary seventy-year-old man, is here explaining how he finds himself carrying an unknown crippled child out of a railway station. (A couple of pages later it will transpire that this child is not a real child at all, but a phantasm who swiftly transforms herself into the eponymous Sylvie, a metamorphosis that comes as no surprise in a work that habitually switches between realism and fantasy.) Here, in the middle of a story that presents the pairing of the old man and the little girl as the most natural thing in the world, the narrator provides an instance of the immediate and irresistible attraction between the two figures, and claims that when he offered assistance to the child, he was necessarily operating under the dictate of a spontaneous, rather than a reasoned, response.

This episode is of interest not only for the narrative strategy that facilitates physical contact between these two particular categories of bodies, but for the analogy deployed as a preemptive justification of the act. After a tortuous consideration of paradoxical etymologies, the narrator prepares the ground for the explanation of his instinctive utterance by citing, as a parallel case, one of the most familiar examples of a reflex: "Closing one's eyelids, when something seems to be flying into the eye, is one of those actions." Here is a connection, albeit a challengingly complex one, between Carroll, fiction, little girls, and the realm of the camera: offering to hold the girl is made equivalent to the way in which potential optical damage is averted by the involuntary blink. In one arena, pleasure is gained, and in the other, pain is avoided: both scenarios effect the capture of an image, either in the arms, or behind momentarily closed eyelids that shut the dangers of the world out of the picture. In both cases, the action is presented as transcending personal choice.

And yet there is a major flaw in this chimerical vision of Carrollian coherence. The fact that the blinking of an eye actually demonstrates the opposite action to a camera exposure—the eye closes for an instant; the shutter opens—is far less troublesome to any projected constructions than the recollection that the equipment used by the Reverend Charles Lutwidge Dodgson[2] throughout his twenty-four years of photographic practice did not "blink" to capture images. On the contrary, taking pictures with his chosen medium, the collodion or wet-plate process, demanded what now seem to us extraordinarily long exposure times. "I took a first-rate photograph only a week ago, but then the sitter (a little girl of ten) had to sit for a minute and a half, the light is so weak now," Carroll mentioned in a letter of December 1877;[3] even in the summer months, which constituted the true sunlit photographic season, a small, fidgety, and impatient child might be required to remain stock-still for sixty seconds or more. While Carroll's mock-medieval legend, "The Ladye's History," claims that the "merveillous machine . . . took manie pictures, each yn a single stroke of Tyme" (1003), the actual facts of the matter are more honestly laid out in the Longfellowian meter of his "Hiawatha's Photographing": pictures had to be taken "With the calm deliberation / The intense deliberation / Of a photographic artist"—or not at all (772).

This faulty analogy between the blink of an eye and photography encapsulates in grosser form one of the major problems that the critic Lindsay Smith has exposed.[4] Forgetting, or otherwise neglecting, both the technical and philosophical circumstances of nineteenth-century photography has been, Smith claims, a besetting tendency of twentieth-century discussions of the form. Writers have either occluded photography's history, or assumed that its beginnings are resolutely uncomplicated—that it offers a single point of origin in normative realism that will only later be challenged and questioned by avant-garde experimentation in the 1920s. To Smith, even the much cherished and clearly indispensable *Camera Lucida*, Roland Barthes's lyrical and poignantly beautiful meditation upon the medium, is predicated on an entirely essentialist view of photography.[5] It is Smith's mission to problematize and complicate this view, to reveal that material choices and complex questioning did indeed accompany photography from its very inception.[6] Our dehistoricized camera-click must be corrected, therefore, and we need to find a more properly historical way to connect this chapter's special topic of Carroll, little girls, writing, and photography to the general project of revealing the nineteenth-century fantasy of original femininity.

If we must give up the click and the blink when thinking about Victorian photography, we can still, it seems, keep a close hold on the child. Smith's work, in common with Carol Mavor's *Pleasures Taken: Performances of Sexuality and Loss in Victorian Photographs*, is fascinated by the fact that seeing the history of photography and the history of the child through the same viewfinder is not only possible, but inevitable. As Mavor puts it, "The child and the photograph were commodified, fetishized, developed alongside each other: they were laminated and framed as one."[7] Certainly the dates fit rather nicely. Although, as we have already investigated, interest in the idea of the child and all that might pertain to it had been steadily growing from the eighteenth century into the nineteenth, it is still fair to say that the Victorian era constitutes the concept's heyday. Photography is even more of a quintessentially Victorian invention. Just after Britain's young queen came to the throne, two Frenchmen, Niepce and Daguerre, had finally discovered how to make permanent the images of the camera obscura.[8] Daguerre's patented process, which employed iodized silver plates, was made public in Paris in 1839, while over in England William Henry Fox Talbot registered his own "calotype" process in 1841: the first phase of photography had begun. The 1850s witnessed a number of scientific and legal developments that enabled the new invention to reach a much wider constituency: not only did Daguerre and Fox Talbot's patents expire in 1855, but a new and patent-free process had been introduced in 1851 by Frederick Scott Archer. This was the collodion, or wet-plate, method, which, although messy, complicated, expensive, and time-consuming, was to garner a new crop of enthusiastic amateur practitioners, including Carroll, Julia Margaret Cameron, and Lady Clementina Hawarden. Professional photography also grew by leaps and bounds: the "Carte de visite" format, first patented in France in 1854, and then introduced to Great Britain three years later, encouraged a vogue for portrait photography and the establishment of photographic studios all over the country. Further important developments occurred toward the end of the century. In 1873 Colonel Wortley greatly simplified the collodion process by offering manufactured dry plates for sale; Kodak appeared on the scene in 1888 with the first reasonably prized and technically manageable cameras. This new technological art form, then, was born at the beginning of Victoria's reign, and by its close had reached a position of ubiquitous popularity.

If photography and the concept of the child share the distinction of being properly Victorian obsessions, they are also linked in other important ways. For one thing, photography was frequently imaged in contemporary writing as a radically "new child" abroad in the world: to Wiertz in 1855, the daguerrotype was an "infant prodigy" who one day would find Genius seizing it "by the scruff of the neck and shout[ing]: Come with me, you are mine now! We shall work together!"[9] In similar fashion, a reviewer of the 1856–57 Photographic Exhibition in London presented photography as "Art's youngest and fairest child; no rival of the old family, no struggler for wornout birthrights, but heir to a new heaven and a new earth."[10] More significantly, the connection between photography and the child was solidified by the fact that this "infant" apparatus was very frequently pointed at real children. Although the earliest daguerrotypes and talbotypes tended to feature landscapes, architecture, and botanical specimens, the second wave of photography, both amateur and commercial, became much more interested in the portrait genre, of which child portraiture formed an important subsidiary. From the mid-1850s onwards, photographs of children constituted a significant proportion of the output of practitioners specializing in what we might call "art photography": the highly familiar images of Carroll and Cameron may spring to mind first, but many other artists, including Oscar Rejlander and Henry Peach Robinson, regularly composed child studies. In the growing world of commercial photography, children of all ages were escorted to professional studios, propped against pillars, wedged into chairs and sofas, and screwed into neck braces to secure the necessary immobility for their own photographic portraits, or pinioned in the embrace of their loving parents for the perfect family group. Once Kodak brought "snapshot" photography within the reach of any moderately comfortably-off individual, the camera was pointed with ever-increasing insistency at the children of the family. Such fervor, of course, continues unabated into our own historical period, in which it is estimated by the major photographic companies that over 70 percent of film stock is exclusively devoted to this particular subject.

The origins of the evident love affair between photography and the child have only recently begun to receive the full attention they deserve. At the vanguard of this scrutiny, Smith focuses her investigation by making strategic returns to the two most cited essays in photographic theory—namely Walter Benjamin's "Small History of Photography" and Barthes's *Camera Lucida*.[11] At the heart of each essay lies a photograph that seems to encapsulate for the writer the essential beauty, magic, and mystery of the medium. Benjamin's photograph is a picture of a very young Franz Kafka—"There the boy stands, perhaps six years old, dressed up in a humiliatingly tight children's suit overloaded with trimming, in a sort of conservatory landscape"[12]—while Barthes eventually finds what he has been looking for in a photograph of his mother, taken when she was five years old. Posed with her seven-year-old brother, the little girl is seen "at the end of a little wooden bridge in a glassed-in conservatory, what was called a Winter Garden in those days."[13] While Smith is rightly attentive to both critics' own theorizations of why these images have such power to move, yoking the two exemplary photographs together forces us to consider a more historically specific question: why should it be that these two seminal twentieth-century discussions are grounded in two nineteenth-century photographs of children?[14] Smith's various answers to this question are fascinating and wide-ranging, encompassing a number of psychoanalytical and historical explanations with equal flair. For my own purposes, I wish to consider the numerous different ways in which photography, in its founding decades, coincides not just with a general notion of "the child," but with the highly specific historical version thereof that we have been examining. The next section of this chapter argues that photography and the child, as imagined at the midpoint of the nineteenth century, are caught up in exactly the same complex web of constructions. Variously challenging the divisions between past and present, fantasy and reality, imagination and materiality, self and other, and, as we shall see when we come to examine the case of Lewis Carroll more particularly, masculinity and femininity, photography and the Victorian child are each other's perfect complements.

That *Camera Lucida* should neglect to provide a thoroughgoing historical account of photography's evolution is not, after all, very surprising. Put simply, the single most startling fact about the medium is as evident in yesterday's casual snapshot as in the very first daguerrotype, even if the former's exposure time is a fraction of the latter's: any and every photograph captures, in an indexical form, an absolute image of a real moment of time and thus automatically excerpts an actual instance of presentness from the temporal flow and consigns it to the past.[15] The moment of past reality is made material, transferred onto a piece of card that we can gaze at and hold in the present tense. For Barthes, any photograph, from the nineteenth or the twentieth century, is "reality in a past state: at once the past and real." The important change comes not within the medium over the years, then, but to the world that first witnesses its abilities:

> Perhaps we have an invincible resistance to believing in the past, in History, except in the form of myth. The Photograph, for the first time, puts an end to this resistance; henceforth the past is as certain as the present, what we see on paper is as certain as what we can touch. It is the advent of Photography, and not, as has been said, of the cinema, which divides the history of the world.[16]

For Barthes, photography not only introduces a new era, but has "some historical relation with what Edgar Morin calls the 'crisis of death' beginning in the second half of the nineteenth century."[17] After all, each and every photograph contains within it the possibility of reminding us of our own existence within the temporal flow, and thus of our own mortality. The death of time in the photograph images in little the real death that awaits us all. In chapter 2 we considered the combination of the luminous beauty of four young girls and the shriveled leaves of a dying season, captured in the last light of the declining day, in Millais's *Autumn Leaves*, which provokes a meditation upon the passage of time, on the evanescence of the moment and the inevitability of decay. Millais creates these thoughts through his choice of theme, and through the artistic vision and painterly skill, not to mention the sheer time and effort, that he expends to make his idea both accessible and powerful to the viewer. What Millais accomplishes through conscious desire in *Autumn Leaves* is achieved unconsciously by even the most banal of photographic prints: through the simple mechanics of its technological process, the photograph automatically makes a profound statement about the nature of time.

If every photograph is thus invested with an inherent ability to promote thoughts about the past and the present, and about life and death, certain photographs, by virtue of their subject matter, are capable of intensifying this effect to an almost painful degree. While we may identify abstractly with the notions of temporality that inform all photographs, we are likely to have stronger feelings when confronted by an image that in some way reminds us of ourselves. Photographs of human beings thus have the potential to speak more directly to our sense of mortality: the normal movement of a breathing body like our own is reduced to deathlike stillness; a moment of real existence is captured to tell us, ever after, that that moment of human life existed, and exists no more. When the camera is pointed at a child, these messages become still more insistent. Depending on the associations carried by the figure of the child in any given historical and cultural period, such effects, as will be seen, may be more or less pronounced, but a number of features appear to transcend such specificity, at least within photography's relatively short history to date. For one thing, the experience of identification is harder to avoid: all adult viewers of a photograph of a child have themselves been children. Moreover, the relationship between the child subject and the image of death that is inescapably carried by its photograph is that much more jarring, because, as Smith notices, in the normal course of human lives, the child is further away from its real death than any depicted adult.[18] Finally, although there is inevitably some degree of cultural construction in the division between child and adult, the rapid changes of growth within childhood's brief estate (ten, twelve, fourteen, sixteen years?) make it seem far more evanescent to us than adulthood, with its long, less-differentiated stretches: consequently photography's ability to make still a being who is hurtling toward its next stage of development is all the more marked. "Only the camera can keep up with the velocity of children," remarks Mavor, reminding us of J. M. Barrie's poignant observation about his beloved and much-photographed Llewelyn-Davies boys: "They had a long summer day, and I turned round twice and now they are off to school."[19]

Photographs of children, then, for us as much as for the Victorians, have the potential to double the inherent signifying powers of the medium. Our nineteenth-century predecessors, however, were in a position to appreciate a still more compelling synergy between their ways of looking at children and the productions of their newest technological enthusiasm. For at least the first two-thirds of the nineteenth century, the child was predominantly perceived in a retrospective and feminized, rather than an anticipatory and masculinized, mode. Consequently, the child tended *not* to be seen in relation to his own adulthood—a perspective that would have viewed him as an incipient adult, the germ, the potential of what is to come, and thereby associated with vigor; vitality; the promise or danger of the future. If the child had been imagined thus as an active figure of forward movement, no real "fit" between this construction and the new photographic medium would have emerged. As events transpired, however, the formal properties of the Victorian invention brought it, coincidentally, into exact register with a philosophically congruent perception of the child. Although our ideas about childhood have shifted over time, enough of this original sympathy persists to make the ensuing working partnership of the child and the photograph continue to seem natural and inevitable. Back in the nineteenth century, though, the similarities between figure and medium, and more especially, the way in which an adult might look at one or the other, were much more pronounced.

The photograph, I maintain, participates in the same fantasy that informs the response to the girl investigated in this study. To recap: in this period, ideal childhood is generally imagined as a wholly separate estate from adulthood, a pitifully brief era of bliss and innocence, which is lost forever at the onset of maturity. The child itself is viewed from the perspective of an adult looking backwards and is therefore an essentially nostalgic construction, associated with the past, often with stasis and sealed perfection, and very frequently with death. As in the case of Little Nell, the child is perceived as existing within her childhood not for her own pleasure or purposes, but as a service to surrounding adults. Simply through their presence, children offer the best possible opportunity for adults to reconnect to their imaginary pasts, to the fantasy era of their own idyllic childhoods. A girl, furthermore, radically distant from an adult male by virtue of her physical difference, more perfectly represents the safe, feminized, time of the nursery from which he has been irrevocably banished.

The myth of original femininity thus involves a willed belief in that which is both untrue and impossible. Single-exposure photography, on the other hand, is a medium that records that which actually happened.[20] Nevertheless, within these parallel realms of fantasy and reality the little girl and the photograph play exactly the same role: in their material physicality, both substantiate the past while simultaneously declaring that it is resolutely over and done with. In Barthes's words, the two presences show us "what has been."[21] When the photograph carries the figure of a girl, the retrospective mode is invoked twice over: looking at the picture, the Victorian gentleman sees both a real representation of his imaginary former self and a true image of the impossibility of returning to the sealed idyll of that girlish childhood. Simultaneously supplying and denying connections, the photograph of the girl combines fantasy and reality, past and present, self and other, femininity and masculinity. For Lewis Carroll, the most celebrated nineteenth-century photographer of little girls, the combination is practically mesmerizing.

The reasons why Carroll should be a principal subject not only of a chapter on nineteenth-century photography but of this study as a whole seem almost too obvious to mention. In the race for the title of the Victorian era's most famous (or infamous) girl lover, Carroll pips Ruskin at the post: although both men's fascination with little girls is well known, Carroll's predilection has been more firmly fixed in the public mind because of the simple fact that he also created one of the most fascinating little girls of all time.[22] In all her different and associated forms—underground and through the looking glass, textual and visual, drawn or photographed, as Carroll's brunette or Tenniel's blonde or Disney's prim miss, as the real Alice Liddell, the dean's daughter, or imaginary beggar, in novel, poem, satire, play, film, cartoon, newspaper, magazine, album cover, or song—Alice is the ultimate cultural icon, available for any and every form of manipulation, and as ubiquitous today as in the era of her first appearance.

Carroll's famous literary creation is of course a no less popular focus in the field of critical analysis. The inescapably connected topic of Carroll's relationships with real little girls has also generated a comparable amount of scrutiny. For those who wish to map the contours of the don's desires, both his public, and more especially his voluminous private, writings provide acres and acres of relevant territory. Letter after letter, journal upon journal, dedicatory poem and book inscription bear witness to Carroll's ceaseless pursuit of juvenile feminine company. Matching Carroll's tenacity are the considerable numbers of critical and biographical commentators who worry over the manifold evidence of obsession and pose the same circular questions—Is it innocent? Is it sexual? Is it sexually innocent? Is it innocently sexual? The answers proposed to these inquiries range from outraged denials of any impropriety even in the private recesses of Carroll's fantasies,[23] to a gleefully malicious accusation of criminal behavior: apparently relishing his own imaginary daring in dispersing "the odour of sanctity" around the "honoured author," one critic com-

137

ments decisively, "Today, . . . [Carroll] would find himself in Wormwood Scrubs,"[24] one of London's major prisons. Because it will never be possible to pin down exactly either what Carroll may have done, or what he may, consciously or unconsciously, have wanted to do, the interpretive dance has no reason ever to come to an end.[25]

All in all, then, Carroll is evidently at the heart of the matter when we think about girls in the nineteenth century, and he is just as much there when we think, more anxiously, about men and girls in the nineteenth century. He is, of course, there as well in my title's allusion to Wonderland, a place that provides a highly convenient hook upon which to hang this investigation. But Carroll turns out to be the most recalcitrant and unaccommodating of figures. He seems to demand star billing within this book, but his resolute avoidance of reconstructive autobiography makes it hard to turn him into its exemplary case study. Unlike De Quincey or Ruskin, Carroll eschews the kind of self-fashioning that speculates on the relationship between the child and the man. But if Carroll produced no avowed autobiography, he undoubtedly left a staggering amount of other personal writings. Unsurprisingly, these materials have been frequently explored and augmented by memoirists and biographers, who, on the whole, have been keen to construct a life story that seems in sympathy with the general patterns explored in this book.[26] A crude schematic plan of the usual versions of Carroll's life—an idyllic childhood, followed by a painful adolescence, and an unfulfilled maturity, enlivened only by connections to little girls—certainly appears to provide fertile ground for the growth of a regressive fantasy.

Traditional Carrollian biography runs as follows. Bountifully provided with sisters (seven in all), the young Charles Dodgson was the beloved eldest son of an adored mother and a revered clerical father, and his earliest days in the family garden are depicted as exceptionally happy and filled with imaginative games. The subsequent expulsion from this Edenic period into the horrors of the exclusively male and abusive world of a public school seems to have been even more distressing for Carroll than it had been for De Quincey: to support this view, biographers generally cite a revealing comment Carroll made to his diary in 1857. Remarking with approval on another public school's provision of a "snug little bedroom" for each pupil, Carroll then apparently offers a rare and troubling glimpse of the unhappiness of his own teenaged years: "From my own experience of school life at Rugby I can say that if I could have been thus secure from annoyance at night, the hardships of the daily life would have been comparative trifles to bear."[27] Christ Church, Oxford, which he joined as an undergraduate, and where he subsequently became a sublibrarian and then a mathematics don and an ordained clergyman, is generally seen as a much safer bolt-hole: Carroll never married, and the college served as his primary home until his death. This ostensibly tranquil existence, however, is complicated for the biographers by the fact that Carroll's diary entries persistently record feelings of dissatisfaction, guilt about his lack of progress, and the fear of unworthiness.

In the accepted accounts of Carroll's life, his true periods of adult happiness are imagined to have been generated by the company, or the inspiration, of girls. It is easy to make the case that his experience with real girls was closely tied to his imaginary girl both at her inception and ever after. The public response to *Alice in Wonderland* (1865) and then to *Through the Looking-Glass and What Alice Found There* (1871) created tremendous excitement within the don's life: biographers are fond of claiming that although in some ways he rigorously policed the division between his two identities, he frequently used his fame as Lewis Carroll to further Charles Dodgson's attempts to befriend little girls. At the very center of the famous Lewis Carroll story lie the days spent with Alice Liddell, but numerous biographers are keen to demonstrate that once she passed out of his life and into adolescence, the "Dream-child" was replaced by other little girls. The comic letters, the teasing exchanges, and the hours with the photographic equipment continued unabated; days at the seaside and trips to the theater stood in for the immortalized rowing expedition up the river to Godstow. In the context of an otherwise sedate and uneventful adulthood, it is Carroll's relationships with girls, both real and fictional, that apparently created the true energy of his life.

If we accept this version of Carroll's life, then it is no great stretch to hypothesize that this child-chasing don was on an impossible quest to catch the child he himself had once been: in such a vision, Carroll's immersion in croquet games on the deanery lawn with Lorina, Alice, and Edith Liddell can then be diagnosed as an attempt to recapture the happiness of the lost parsonage garden of his own childhood.[28] From this point onwards, it is admittedly hard to make a straightforward case that Carroll regards his former self as feminine, but we could nevertheless move some distance toward this conclusion by devious routes. For instance, we can focus on the following conundrum: Carroll's writings simultaneously display a longing for a return to childhood, and a violent rejection of all children who happen to be male. A stanza he wrote when only twenty-one years old was included in a volume of poetry he published nearly forty years later:

I'd give all wealth that years have piled
   The slow result of Life's decay
To be once more a little child
   For one bright summer day.

$(861)^{29}$

In the wake of Wordsworth's mighty *Ode*, such sentiments are entirely conventional in this period, but they nevertheless sit awkwardly alongside Carroll's other, assertively unromantic, references to the "little child" he actually had been. To be sure, when Carroll declares that "as a little boy, I was simply detestable,"[30] he is simply adding to the litany of boy abuse that forms a regular feature of his published texts and his private correspondence alike.[31] With lisping Bruno practically the only exception to his self-imposed rule, boys in Carroll's oeuvre are, in his own words, "a mistake," and certainly "not an attractive race of beings."[32] The unfortunate boy baby who turns into a pig in Alice's arms[33] (all to the good, she thinks, as "it would have made a dreadfully ugly child" [64]) reappears in much more hideous form in *Sylvie and Bruno*'s boy-cum-porcupine, the vile and vilely named Uggugg. But what are we to think when we place Carroll's apparent rejection of his *own* boy self next to that desire to recapture "vanish'd summer glory" which pervades much of his poetry, not least the prefatory verses to the two *Alice*s? If we take the poet's longing to regress seriously, can we then conclude that he wishes to return not to a distastefully porcine boyhood, but to an entirely phantasmal girlhood?

The past few paragraphs show what can be stitched together, in the absence of the whole cloth of a thoroughgoing autobiography, to connect Carroll to the male fantasy of original femininity. But is it possible to think of Carroll's lack of interest in the conventional form of self-commemoration as something other than a frustrating gap to be inadequately filled by critical speculation, biographical and otherwise? Could there be more productive ways to think about his resistance to the genre? The remainder of this chapter asks whether the work of autobiography—which is to say, the act of imagining the present self in relation to the former self—is effectively performed by other means within Carroll's oeuvre. As has already been discussed, the photographic form has an inherent ability to present a relationship between that which is and that which has been: Carroll's photographs of little girls, at their most effective, not only invoke this duality but also have the power to combine any number of others, especially the key oppositions of adult and child, self and other. On one notable occasion Carroll was also able to achieve this effect in his other chosen medium of expression: the central portions of *Alice in Wonderland* present an omnifaceted juvenile feminine lead, a little girl who is everything and its opposite, and who breaks down the division between old and young, big and little, powerful and powerless. By way of contrast, I turn in conclusion to a series of tableaux in Carroll's fiction that display a much more obvious and conventional relationship between youth and age. Despite the fact that these moments are presented in a quasi-photographic mode, the absence of photography's tacit ability to invoke two temporalities is sorely felt: adult and child alike are fixed in rigid and conventional positions and denied the complex play that energizes Carroll's best work. While De Quincey and Ruskin constructed personal narratives that linked the mature male writer to the fantasized feminine self of childhood, Carroll chose quite a different form of commemoration: for this Victorian gentleman, the precious relationship between the old man and the little girl is most successfully represented when the former individual is utterly effaced and excluded from the picture.

To illustrate the photographed girl's signifying power, any one of Carroll's stack of girl studies would serve the purpose: the image of the lovely girl, fully real yet fully lost, makes manifest the fantasized and feminized perfection of the former self. In the vast majority of cases, Carroll's relationship to the image is everywhere and nowhere.[34] As the photographer, he creates the picture, and as its subsequent owner, he has the ability to look at it whenever he wishes, but there is no explicit representation of his controlling presence within the photograph. For Carroll, the effacement of the adult male appears to allow him to invoke the liberating fantasy of the little girl's power[35]—to create a little girl, we might say, who not only has the ability to confound temporality by bringing the past self vividly and magnificently into the present, but who can also challenge any other imaginable opposition.

Figures 8, 9, and 10—*Agnes Grace Weld as Little Red Riding Hood* (1857), *Alice Liddell as a Beggar-Child* (c. 1858–59) and *Portrait of Evelyn Hatch* (c. 1878–79)—are three highly familiar images in the worlds of Victorian studies and art history and have been subject to numerous intelligent and interesting critical analyses.[36] The earlier two pictures are the evident result of the photographer's fondness for dressing-up games and "make-believe," while the late study is the most infamous example of the little girl in her "favourite state of nothing-on," to quote Carroll's self-protective (or self-deluding?) periphrasis.[37] Despite this difference, the

141

photographs share a range of significant characteristics. Looking directly at the lens, all three girls confront the viewer by appearing to making deliberate eye contact. Any preconceived notion of the submissive docility of the diminutive Victorian miss is thus thrown into question: Agnes, Alice, and Evelyn are evidently little girls who don't behave as little girls should. In each case, the pictured girl further complicates the photograph's inherent ability to question dualities.

Emerging out of the dense ivy of the photograph's background, Agnes is a disturbingly hypnotic figure. While the proffered basket seems to suggest openness and solicitation, the withholding Napoleonic right hand, and more definitively, the girl's expression (the ominously hooded eyes, down-turned mouth, and creased forehead) signal a ferocious denial of reciprocity, even as we are held in thrall by that gaze. Mavor comments succinctly on the ways in which the photograph of Agnes attacks any straightforward apprehension of the narrative in which she is ostensibly placed: "Hers are the eyes of the wolf that has presumably just eaten her grandmother; we wonder whether she has eaten the wolf, and whether she is about ready to eat us up."[38] This is a Little Red Riding Hood who has no need of the assistance of any ax-toting woodcutter. Despite her evident childishness (notice those daintily placed button-boots), Agnes exudes a mysterious power that is both adult and feral.

The photograph of Alice Liddell as a beggar repeats some of the dynamics of the earlier picture. This time, the act of solicitation is made overt: pretending to be begging, Alice and her cupped right hand appear to ask for our charity. Once again, however, the gesture of supplication is defiantly undercut, not only by the child's cockily assertive stance (that left hand resting on the hip), but more obviously by the arrogant confidence of Alice's coolly appraising gaze. While Agnes disrupts the familiar narrative of a folktale, Alice works to destabilize the massive divisions and inequities of Victorian society: an evidently well-fed, clean, and glossy-haired child of the upper middle classes puts on artfully disordered rags and pretends to occupy the lowest stratum of all. Making an ugly social reality visually seductive (for Tennyson, this was the most beautiful photograph he had ever seen), the joint playacting of photographer and subject also disturbs any number of other binaries. Not the least of these for late-twentieth-century commentators was the question of the photograph's simultaneous relation to constructions of both innocence and sexuality.[39] Alice's revealed flesh, and, much more disturbingly, the knowingness of her appeal to the viewer, have made it very difficult for most critics to see this simply as a lovely photograph of a seven-year-old girl.

FIGURE 8. Lewis Carroll, *Agnes Grace Weld as Little Red Riding Hood* (1857). (Gernsheim Collection, Harry Ransom Humanities Research Center, University of Texas at Austin.)

This difficulty has been considerably heightened since Morton N. Cohen brought to light four nude studies of little girls, apparently the only remaining examples of Carroll's extensive work in this mode.[40] Of the four photographs, all of which were colored in and given fanciful painted backgrounds, only the *Portrait of Evelyn Hatch* is arresting: here a very young girl takes on the erotic pose of an odalisque, of a courtesan, and, through the overlaid oil paint, meets our gaze with calm self-possession. As in the photograph of Alice, adult sexuality is signaled even as the immaturity of the child's body seems to deny the possibility of such a message. Child and adult, innocence and experience, however, are not the only oppositions called into question by this photograph. Evelyn also seems to straddle the boundary between animal and human, between reality and the dream, and nature and artifice.[41]

All three photographs, then, share the ability to confound distinctions: the little girl is made mesmerizingly enigmatic by her ability to be both a thing and its opposite. Although the pictures are obviously the result of an unequal partnership between Carroll and his models, it will never be possible to say exactly how wide that inequity may have been on any given occasion: did the photographer stage-manage the whole show, or was something always intrinsically of the girl's own making? Such questions may be unanswerable, but it certainly appears that Carroll had no wish to represent within these photographs any trace of his own dominant role. In consequence, because she herself lays claim to adult power, the little girl is never diminished, or otherwise defined, by a relationship to an adult presence that stands outside of her. In Carroll's photographs of girls, the form's technical ability to combine past and present within a single image is complemented by the subject's simultaneous existence within the realms of childhood and adulthood.

The photographic medium, then, offered Carroll both satisfaction and the freedom of self-effacement: the relationship of the adult male and the little girl could be captured without the necessity of bringing the man into frame. Only once in his career did Carroll manage to achieve a parallel feat within the genre of creative fiction. *Alice in Wonderland* presents us with a little girl of most remarkable abilities. In chapter 1 we learn that "this curious child was very fond of pretending to be two people" (21); certainly, as the story progresses, Alice gets the opportunity to play an astounding variety of roles. Just as the photographs of Agnes, Alice, and Evelyn invoke and defy conventional stereotypes of demure Victorian maidens, the Alice of Carroll's first fantasy narrative rarely signifies only one thing: sometimes huge, sometimes tiny, powerful then powerless, pa-

FIGURE 9. Lewis Carroll, *Alice Liddell as a Beggar-Child* (c. 1858–59). (Gilman Paper Company Collection, New York.)

FIGURE 10. Lewis Carroll, *Portrait of Evelyn Hatch* (c. 1878–79). (The Rosenbach Museum and Library, Philadelphia, and A.P. Watt Ltd. on behalf of the Trustees of the C.L. Dodgson Estate.)

tronizing then patronized, she constitutes, at different times, both terms of any given opposition.

Most particularly, thanks to the dizzying shifts in her experiences, the Alice of the central portion of the tale never occupies for very long a state we could confidently designate as the child's position.[42] Thus we find no stable representation of the relationship between little girl and mature man that has so frequently engrossed our attention in this study: Wonderland is no country for old men. Although Alice has a series of encounters with figures whom one could try to force into the older male role (the White Rabbit, the Dodo, the Caterpillar, the Cheshire Cat, the March Hare, the Hatter, the King of Hearts, the Gryphon, and the Mock Turtle, to name the likeliest suspects), the balance of power is never weighted with any certainty or for any length of time in their favor. Alice's frequent comments about eating remind us that a little girl is just as likely to devour as to be devoured, while her equally frequent changes in size destroy the conventional arrangement in which an older male can be sure of being bigger than a young female. Indeed, the conception of age's relation to youth is literally inverted in the story's prime representation of an old man, which appears in Alice's idiosyncratic rendition of "You are old, Father William":

146

"You are old, Father William," the young man said
  And your hair has become very white;
And yet you incessantly stand on your head—
  Do you think, at your age, it is right?"

(50)

Parodying the very idea of the august dignity of enfeebled old age, the
verses reveal that not only is Father William in the habit of performing
headstands, but also of turning somersaults, munching down a goose,
bones, beak, and all, and balancing an eel upon his nose. And while
elderliness is not marked by regretful weariness, neither is Alice's youth
venerated for its appealing sweetness, at least not during her adventures
underground. Because the relationship between the heroine and Wonderland's supposedly "adult" figures is constantly changing, the idea of Alice
as a child promotes neither nostalgia nor sentimentality within the story
itself.

It is undeniably true, however, that a very different note is struck both
in the prefatory poem and the tale's denouement.[43] The poem, which apparently commemorates that first telling of the story to Alice, Lorina, and
Edith Liddell, quite deliberately casts the "golden afternoon" into a long-
lost past, so that childhood is seen from an adult's vantage point.[44] Alice
Liddell, apparently no longer a child, is exhorted to take the "childish
story":

  And, with a gentle hand,
Lay it where Childhood's dreams are twined
  In Memory's mystic band.
Like pilgrim's wither'd wreath of flowers
  Pluck'd in a far-off land.

(12)

A similar movement occurs at the very end of the story proper. Narrative
attention switches to Alice's ploddingly pedestrian sister, who dismisses
our heroine with the words, "It *was* a curious dream, dear, certainly; but
now run in to your tea: it's getting late" (118). First dreaming, in a remarkably unsororal fashion, of a seductively childish Alice with "tiny
hands," "eager eyes," and "that queer little toss of her head to keep the
wandering hair that *would* always get into her eyes" (119), the sister then
proceeds to find tediously plausible "explanations" for each of the wild
and wonderful emanations of the little girl's story. Then, in the same way
that the poem splits Alice Liddell into the remembering adult and the
remembered child, the sister's closing thoughts create a grown-up Alice
looking back:

147

Lastly, she pictured to herself how this same little sister of hers would, in the after time, be herself a grown woman; and how she would keep, through all her riper years, the simple and loving heart of her childhood; and how she would gather about her other little children, and make their eyes bright and eager with many a strange tale, perhaps even with the dream of Wonderland of long ago; and how she would feel with all their simple sorrows, and find a pleasure in all their simple joys, remembering her own child-life, and the happy summer days. (119)

This is one of the moments of anticlimactic conventionality in *Wonderland*'s final pages; the sister's saccharine celebration of Alice's "simple and loving heart" certainly rings false to those of us who have enjoyed our heroine's various displays of curiosity, timorousness, tactlessness, snobbery, petulance, self-aggrandizement, and downright bad temper in the preceding twelve chapters. Only in Wonderland's frame, constricted by either the real presence of her elder sister or the imagined presence of her own adult self, is Alice limited to the performance of an alternatively coquettishly adorable or angelically innocent childishness.[45]

In the context of our examination of the inherent signifying powers of the photographic medium, extremely interesting issues are raised by the narrative's closing with the sister's "*pictur*[ing] to herself" a grown-up Alice surrounded by little children. In subsequent prose works Carroll becomes increasingly fond of creating still scenes that seem to mimic the photograph, or at least the way in which a photograph allows us to gaze steadily at the little girl in repose: *Through the Looking Glass* and *Sylvie and Bruno* contain numerous tableaux constructed along these lines. In these instances, however, Carroll always includes, in one way or another, a version of an adult presence, with the result that the child becomes fixed in the position of the child and loses the flexibility of the most successful of his photographs and the first Alice. Carroll's fantasy literature becomes progressively less daring and interesting over the course of his writing career: it is his attempt to reproduce photography's ability to capture both the lost and the present self, both child and adult, that allows a disabling sentimentality and nostalgia to flood in.

When Alice makes her second trip to a realm of fantasy, the conditions of her contract have been significantly diminished: the radical potential of Wonderland all but disappears in the Looking Glass world. Now she is a mere pawn in the game of chess that forms the story's governing conceit, maintaining little-girl stature and demeanor throughout her travels, even when she gains the crown of a queen in the final square. One of the primary reasons this happens is that the tendency to delimit child-hood, so evident in the frame but not the experience of Wonderland, creeps into the center of this later story. Once again, this occurs when the child is placed in diametric opposition to an adult: Alice is circumscribed twice over when she is put in relation both to her grown-up self and to an older male.

At first glance, *Through the Looking Glass* appears to repeat *Wonderland*'s tendency to turn the gravitas of the older male on its head: Humpty Dumpty's massively overdetermined fall inevitably follows his overweening pride, while the White Knight seems constitutionally unable to keep himself, or his belongings, upright. "The more head-downwards I am, the more I keep inventing new things," he tells Alice, who is singularly unimpressed by his upside-down sandwich box (223). The White Knight's song—the "name" of which is "The Aged Aged Man"—once again inverts conventional reverence for the old, this time by guying Wordsworth's lament for the ancient Leech Gatherer, "Resolution and Independence." But the tableau of the older man and the little girl that is composed when Alice stops to listen to the White Knight is the point of entry for a very particular brand of sentimental nostalgia.[46] The simple progressive temporality of Alice's experience in the Looking Glass world is suddenly disrupted, and we are transported into her future life:

> Of all the strange things that Alice saw in her journey Through The Look-ing-Glass, this was the one that she always remembered most clearly. Years afterward she could bring the whole scene back again, as if it had been only yesterday—the mild blue eyes and kindly smile of the Knight—the setting sun gleaming through his hair, and shining on his armour in a blaze of light that quite dazzled her—the horse quietly moving about, with the reins hanging loose on his neck, cropping the grass at her feet—and the black shadows of the forest behind—all this she took in like a picture, as, with one hand shading her eyes, she leant against a tree, watching the strange pair, and listening, in a half-dream, to the melancholy music of the song. (224–25)

The moment's immediacy is transformed into a Wordsworthian spot of time: we are given a double vision of the child watching the adult Knight, and the adult Alice who is remembering. Making allowance for the slight movements of the horse, and the blue of the Knight's eyes, we could be glancing with her at a black-and-white photograph from long ago. When we return to the present tense of the tale, Alice is resolutely unmoved—she listens to the ballad "very attentively, but no tears came into her eyes"

(225)—but we can no longer look at our heroine in quite the same way again. As in Wonderland's framing materials, Alice has been diminished by the appearance of that imagined adult self, but this scene pushes her delimitation still further. Sentiment pours in at the precise moment when Alice is brought into relation with a nostalgic older man: feeble and foolish though he seems, the White Knight stands as an early representative of a conception of melancholy adulthood that comes to dominate Carroll's writing, and that forms the counterpoint to an equally engrossing obsession with angelic feminine childhood. Only the Alice seen from the distance of adulthood is encrusted with a cloying sweetness, but it is this sugary avatar of the little girl who eventually wins top billing as the heroine of *Sylvie and Bruno*; shaved of his more ludicrous eccentricities, the White Knight returns to play the role of that work's weary narrator.

The split between childhood and adulthood, or, more concretely, between little girls and old men, that inveigles its way into Alice's world finds full representation in Carroll's last long works, *Sylvie and Bruno* (1889) and *Sylvie and Bruno Concluded* (1893).[47] Dwarfed by the gigantic reputation of *Alice in Wonderland* and *Through the Looking Glass*, this two-part fantasy novel has largely been neglected, or, if examined at all, castigated for its sickly sentimentality, its confusing shifts between the fairy-tale countries of Outland and Elfland and the more conventionally novelistic world of Elveston, the noxious baby talk of the boy Bruno and the feeble conventionality of its eponymous heroine.[48] Within this present study, however, *Sylvie and Bruno* finds a natural home. This is the one text of Carroll's that persistently presents the pairing of man and girl, and that participates fully in the paradigm we have examined most recently in Ruskin's *Ethics of the Dust*: once again the old man is associated with the troubled and enervated world of the present day, while the little girl is just as firmly linked with the jewel-like perfection and purity of long ago. Furthermore, it is a work that uses the vision, or the transfiguring sight, as a narrative trope.

Inasmuch as they reproduce familiar patterns, *Sylvie and Bruno*'s constructions of the opposite but complementary figures, the old man and the little girl, can be sketched fairly briefly. Carroll heightens the difference between the two parties by making his narrator excessively aged and enfeebled—not only is the old gentleman afflicted by "[t]hree score years and ten, baldness and spectacles" (291), but he is also a demoralized invalid. It is no act of chance that he is reading a book entitled *Diseases of the Heart* when we first meet him on his journey down to the country to stay with a doctor friend, for the narrator is essentially heartsick in both a medical and an emotional sense. "Life and its pleasures," he says wearily, "seem like a mine that is nearly worked out" (426). Certainly the real world in which the narrator exists shares this general air of lassitude and depression: in the vision of contemporary life that *Sylvie and Bruno* takes surprising pains to represent, England is riven by unequal distribution of income, and the impoverished working classes are plagued by drunkenness, cruelty, and disease. In complete contrast stands Sylvie, who is not only a young, fresh, and beautiful creature from the novel's other realm of fairyland, but is also connected to the pure and noble world of earlier times. And just as Ruskin's girls in *The Ethics of the Dust* are crystals, so is Sylvie represented by a flawless precious stone—in this case, the blue and red, heart-shaped gems of twin lockets, inscribed with the words "All-will-love-Sylvie" and "Sylvie-will-love-all," which turn out in the end to be one and "the *same* Jewel all the time" (674). The jewel's message of the reciprocity of loving and being loved is Sylvie's own, and she alone possesses the power, through her affectionate heart and simple faith, to cure the narrator's heart.

In the course of *Sylvie and Bruno*'s general quest to demonstrate the power of love, Carroll uses the device of the vision in various different ways: sometimes it functions to transport the narrator between the work's two domains, and at others to strengthen the links between the characters of these paired realms. In one of the early instances of this latter phenomenon, the narrator is sitting on a train, trying to "think the veil away"—which is to say, to discover by the power of thinking whether the concealed face of the young woman opposite to him is "pretty" or "plain" (272). For a while, we learn, "the dimly-seen oval remained as provokingly blank as ever," but eventually "there *was* a result: ever and anon, the veil seemed to vanish, in a sudden flash of light: but, before I could fully realize the face, all was dark again. In each such glimpse, the face seemed to grow more childish and innocent: and, when I had at last *thought* the veil entirely away, it was, unmistakably, the sweet face of little Sylvie!"(272). At another juncture, the narrator attempts to explain how intense a feeling he is experiencing by comparing it to the effect of a powerful vision: "I had felt such a pang only once before in my life, and it had been from *seeing* what, at the moment, realized one's idea of perfect beauty—it was in a London exhibition, where, in making my way through a crowd, I suddenly met, face to face, a child of quite unearthly beauty" (624–25).

In *Sylvie and Bruno* the ultimate sight is always that of the beautiful little girl, yet because of the dominant presence of our old-man narrator, we never see her without also being aware of his gaze. Consequently, it is perhaps not surprising that the work's primal scene, the moment when both the narrator and the reader see Sylvie for the first time, doubles this look: the mature man is both inside and outside the frame:

> The Warden, a tall and dignified man with a grave but very pleasant face, was seated before a writing table, which was covered with papers, and holding on his knee one of the sweetest and loveliest little maidens which it has ever been my lot to see. She looked four or five years older than Bruno, but she had the same rosy cheeks and sparkling eyes, and the same wealth of curly brown hair. Her eager smiling face was turned upwards towards her father's and it was a pretty sight to see the mutual love with which the two faces—one in the Spring of Life, the other in its late Autumn—were gazing on each other. (267)

Although initially it might seem as if the father-and-daughter relationship will provide the key to understanding the meaning of the work's man-and-girl tableaux, the language of paternity tends to be conspicuous in its absence from subsequent repetitions of this embrace.[49] This "pretty sight" instead establishes that in *Sylvie and Bruno* the "mutual love" of spring-time females and late-autumnal males is indeed the highest form of love. Right up until the very last moments of the story, when the "vision" of Sylvie is "fast slipping from [the narrator's] eager gaze" (674), we continually see the little girl either through the eyes of an old man, or in the arms of an old man, or both simultaneously. If Carroll's photographs for the most part exclude any figure who could conceivably stand for his adult self, this late work takes exactly the opposite tack. *Sylvie and Bruno* seems entirely unable to look at a little girl without also showing us the old man to whom she is unbearably precious.

Lewis Carroll's participation in the fantasy of lost girlhood reveals that the act of representing the relationship between past and present selves can be achieved in forms other than conventional autobiography. In claiming that the photograph of the little girl allowed the male viewer to see both that little girl *and* his former self, I have been arguing that one of the reasons for Carroll's fascination with this new medium was its ability to represent this doubleness in one person: he could thus be present without being present. When Carroll separates out the elements of the fantasy into its constituent parts and gives written descriptions of the little girl in relation to the older man, the effect is radically different. The ambiguities of Carroll's single figures are infinitely superior to the fixity of his adult-and-child tableaux: the former shimmer with tantalizing complexity, while the latter founder in the worst kind of cloying sentimentality. In this light, Carroll's decision to avoid autobiography becomes at the very least an aesthetically wise choice: his is an art that thrives on self-effacement.

A "New 'Cry of the Children'": Legislating Innocence in the 1880s

> Quelle dommage that the world isnt composed entirely of little girls from 6–12.
>
> . . . since it is merely an English ~~convention~~ tradition which assumes Heaven knows why? that a girl is not Amabilis when she is at her most amiable age.
> *(Ernest Dowson, letters to Arthur Moore, August 1890, January 1892)*[1]

A strange story of an early-morning collision on deserted city streets appears in the opening pages of Robert Louis Stevenson's most popular novella. It is the reader's first introduction to Dr Jekyll's depraved alter ego, the diminutive but malevolent figure of Mr. Hyde:

> I was coming home from some place at the end of the world, about three o' clock of a black winter morning, and my way lay through a part of town where there was literally nothing to be seen but lamps. Street after street, and all the folks asleep—street after street, all lighted up as if for a procession, and all as empty as a church—till at last I got into that state of mind when a man listens and listens and begins to long for the sight of a policeman. All at once, I saw two figures: one a little man who was stumping along eastward at a good walk, and the other a girl of maybe eight or ten who was running as hard as she was able down a cross-street. Well, sir, the two ran into one another naturally enough at the corner; and then came the horrible part of the thing: for the man trampled calmly over the child's body and left her screaming on the ground. It sounds nothing to hear, but it was hellish to see.[2]

The tale, told by a Mr. Enfield, constitutes one of only two moments in the entire text in which Mr. Hyde's proclaimed wickedness is actually provided with some kind of content.

The second of these instances presents us with a new observer, and a different perspective, for instead of overhearing one man's words to a friend and kinsman, we read a third-person version of a maidservant's eyewitness account. The preexisting psychological states of the two spectators are, furthermore, diametrically opposed: while Enfield is evidently uneasy in the lamplit metropolis, the young woman takes such a romantic delight in the beauty of the city by full moon that "never had she felt more at peace with all men or thought more kindly of the world" (46). Nevertheless, despite these initial distinctions, the structure of the outrages they each observe remains remarkably constant. Once again, two people come up against each other on a common thoroughfare: this time the maid "became aware of an aged and beautiful gentleman with white hair drawing near along the lane; and advancing to meet him, another and very small gentleman" (46). Although the two figures do not collide with the force that marked the encounter between girl and little man, violence swiftly ensues. In a moment Mr. Hyde is again "trampling his victim under foot," and on this occasion proceeds to "hail[] down a storm of blows, under which the bones were audibly shattered and the body jumped upon the roadway" (47). The two scenes that define Mr. Hyde's "insensate cruelty" in this work, then, are both enacted upon London's nocturnal streets: in quick succession, a little girl is stamped on, and a venerable old man is stamped out of existence.

Stevenson wrote *Dr Jekyll and Mr Hyde* in the fall of 1885, a couple of months after he, in common with the bulk of London's citizens, had been gripped by a sensational newspaper series and the unprecedented public scandal it created.[3] For four days in July, the *Pall Mall Gazette* had published a shocking exposé of child prostitution in London under the lurid title of "The Maiden Tribute of Modern Babylon." The series purported to represent the complete and accurate findings of four weeks of intense and grueling research in the capital's seamy underworld by the crusading journalist W. T. Stead and his dedicated team of investigators. Stead was quite candid about his motives for bringing such matters to public attention: he and a collection of like-minded reformers were determined to ensure that the Criminal Law Amendment Act, a piece of legislation that had for the past four years failed to make its way through Parliament, would finally become law. According to its own expressed aims, the *Pall Mall Gazette*'s campaign must be judged entirely successful, for the general outrage it incited resulted in the swift passage of the bill through both houses the following month, culminating in the act's receipt of the Royal Assent on August 14, 1885.

While Stevenson's decision to set his tale in a dark and nightmarish London labyrinth suggests a local debt to the corrupt metropolis created in Stead's series, current critical readings of *Dr Jekyll and Mr Hyde* are most likely to sense one particular connection between the text and its immediate historical context. Although the Criminal Law Amendment Act primarily concerned itself with the extension of the state's powers to protect young girls, most notably in its raising of the age of consent from thirteen to sixteen years of age, it also included a number of other significant measures. A late addition by the member of Parliament for Northampton, Henry Labouchère, effectively criminalized all forms of sexual congress ("gross indecency") between males of any age and instituted a sentence of two years imprisonment, with or without hard labor. In the light of Eve Sedgwick's groundbreaking theories about male homosociality and homophobic panic, a work like *Dr Jekyll and Mr Hyde* now seems entirely invested in issues of male-male desire: it simultaneously presents an almost wholly male society organized around bonds of friendship and becomes hysterical about the idea of what is, after all, one man inside another man.[4] Stevenson's story, then, just as much as Wilde's slightly later *Picture of Dorian Gray* (1895), can justifiably be seen as a literary emanation of the same historical and cultural conditions that produced the Labouchère amendment.

At this juncture, however, I am interested in suggesting a rather different reading that tends more toward the allegorical than the strictly historical.[5] Although *Dr Jekyll and Mr Hyde* makes no connections, narrative or otherwise, between the two signal victims of Hyde's brutality, the bond must be forged, so as to focus once again on the pairing of the little girl and the old man, the two major players in the story traced throughout this project. What is it about the complex debates and events of the summer of 1885 that effectively tramples the life out of these two previously cherished figures? Posing the question in this fashion is dangerously glib: to suggest that the paradigm we have been following through the nineteenth century collapses over the course of a couple of months in a single year implies far too simplistic a causal model and an overly schematic understanding of historical processes. Nevertheless, the heightened atmosphere of July and August 1885 may well be considered and presented as an encapsulation of the manifold tensions that had been rising ever since the focus on the little girl began. When the "long[ing] for the sight of a policeman," to use Enfield's words, becomes so intense that the law itself must officially define and control girlish innocence, then the little girl's reign is definitely over, and her privileged relation with the gentle and nostalgic older man comes to an abrupt end.

"The Maiden Tribute of Modern Babylon" emits the last gasp of the myth of ideal girlhood, a myth that had contained the power to solace and delight the Victorian imagination. Before scrutinizing the complicated ways in which Stead's narrative simultaneously exploits and destroys the idea of the innocent girl, I want to take a moment to review her history. The ideal little girl of the nineteenth century could trace her lineage back to the concepts of childhood developed on the one hand by Locke and Rousseau, whose philosophical writings established the child as a pure point of origin, preexisting the divisions both of class and sexuality, and on the other, by the strains of Evangelically influenced Christianity that rejected Calvinistic notions of original sin. The early Victorian period, borrowing most immediately from Wordsworthian constructions of childhood, adopted a feminized version of this pure child as a figure of national fantasy: relentlessly consigning the private, the tender, the personal, and the protected to a female domain, domestic ideology inevitably recast the ideal child as a little girl. The repeated reimagining of male childhoods as feminine eras, whether in autobiographical, fictional, or other kinds of works, argues for the important presence of a personal fantasy within this wider construct. However, the close of the nineteenth century witnesses a definitive change. Modes of depicting remembered childhood are transformed: at the moment that the idea of the girl is severed from the concept of impenetrable perfection, the boy child and a host of alternative associations march into view.

The heroine of "Maiden Tribute of Modern Babylon" occupies an important place in the story of the little girl's fall from grace. Both Stead's series and the age-of-consent legislation constitute the end point of a process that we have already seen at work in the early Victorian debates about exploitative child labor. The reports produced by the Royal Commission on Children's Employment in 1842–43 invoked the idea of the ideal girl in order to show exactly how far from ideal were the lives experienced by certain little girls laboring in the nation's burgeoning industries. This tactic of bringing the cherished image into relation with the working girl turned out to be a perilous enterprise (see chap. 2). Close focus on the brutalized physical existence of the laboring girl effectively sexualized her body and placed her ideal sister in a position that threatened her fundamental premises altogether. If she were different from the working girl, then her ideality would be revealed to be dependent upon her material and social underpinnings, and her claim to classless universality was a sham; if she were the same as the working girl, then she too was irremediably sexualized.

Essentially irresolvable though these conflicts were, they did not gain sufficient power to destroy the concept of the ideal girl there and then.

157

On the contrary, the little girl's popularity climbed steadily in the Victorian era, reaching its height in the novels of Dickens, the paintings of Millais, and the works of Lewis Carroll. In 1885, however, the ideological tensions embedded in the child labor scandal of the 1840s returned with a vengeance. Although the commissioners' rhetoric in 1842–43 had linked the workplace to a brothel through the force of analogy, the abused child under scrutiny in that period was of course not actually a streetwalker, but a pathetic industrial drudge, toiling in squalid machine-sheds or pushing corves in dripping Yorkshire mines. Encounters with girls who were merely "like prostitutes" had been bruising enough to the nineteenth century's favorite icon. When the ideal girl is forced into relation with real prostitutes in the underground empire of vice in "Maiden Tribute," the strain proves fatal.

Although W. T. Stead strategically presented his shocking findings as if he were exposing a hitherto unexamined canker within the body politic, it is important to recognize that the issues and concerns that convulsed the capital in 1885 had already been receiving some degree of attention for at least the past fifty years. Back in the 1830s the attempt to save girls from entrapment in brothels was evident in the work of the Guardian Society and the London Society for the Protection of Young Females, while Lord Ashley's call in 1838 for legislation constituted the first stirrings of parliamentary interest in this troubling area. An Act to Protect Women under Twenty-One from Fraudulent Practices to Procure Their Defilement was finally passed in 1849, but its provisions, weakened by repeated objections over the intervening years, were generally agreed to be useless in practice.[6] At this point, discussion about the necessity of raising the age of consent had not yet become part and parcel of the call for increased protection of girls at risk: the watershed age of twelve had been the legal limit since at least the thirteenth century, when it was first recorded in legislation, and was reaffirmed in the Offences against the Person Act of 1861.[7] The demand for a change to the legal age did not come to the fore until the wave of opposition to the highly repressive Contagious Diseases Acts brought the problem of prostitution to much wider attention.

First introduced in 1864, and then extended in 1866 and 1869, these acts sought to limit the spread of venereal disease amongst soldiers and sailors by authorizing the police in designated garrison towns and naval ports to apprehend any woman suspected of prostitution. If the woman, after a compulsory medical examination, were found to be infected, the acts empowered the Lock Hospital to detain her, against her will if necessary, for up to nine months. The acts excited considerable controversy: the feminist movement for their repeal, led by Josephine Butler, and supported by John Stuart Mill, condemned them on the grounds that they interfered with a woman's civil liberties, gave arbitrary powers to plainclothes police, represented the condoning of vice by the state, and, above all, stood as the apotheosis of the double standard of morality. To Butler and the growing numbers of concerned individuals in social purity movements, the government was evidently tackling the problem of prostitution in society both in a misguided and an immoral fashion if it only ever levied punishments on the female supplier, and never the male customer. Consequently, when she stood up before the Royal Commission on the Contagious Diseases Acts in March 1871, Butler made a powerful pitch for the raising of the age of consent, arguing that efforts to prosecute those who lured young girls into vice would be entirely ineffectual until Great Britain made it illegal to have sex with them:

> Seduction must be punished. At present, for the purpose of seduction, and of seduction only, our law declares every female child a woman at twelve years of age. I am ashamed to confess to such a shameful state of the law before you gentlemen, but a child is a woman, for that purpose alone, at twelve years of age. I know from my experience amongst this class of women how many have become so from that cause. . . . Our law declares a girl of twelve a woman. On this Parliament could and should act. The age of consent must be raised.[8]

The royal commission's report, published in July of the same year, appeared to agree with Butler on this issue, to the extent of recommending "the absolute protection of female children to the age of fourteen years, making the age of consent to commence at fourteen instead of twelve as under the existing law."[9] Soon this recommendation was to be included in one of the supplemental clauses of the bill that was the result of the commission's labors. A Bill to Repeal the Contagious Diseases Acts and for the Better Protection of Women (commonly known as "Mr Bruce's Bill," after the home secretary who rather reluctantly introduced it) came before the Commons on February 13, 1872, but had already caused dissension within the ranks of those who ostensibly supported abolition. In the opinion of Butler, for instance, the new bill did not repeal but rather extended the principles of the Contagious Diseases Acts, albeit in a weaker and modified form, from the original thirteen towns to the entire country: consequently she could not consider the legislation acceptable, even if its raising of the age of consent would be a definite improvement to the existing state of affairs. After complicated debate, the two most prominent abolitionist associations also found it impossible to support the bulk of the bill's measures. In the face of this reaction, and unwilling to provoke controversy in the run-up to a contentious by-election, Prime Minister Gladstone decided to withdraw the bill entirely. Over the next three years, the raising of the age of consent was continually deferred, meeting opposition both from those who were unwilling to differentiate between the legal ages of marriage and consent, and those who argued passionately against any increase "on the ground," as Butler recorded in disgust, "that their sons would be placed at a great disadvantage."[10] Finally, a modest raise to the age of thirteen was enshrined in legislation in 1875.

The next important move in this area began to gather steam at the end of the decade, when the social purity campaigner Alfred Dyer took it upon himself to investigate allegations of "white slavery" in the export of young English girls to Belgian brothels. In response to his findings and pressure from the newly formed London Committee for the Suppression of the Traffic in British Girls for the Purposes of Continental Prostitution, a House of Lords select committee was convened in 1881 "to inquire into the law for the protection of young girls from artifices to induce them to lead a corrupt life, and into the means of amending the same."[11] Out of this inquiry, in addition to measures to render this foreign trade illegal, came the more general and wide-reaching recommendation that the age of consent be raised from thirteen to sixteen. Various versions of a Criminal Law Amendment bill were drawn up over the next few years, but once again they ran into continual difficulties in parliamentary debates. Without widespread public support, age-of-consent legislation looked likely to founder in interminable confusion. Only when W. T. Stead turned the focus from the abuse of English girls abroad, to the problem of child prostitution in the heart of England's capital city, did the emotional temperature of the debate begin to rise to fever pitch.

"Let me conclude the chapter of horrors by one incident," wrote Stead on July 6, 1885.[12] The story Stead chose as the finale to the first shocking installment of "The Maiden Tribute of Modern Babylon" was, he claimed, "only one of those which are constantly occurring in those dread regions of subterranean vice in which sexual crime flourishes almost unchecked," and told the tale of "A CHILD OF THIRTEEN BOUGHT FOR £5." I pick up the narrative midway into its third paragraph:

Lily was a little cockney child, one of those who by the thousand annually develop into servants of the poorer middle-class. . . . Her experience of the world was limited to the London quarter in which she had been born. With the exception of two school trips to Richmond and one to Epping Forest, she had never been in the country in her life, nor had she ever seen the Thames excepting at Richmond. She was an industrious, warm-hearted little thing, a hardy English child, slightly coarse in texture, with dark black eyes, and short sturdy figure. Her education was slight. She spelled write "right," for instance, and her grammar was very shaky. But she was a loving affectionate child, whose kindly feeling for the drunken mother who sold her into nameless infamy was very touching to behold. In a little letter of hers which I once saw, plentifully garlanded with kisses, there was the following ill-spelled childish verse:—

As I was in bed
Some little forths (thoughts) gave (came) in my head.
I forth (thought) of one, I forth (thought) of two;
But first of all I forth (thought) of you.

The poor child was full of delight at going to her new situation, and clung affectionately to the keeper who was taking her away—where, she knew not.

The first thing to be done after the child was fairly severed from home was to secure the certificate of virginity without which the rest of the purchase-money would not be forthcoming. In order to avoid trouble she was taken in a cab to the house of a midwife, whose skill in pronouncing upon the physical evidences of virginity is generally recognized in the profession. The examination was very brief and completely satisfactory. But the youth, the complete innocence of the girl, extorted pity even from the hardened heart of the old abortionist. "The poor little thing," she exclaimed. "She is so small, her pain will be extreme. I hope you will not be too cruel with her"—as if to lust when fully roused the very acme of agony on the part of the victim has not a fierce delight. To quiet the old lady the agent of the purchaser asked if she could supply anything to dull the pain. She produced a small phial of chloroform. "This," she said, "is the best. My clients find this much the most effective." The keeper took the bottle, but unaccustomed to anything but drugging by the administration of sleeping potions, she would infallibly have poisoned the child had she not discovered by experiment that the liquid burned the mouth when an attempt was made to swallow it. £1 1s. was paid for the certificate of virginity—which was verbal and not written—while £1 10s. more was charged for the chloroform, the net value of which was probably less than a shilling. An arrangement was made that if the child was badly injured Madame would patch it up to the best of her ability, and then the party left the house.

From the midwife's the innocent girl was taken to a house of ill fame, No. ———, P-street, Regent-street, where, notwithstanding her extreme youth, she was admitted without question. She was taken up stairs, undressed, and put to bed, the woman who brought her putting her to sleep. She was rather restless, but under the influence of chloroform she soon went over. Then the woman withdrew. All was quiet and still. A few moments later the door opened, and the purchaser entered the bedroom. He closed and locked the door. There was a brief silence. And then there rose a wild and piteous cry—not a loud shriek, but a helpless, startled scream like the bleat of a frightened lamb. And the child's voice was heard crying, in accents of terror, "There's a man in the room! Take me home; oh, take me home!"

· · · · ·

And then all once more was still.

That was but one case among many, and by no means the worst. It only differs from the rest because I have been able to verify the facts. Many a similar cry will be raised this very night in the brothels of London, unheeded by man, but not unheard by the pitying ear of Heaven—

For the child's sob in the darkness curseth deeper
Than the strong man in his wrath

As Judith Walkowitz comments in her discussion of the *Pall Mall Gazette* furor, "historians . . . have tended to focus on one of three issues: the reliability of Stead as a narrator (whether or not he told the 'truth'), his sexual psychology (his status as a latter-day Puritan whose 'repressed sexuality' was the 'motive force' of his activities, according to Havelock Ellis); or the impact of the 'Maiden Tribute' and the legislation it provoked on class politics, the idea of childhood, and the political economy of sex."[13] Lily's story, carrying the major themes of the entire series in its compressed and rhetorically hybrid narrative, yields material for all three areas of discussion, but it also does a great deal more. First and foremost, the pathetic tale functions as a kind of explanatory primal scene for the horrors to come in the subsequent editions of the *Gazette*: the terrible blight of teenaged prostitution that spreads across the metropolis finds its origin, in Stead's account, not in grinding poverty's lack of alternatives, but in the rape of an unwitting and drugged innocent. Delivered up to the lust of the shadowy aristocratic villain in the Regent Street bedroom by the betrayal of a triumvirate of working-class women (the most calumniated member of which is the child's own mother), the thirteen-year-old girl is inevitably ensnared in the net of vice and is presented as having no choice but to continue in the course that has been forced upon her. The class drama in Stead's narrative is anything but subtle: in a land beset by upper-class evil, it is up to the honest and decent citizens of England to rescue the daughters of the working class by insisting that their government pass legislation that will protect the powerless, and constrain the evil desires of the powerful. When the Criminal Law Amendment Act was passed the following month, the *Pall Mall Gazette* was triumphant. The wicked seducer whose desires were aroused by the body of a thirteen-year-old virgin was now threatened by the full majesty of the law; the innocence of girls like Lily was at last officially protected.

The tale of Lily's rape offers exceptionally rich opportunities for the analysis of Stead's rhetorical strategies because this happens to be a story that Stead was not only reporting, but that he himself had constructed. In whatever way the original readers of that day's *Pall Mall Gazette* may have understood the newsprint in front of them on July 6, 1885, they knew in a matter of weeks that "Lily" was not "Lily" at all, but a girl called Eliza Armstrong, and that she had not been raped, because the man who had entered the bedroom in Regent Street was not a vicious aristocratic seducer, but Stead himself. The potential rape of Lily was certainly a set piece, not least in the sense that Stead had set it up purely to show that such things could be done. A complex chain of events had brought the "truth," or at least, a different version of the story, to light. After neighbors of Eliza Armstrong's mother recognized some of the circumstances of the newspaper story and harangued her in public, Mrs. Armstrong started proceedings to get her daughter back, arguing throughout that she had not sold her into prostitution but had truly believed that Eliza was taking up a position in domestic service. In the resultant, much-publicized, court case, Stead was accused, with three of his assistants and the reformed "old procuress" and the abortionist/midwife, of various combinations of abduction and, on account of the medical examination, indecent assault. The outcome of the case appeared to support Mrs. Armstrong's claims. Stead and one of his assistants were found guilty of abduction, and sentenced respectively to terms of three months and one month of hard labor, while the two working-class women received much longer prison terms on the assault charge.

Whether or not this resolution of the saga established the truth of what had happened, or indeed, represented fair and equitable decisions for each of the participants, is a complicated and important question in its own right.[14] In this particular analysis, however, these circumstances primarily show that we are entirely justified in regarding "Lily's Story" as a strategically constructed artifact. Although the peculiarity of the events behind the narrative will occasionally demand attention (for instance, how are we to understand Stead's positioning of himself in the story? Whatever made him believe that he had the right to subject a little girl to an unnecessary and frightening examination?), the text itself is our primary focus.

But what kind of a text is the "Maiden Tribute"? Walkowitz's reading of the series as a narrative shrewdly analyzes its generic instability, paying especial attention to its formal debts both to melodrama and pornography. Lily's story unsettles us almost as much in its combination of incompatible narrative conventions as in its subject matter: on the simplest level, the sensationalist mode of "the very acme of agony" coexists uneasily with the bald matter-of-factness of such statements as "if the child was badly injured Madame would patch it up." Over and again, we are witness to the strange meeting of the self-proclaimed frankness of Stead's reportage with a variety of avowedly fictional forms. Perhaps the oddest move in this story is the unacknowledged revisiting of one of literature's most famous rapes, the tale of *Clarissa*. Clearly Stead's foolish procuress is following her eighteenth-century script too closely when she tries to administer chloroform as if it were laudanum, the "London milk" used to drug Richardson's heroine.[15] The pattern of similarities and discontinuities between the two stories is intriguing. For instance, although Richardson's "innocent girl" had also been led unwittingly into "a house of ill fame" nearly a century and a half earlier, the two victims are obviously of dissimilar ages: Stead's text could not take more pains to show that Lily can only be seen as a child, while Clarissa, in effect, becomes a young girl only after the rape, and then, purely through an act of will.[16] But the actual moment of the rape remains as inexpressible for the journalist as it did for the novelist—only a suggestive absence, marked by a typographical ornament, fills the lost segment of time, the period of the heroine's transformation from one kind of person to another. Of course, in this instance, the reason that Stead "can go no farther" turns out to be significantly different from Lovelace's predicament. The ornament, in pretending to represent the unrepresentable, actually covers the fact that there is nothing to represent. The moment of truth in the "Maiden Tribute" did not see the fulfillment of the aristocratic rake's desires, but the unveiling of Stead's masquerade as aristocratic rake, and his assumption of the role of savior that he himself had made necessary.

While these novelistic echoes place the "Maiden Tribute" in a literary continuum, the series' arrogation of the style of the official report shows it working in a register with a very different relation to truth. Adopting a variety of quasi-governmental stances, Stead attempts to convince his readers that this commercial enterprise is actually the people's equivalent of a parliamentary investigation (a necessary strategy, the journalist would have us believe, given that Westminster harbors corrupt aristocrats). Occasionally the results of this posturing are almost laughably bathetic: in Lily's story of "nameless infamy," the specificity of the narrator's indignation about the overpricing of that vial of chloroform sounds a ludicrous note. Stead as weights-and-measures inspector, with his insistence on value for money and the sanctity of pounds, shillings, and pence, however, takes a minor role in comparison to Stead the lofty commissioner. Indeed, Stead dubs his entire endeavor "a Special and Secret Commission of Inquiry" from the outset (he himself is its "Chief Director") and borrows numerous features from the royal commission format, most notably the case history. If the content of Lily's story repeats the ideological conflicts that invigorated the furor in and around the Royal Commission on Children's Employment of 1842–43, the fact that the "Maiden Tribute" mimics the form of the government inquiry already constitutes one of the bonds that ties the two scandals together.

Moving from questions of form to those of content, we can see that a more specific link between Stead's work and that particular royal commission is forged by the citation at the end of Lily's story of the last two lines of Elizabeth Barrett's "Cry of the Children": "For the child's sob in the darkness curseth deeper / Than the strong man in his wrath." (For a discussion of the poem's inspiration by the government report, its fashioning as a modern revision of Wordsworth's highly influential *Intimations Ode*, and its important part in pushing through the Factory Act of 1844, see chapter 2.) The emotive language of "The Cry of the Children" appears twice in the "Maiden Tribute": in the third installment of the series, Stead returns to the poem, the nineteenth century's most impassioned and most celebrated critique of child labor, to quote its penultimate stanza. In this later instance, the connection between the campaign to regulate children's employment in mines and factories and the present work in hand is made explicit. Prefacing the verse with the words, "Well may [the child victims of vice] scream—far worse their lot than the little slaves of the loom of whom Mrs. Browning says . . ." (July 8), Stead both identifies the poet and the poem's historical source and makes the point that although the two situations are similar enough to justify the comparison, the plight of today's exploited children is in fact much more severe.

Stead's first use of the poem raises far more complicated issues. There is no sure way of telling how many of the *Pall Mall Gazette*'s readers would have recognized this brief and unlocated quotation. Even those that did, and who assumed that Stead expected them to connect this outrage with the earlier scandal, may not have realized how their reading of these lines was definitively altered by the surrounding context. Without knowing the poem, or having it available for immediate reference, the reader is inevitably struck by the absolute appropriateness of the two lines to the situation that has just been described. Although Barrett's child had been sobbing in the darkness of the mine, the first quoted line now seems to refer directly to Lily's terrified bleat in the darkness of the Regent Street bedroom. More damaging to the poem's original meaning, however, is the inevitable transmogrification of "the strong man in his wrath." When the poem, or even the final stanza, is read as a piece, it is clear that the strong man figures only as a counterexample of one who might also call for heavenly vengeance. But the suggestive brevity of the two-line extract forces a new interpretation: if the child sobbing is easily identifiable as Lily, then the strong man corresponds to the only male position that has been established in the preceding narrative—that of the purchaser, the rapist. Accepting that male sexual desire might encompass wrathful cursing comes as no stretch for readers who have just been exposed to the idea that the violator of virgins is of the type who, when "fully roused," finds a "fierce delight" in "the very acme of agony on the part of the victim."

In its original historical moment, Barrett's poem had averted its glance from the troublingly explicit visions of working girls' bodies that had stood out in its source document, the report of the royal commission. The little worker in "The Cry of the Children" was depicted not as a physical presence in her own right, but as an abused version of the ideal girl, who could easily be restored to her true self by the forces of compassionate intervention. But if Barrett was able to avoid the sexualizing tendencies already present in the debate in the 1840s, the snippet of her poem that is drafted into Lily's story has no defenses whatsoever: now the little girl is placed in an explicitly sexual position.

The transformation experienced by Barrett's poetical child in this excerpt encapsulates the larger phenomenon of the sexualization of the ideal girl in the "Maiden Tribute." Yet how doggedly Stead invokes the Victorians' most cherished concept in the face of recalcitrant evidence! Although

Stead is dealing almost exclusively with impoverished urban children, he is keen to show that his girls are as loving and giving, and as prone to value flowers and poetry, as any genteel Little Nell. Rejecting those portions of the ideal girl's prescription that do not suit his polemical strategies, Stead is equally liable to augment the formula: although ultimately he finds it more useful to emphasize the mental, rather than the physical, immaturity of the girl, he is not averse to throwing the odd "fact" from new medical theories about puberty into the mix. All in all, the "Maiden Tribute" strives to present us with an innocent little girl who is entirely unable to protect herself and must therefore be protected by legislation. This stress both on the girl's sweetness and her vulnerability inevitably determines the depiction of the other players in the drama of violation, and ultimately proves to be a counterproductive move. By lifting the girl at risk away from her class trappings, Stead makes it seem as if all girls are equally threatened. Just as significantly, his insistence on the omnipresence of the sexual threat to little girls sets up the young virgin as the most sexually desirable object in the world.

When Lily is first introduced to us, Stead seems torn between his desire to give an accurate assessment of her class position and his hope that we will immediately recognize the true signs of exemplary girlhood that lie within her. Designating his subject as "one of those who by the thousand annually develop into servants of the poorer middle-class," the journalist shows an acceptance of the status quo that seems untinged, at least in this instance, with any shades of critical irony—rather, the phrase "annually develop" appears to stress both the inevitability and the naturalness of the process. Class markers return to punctuate the text at regular intervals and coexist uneasily with Stead's insistence upon the girl's ideality.

A concept of "naturalness" is more pointedly used in this passage to connect Lily to the carefree rural world that had been the ideal girl's especial habitat from the moment of her conception onwards. The materials at Stead's disposal are not particularly amenable, but he can at least endow the real "Eliza" with a flowery name: redolent of purity, innocence, and whiteness, a "Lily," according to the biblical text, should also be far removed from the necessity of toiling for her living, in the sculleries of the homes of "the poorer middle class" as much as anywhere else. The ruralization of Eliza Armstrong does not end here, however. When Stead sums up Lily's thirteen-year history in a couple of sentences, he concentrates chiefly not on what has happened, but on what has not. Emphasizing that "[w]ith the exception of two school trips to Richmond and one to Epping Forest, she had never been in the country in her life," the writer

167

both establishes these three days as the highpoints of her existence and implies that the child has been unjustly kept away from what should be her natural due. Pining instinctively for the green fields and trickling rills she has no real reason to know (in this light, even the filthy Thames seems to get cleaned up into a desirable destination), the little girl, ever cheerful, must make the best of her brickish surroundings. If there are no daisies to string into chains, then she will "garland" her little letters with kisses.

Stead strives to bring his urban girls into contact with nature, or rather with a concept of nature that is as decorative and unthreatening as the flower that provides its most apt symbol. In some cases, the disastrous outcome of what should be the joyous (and entirely chaste) reunion of girl and countryside is proof positive of the utter evil of the world under examination. Consider his second case: "A young man, determined to ruin a girl, takes her out for a trip into the country. The girl, tired and exhausted, sits down in a wood. He sprinkles an ounce of chloroform over a bunch of flowers and presses it over her face. She becomes unconscious, and he has his way" (July 13). Stead's emphasis upon the intrinsic innocence and modesty of girlhood would of course never allow al fresco sex to be a romping combination of buxom wenches and inviting haystacks: instead we witness a dastardly drama of a calculating seducer, an inert body, and modern methods (chloroform sales must have been brisk in 1885). When the ideal girl's favorite accoutrements are used as instruments of her destruction, then things really have gone too far.

A more poignant, because less sensational, combination of girls and flowers is wrought in the story of Emily, "a child-prostitute who, at the age of eleven, had for two years been earning her living by vice in the East-end" (July 8). The description by Stead's "informant" reads in full:

> Emily.—Short of her age, broad and stout, with a pleasant face with varying expression; sometimes a fearfully old look, and sometimes with the face of childhood; she told me she had never had a toy in her life or ever been in a garden. I found her to be fearfully diseased and sent her to the Lock Hospital. She was there about six weeks. Returned looking fat and well, but odd in her ways, her mind fearfully fouled by the life she had led, and which she liked to talk about. Some one called her "the Demon Child," and it was an apt name for her. Offended, she would scream as if she was being murdered [even] if no one touched her; only a look from some would set her off: no one seemed able to pacify her; if possible she would get away from everybody and lie down close to a large bed of mignonette, and put her head amongst it and become calm. "Just an excuse for idleness and

wickedness," some would say, but I saw her do it dozens of times, and gave directions that she should not be prevented from going into the garden, she was such a child. One day I saw her as usual tear shrieking along the broad walk and away to the path by the greenhouse, sit down under an apple tree, and burying her head in thick grass bloom, subside down and said, "Why do you always run to this corner, little one: does the sweet mignonette do you good, and cure you of being naughty?" "It's the devil makes me so bad," she answered in a moment, "and I think the nice smell sends him away"; and down went her head again.

"Strange that the fragrance of the mignonette should calm the shattered nerves of the demon child, who had probably never before enjoyed the smell of a flower," comments Stead at the end of this oddly touching anecdote.

In the journalist's endeavor to make his readers see all little girls, however befouled, as potential avatars of the ideal, the project of Emily presents far greater challenges to his powers than custom-built Lily. As an established prostitute, Emily has done the deed not once, but possibly hundreds of times, and what to Stead is always the tragic importance of the first seduction has been dissipated by endless repetition. Furthermore, Emily has plied her trade in the solidly proletarian East End, thus giving Stead no opportunity to construct his favorite class narrative of West End vice, in which the dissolute members of the upper echelons prey on the daughters of the poor. Surely the most problematic detail in Emily's story, however, is the admission that "she liked to talk about" her former life on the streets. This fact is utterly unassimilable to the idea of the ideal girl, and consequently Emily is depicted as a "demon child," who may appear to have recovered her health, but is actually terminally ill from a venereal disease that affects far more than the physical being. "The innocent girl once outraged seemed to suffer a lasting blight of the moral sense," Stead opines. "They never came to any good: the foul passion from the man seemed to enter into the helpless victim of his lust, and she never again regained her pristine purity of soul." In the face of these obstacles, Emily's dimly comprehended desire for sweet-smelling flowers, or, more precisely, for the tellingly named mignonette, is the only trace of the ideal girl she never had the chance to be.[17]

Emily's story immediately precedes the second appearance of "The Cry of the Children." The stanza quoted ("Well may those children weep before you") contains the poem's clearest echoes of the *Intimations Ode*, and most forcefully makes the point that through the failure of adults, exploited children are being denied their heavenly ordained relationship with the beauties of nature. Elsewhere, Stead invokes the spirit of the *Ode* when he visits a high-class brothel in the north of London and comes across "a lovely child between fourteen and fifteen, tall for her age, but singularly attractive in her childish innocence" (July 8).[18] Employing one of the comparisons to baby animals of the countryside that, like flower references, pepper his text (remember Lily's "startled scream like the bleat of a frightened lamb"), Stead notes that "the timid glance of a frightened fawn" "still linger[s]" in her eyes. He then describes himself slinking away like "a guilty thing," an adult far more besmirched than Wordsworth's original schema had ever imagined.[19]

While Stead does all he can to link his girls with a natural world they have never experienced, he has no interest in making the countryside a symbol of England's lost past. The connection between little girls and the rural idyll of a bygone era, we recall, formed a crucial feature both of the commissioners' rhetoric and many visual and literary representations of girlhood in the early and mid-Victorian period. Stead has no truck with this temporal dimension for two reasons. In the first place, unlike the government report of 1842–43, the "Maiden Tribute" is reluctant to use labor as the primary problem in these little girls' worlds: consequently a contrast between an imaginary preindustrial Eden and the contemporary workaday world has scant appeal. In the second place, nostalgia is inappropriate because Stead presents child prostitution as if it were a hangover from the worst excesses of medieval feudalism. In keeping with the story's central pairing of the working-class child and the aristocratic rapist, girls of the streets become the modern-day versions of "the female serfs from whom the seigneur exacted the *jus primae noctis*" (July 6). According to Stead, far from being a debased version of a lost golden age, England's present is better than its past because the working man now has the political power to put an end to this unjust treatment of his daughter. The *Pall Mall Gazette*'s readers, it is flatteringly implied, will want to push this reform through, because they, and not the vicious aristocracy, are the true heirs of the Englishman's natural property of chivalric honor. Now that "the hour of Democracy has struck," they will do their utmost to end these abuses. Not only are the Middle Ages rejected in this fashion, but also the past of Arthurian legend ("I am no vain dreamer of Utopias peopled solely by Sir Galahads," runs Stead's proud boast [July 6]) and of classical antiquity, which provides the fundamental myth of the maiden tribute levied to slake the Minotaur's unnatural lust.

But if the little girl in Stead's narrative no longer acts as the most fitting representative of a long-lost rural England, she nevertheless fills many of the other requirements laid down for ideal girlhood in the domestic conduct literature of the early Victorian period. A "warm-hearted little thing," a "loving affectionate child" filled with "kindly feeling" both for her keeper, but more especially, for her undeserving mother, Lily and her demonstrative actions more than fulfill Mrs. Ellis's prescription for girlish behavior, while her versified effusions show that she is fully conversant with the tender alliance between the feminine and the poetic. Stead's inclusion of the contents of that "little letter" might prompt the more suspicious reader to wonder how he came to be privy to such material, or to speculate about how much more of this story might lie behind the newsprint, yet the journalist apparently felt that this sterling evidence (real or constructed?) of Lily's pathetic strivings toward ideality more than justified the risk. Moreover, the essentially puerile verse plays a valuable role in the overall design of the set piece: in sharp contrast to the violent nocturnal scene to which we (and Lily) will shortly be exposed, and which appears to be summed up in the unidentified couplet that closes the drama, her four lines of doggerel set up a touching image of the innocent child in bed, quietly and lovingly thinking of her mother. Reproducing Lily's mistaken spelling, perhaps in an overanxious zeal for verisimilitude, and then obsessively correcting it, Stead simultaneously draws our attention to the child's disadvantageously low origins and celebrates the fact that her true girl nature manages to shine through.

Flowers, rural echoes, loving daughterliness, and flights of poesy aside, Lily's intrinsic claim to ideal girl status stands or falls, in Stead's representation, on the combined qualities of her immaturity and her innocence. Throughout the "Maiden Tribute," the two attributes are always collapsed together: a young girl is innocent because she is young. Stead can barely describe thirteen-year-old Lily without recourse to the noun *child* and the adjectives *little, small*, and *short*. The tendency is not restricted to this particular case history: every female he meets under the age of around twenty-one is presented in terms that suggest childishness, rather than developing, or developed, womanliness. Conduct manuals like *Daughters of England* had encouraged the daughters of the middle classes to make the period of their girlhood as prolonged as possible; forty years later, Stead not only widens the net so that the daughters of the working classes can also be consigned to the position of childhood, but finds new methods to justify his classifications.

The concept of puberty, used to support all manner of different arguments throughout the nineteenth century, had only fairly recently been drawn into the debate about the age of consent. Hoping to promote the idea that the period of parental protection should be extended, both Josephine Butler and Elizabeth Blackwell had helped to make the discrepancy between the age when a girl attained physical maturity, and the age when the law said she could be sexually active, an important focus for the first time in the 1870s.[20] Indeed, Blackwell had tried to bring into play a new concept of "nubility," which she claimed was a distinct physiological stage that came considerably later in life than puberty, and which, in its late arrival, was proof of the human race's superiority over the rest of creation.[21] Stead takes whatever is useful to his campaign from this medicalization of the debate. Certainly the scene in Lily's story in which a midwife-abortionist peers between the legs of the heroine is a significant departure from all previous literary attempts to define the nature of girlhood. In Stead's construction, the hardened old functionary is so struck by the lack of fit, as it were, between the girl's physical immaturity and the sexual act toward which she is helping to dispatch her, that she breaks out of her professional detachment to exclaim, "The poor little thing . . . She is so small, her pain will be extreme." Elsewhere, in "A Close Time for Girls," a heavy-handed comparison between the game laws and the current rules on the age of consent, Stead invokes the weight of medical science in more straightforward fashion:

> Fish out of season are not fit to be eaten. Girls who have not reached the age of puberty are not fit even to be seduced. The law ought at least to be as strict about a live child as about a dead salmon. . . . Scientifically, therefore, the close time should be extended until the woman has at least completed sixteen years of life. (July 8)

As perhaps the uncharacteristic use of the word "woman" in this passage reveals, the age of puberty is something of a red herring in the whole debate: after all, if it turned out that most girls experienced the menarche *before* they were sixteen years old, then, according to this particular argument, the age of consent *should* be set at a lower level. For those reformers who wished to establish a legal age of eighteen, or even twenty-one, then, a concept of a natural link between that watershed and physical "readiness" was distinctly unhelpful. Consequently, both because bodies in general were notoriously unstable, refusing to give hard and fast rules as to when they would mature, and because bodies in particular were unyield-

ingly absolute, in that when they did develop, they manifested incontro-
vertible signs of that maturity, it is much more in Stead's interest to trans-
fer the idea of immaturity from the physical to the mental realm. In so
doing, he finds a way to widen the constituency of his favorite category
of wronged innocents, and to remake the image of girls who would otherwise be entirely unredeemable.

Pages and pages of the "Maiden Tribute" are devoted to proving that
girls (most particularly, of course, those between the ages of thirteen and
sixteen who are currently unprotected by the law) do not have the mental
maturity to understand what they will lose if they agree to their own
seduction. The stupidity of these girls—which is tantamount to imbecility
in Stead's representations—must therefore be protected by becoming formalized: girls do not have the ability to know what it means to consent,
and therefore they should not have the right to consent at all. The reason
that all of the interviewees must be depicted as such absolute dimwits is
not hard to fathom: the fundamental premises of Stead's project are ruined if we are able to imagine that, if not necessarily an intelligent girl,
then at least a girl who is capable of weighing up alternatives, might well
decide that it makes financial sense for her to arrange her own seduction.
The "Maiden Tribute" comes dangerously close to showing such a situation when it tells the story of "a nice, simple, and affectionate girl of
sixteen," a regular Sunday school pupil whose father is "touched in his
wits" (significantly enough) and whose mother is a charwoman (July 7).
Driven by the prospect of the considerable sum of two pounds (which
represents two months' wages to her) and by her sense of obligation to
the apparently benevolent procuress who has been advancing her mother
money for months past, the girl is on the brink of allowing that "friend"
to set up her defloration.

As in the Lily story, Stead is once again playing a complex double role
of potential seducer (the procuress is working for him) and ultimate savior, but this time we are made fully aware of the pious fraud that is afoot.
The tactics in this drama, furthermore, are significantly different because
of the hugely important fact that the heroine is distinctly willing. Thus
Stead must expend tremendous energy to prove that the girl has not the
slightest idea of what she is letting herself in for. "The one thing she
dreaded about being seduced was having to be undressed. Poor child, it
was the only thing she could realize." When Stead, in his attempt to "deter
her from taking the fatal step," informs her that she might become preg-
nant as a result of "los[ing] her maid," the information comes as a bolt

from the blue. Despite all this enlightening discussion, however, and to her interlocutor's "astonishment," "the child persisted that she was ready to be seduced." Consequently Stead is driven to desperate measures:

> "Now," said I, "if you are seduced you will get £2 for yourself; but you will lose your maidenhood; you will do wrong; your character will be gone, and you may have a baby which it will cost all your wages to keep. Now I will give you £1 if you will not be seduced; which will you have?"

The girl responds in the following fashion:

> "Please sir," she said, "I will be seduced."
> "And face the pain, and the wrong-doing, and the shame, and the possible ruin and ending your days on the streets, all for the difference of one pound?"
> "Yes, sir," and she burst into tears, "we are so poor."

We are encouraged neither to respect the girl's simple dignity and steadfastness of purpose in the face of this emotional hectoring, nor to imagine that she has placed the fact of her virginity next to the potential benefit of an extra pound to her family's desperate poverty, and made the painful decision that the latter is the more tangible good. Stead seems unwilling to plumb the depths of what she means by that reply, "We are so poor." Instead he fulminates once again about her stupidity, applying, albeit ironically, a material valuation of virginity that repeats the market logic of the industry he pretends to abhor. "Could any proof be more conclusive," he proclaims in the final sentence of the second day's installment, "as to the absolute inability of this girl of sixteen to form an estimate of the value of the only commodity with which the law considers her amply able to deal the day after she is thirteen?"

As the quotations amply demonstrate, in order to achieve his desired end, Stead twists and turns to transform this girl's story into a tale of wronged innocence, of vulnerability that must be protected at all costs by the caring force of legislation. The previous day's finale had presented no such problems, had raised no irresolvable possibility that brute poverty might be the overwhelming villain in the whole sorry mess. Although Lily comes from a poor background and has a drunken mother willing to sell her for a few coins of silver, we never entertain even for a moment the idea that the girl's consciousness of her own poverty has led her toward the brothel bedroom. "Consciousness," of course, is not a faculty that Lily is allowed to possess, either in its metaphorical or literal sense:

174

because the child is completely ignorant about her destination, the fact that she obviously has no idea about what might be involved in a seduction does not come into the equation, and soon enough, her state of unknowing is transformed from a mental to a physiological condition by the administration of chloroform. Stead thus stages a play in which the question of consent is void of meaning. Even then, he is unwilling to leave well enough alone: although his scenario "proves" that a young girl could conceivably be put in a situation in which she would have no opportunity to say either yes or no, Lily must be represented as having sufficient strength to struggle free of her drug-induced stupor to cry out against the incompletely comprehended threat of "a man in the room." The Sunday school girl's "yes" is meaningless because she does not understand what she is talking about; both Lily's silence and her "no" are meaningless because they have no power to protect her. The only solution to the problem, Stead's drama insists, is to remove the ability to consent altogether: all girls under sixteen must be placed in a category where their individual utterances or silences have no meaning because the state's "no" is preemptive.

Although Lily appears as the epitome of vulnerability in the "Maiden Tribute," her very powerlessness has a powerful effect upon the representation of the other figures in the London underworld. Most importantly, the male in the piece can be no casual roué: the absolute innocence of the girl necessarily transforms the seducer into the ultimate blackguard. Furthermore, the seducer's satisfaction, as constructed in Lily's story, is not an autonomous affair, but very specifically dependent upon the reaction of a slip of a girl—remember that "to lust when fully roused the very acme of agony on the part of the victim has . . . a fierce delight." Throughout Stead's narrative, male sexual desire, and more particularly, aristocratic male sexual desire, has a distant, or, at the most, a circuitous relationship to the man's own physical pleasure; rather enjoyment is derived from the knowledge of despoliation, of the ruination of innocence. Insisting that sex with an unwilling or a willing-because-unaware virgin is the kind of sex that best satisfies this substantial body of men, the "Maiden Tribute" not only makes the young virgin the focus of the drama, but also sets her up as the most desirable figure of all. Wanting his readers to focus on Lily as the archetypal girl at risk, Stead elevates the child virgin to the position of the supreme sexual object, barely acknowledging elsewhere that a desire for sexual intercourse may exist independently of the lust to rend a juvenile maidenhead.

175

As its emotive title suggests, the "Maiden Tribute of Modern Babylon" presents a vision of a city in the thrall of a demonic virginity cult. The conclusion of the third day's installment of the series tells the story of two passionate devotees to the religion:

> As in the labyrinth of Crete there was a monster known as the Minotaur who devoured the maidens who were cast into the mazes of that evil place, so in London there is at least one monster who may be said to be an absolute incarnation of brutal lust. The poor maligned brute in the Cretan labyrinth but devoured his tale of seven maids and as many boys every ninth year. Here in London, moving about clad as respectably in broad cloth and fine linen as any bishop, with no foul shape or semblance of brute beast to mark him off from his fellows, is Dr. ———, now retired from his profession and free to devote his fortune and his leisure to the ruin of maids. This is the "gentleman" whose quantum of virgins from his procuresses is three per fortnight—all girls who have previously not been seduced. But his devastating passion sinks into insignificance compared with that of Mr. ———, another wealthy man, whose whole life is dedicated to the gratification of lust. During my investigations in the subterranean realm I was constantly coming across his name. This procuress was getting girls for ———, that woman was beating up maids for ———, this girl was waiting for ———, that house was a noted place of ———'s. I ran across his traces so constantly that I began to make inquiries in the upper world of this redoubtable personage. I soon obtained confirmation of the evidence I had gathered at first hand below as to the reality of the existence of this modern Minotaur, this English Tiberius, whose Capreae is in London. (July 8)

Even though these monstrous London Minotaurs are presented as extreme cases, the persistent return in "Maiden Tribute" to basic thematics of child sacrifice and depraved bloodlust ensures that the virgin's vulnerable body is placed at the heart of the labyrinth of sexual desire.

Subtle nuances of characterization and gradations of moral culpability have thus no relevance to the central antithesis in "Maiden Tribute," the black-and-white dyad of the deepest-dyed villain and the entirely innocent virgin. Stead, however, not only wants his readers to believe in the absolute wickedness of this encounter, but in addition, and more problematically for the simple clarity of his melodrama, in its widespread and everyday occurrence. It is too much of a stretch to believe that satanically possessed fiends of wickedness also possess the administrative sangfroid to stage-manage the complicated and time-consuming requirements of their overmastering predilection. Consequently, as is demonstrated in the above description of the many and varied activities needed to facilitate Mr. ———'s passion, it is necessary to bring a third term into play. According to Stead, veritable armies of lower-class women (very occasionally the odd male makes an appearance) are at work to ensure that the two parties are brought together. Ever industrious in their pursuit of appropriate quarry (note that image of beating up game in the previous quotation), working-class women in the "Maiden Tribute" lean ingratiatingly across perambulators pushed by naive nursemaids in the parks, dress up as Sisters of Mercy and accost dazed Irish girls fresh off the steamships at the docks, and pose as respectable mistresses of sewing establishments to lure unsuspecting maidens to their doors. Once the raw material is secured, the same women, or their business associates, continue their labors to make sure that the dissolute seducer finds full satisfaction: medical examinations are arranged and conducted to check that *virgos* are indeed *intacta*, underground or padded rooms are booked so that the dastardliest of deeds can be performed without annoying interference, and girls are discreetly escorted to and from the trysting place. Stead's calculatedly misogynistic representation of the sex service industry sounds its deepest note in Lily's story, where, as we have already seen, one of the trio of working-class women who contrives the child's downfall is the child's mother herself. But, on the whole, the "Maiden Tribute" is more interested in impressing upon its readers the sheer size and systematic organization of this thriving metropolis of vice than in drawing them into a familial drama of maternal or sororal betrayal.

While the innocent virgin is both the center and the cause of this massive and thriving sex industry, the thematics of "Maiden Tribute" will not allow her to be represented as a sex-worker herself. It is tempting to argue that if Stead and other social purity advocates had approached the problem of child prostitution in the same way that earlier reformers had addressed the issue of child labor, then the image of the ideal little girl might have had a better chance of survival, albeit in a diminished form. The sex industry, in this hypothetical light, could have been yet one more business whose conditions of employment needed to be regulated in line with other trades that had long since banished children from the workplace, or restricted their hours of entry, and sent them off to the classroom.

The reasons why this point of view was impossible for England in the nineteenth century, or, for that matter, the twentieth century, are of course legion, and I can only touch on a couple of salient points here. Admitting that prostitution, and not just procuration, was indeed an industry would not only have threatened to bring England into line with the Continental perspective, with its heinous and abhorred systems of state control, but, more broadly, would have demanded full-scale recognition of the country's enormous economic and social inequalities. In short, society would have to acknowledge that the day-to-day existence of some of its members was so difficult that prostitution was an acceptable and rational career choice, not the desperate end result of a melodramatic seduction or rape. From this angle of perception, prostitution would either have to be accepted as part of the status quo, or the status quo would have to be altered. In the first instance, an acceptance of the current state of affairs would be forced to include an admission that the ideality of girlhood was strictly an economically contingent construction—society at large would simply have to deal with the fact that while rich little girls enjoyed lives of cocooned innocence, their impoverished counterparts might very well have to head off to the streets to make a living. The second instance, the complete redress of widespread and thoroughgoing inequality, would involve nothing less than revolution.[22] To the social conscience of the 1880s, as profoundly conservative as it was overtly moral, neither of these alternatives was acceptable.

As examination of the "Maiden Tribute" in general, and Lily's story in particular, shows, the real issue of the economic basis of prostitution is obscured in favor of a highly personalized morality drama, in which caring members of society (like Stead) rescue the innocent child (like Lily) from the snares of vice. Although Lily is clearly a working-class girl, Stead lays the blame for her plight not on economics, but rather on a combination of aristocratic male villainy and working-class female opportunism. Although Stead obviously wants to stage the rape scene as a class drama, even stronger is his desire to present Lily as an innocent heroine whose qualities transcend her lowly origins. Because Lily's tragedy is thus organized around her innocence, not her poverty, *all* little girls become implicated in the threat of vice. While daughters of the poor are shown to be especially vulnerable because of the ease with which parental protection can be pared away, Stead's version of events makes it seem possible that any unwary young girl (and all young girls are by definition unwary), rich or poor, who might lose her way somewhere between Regent Street and Piccadilly, would immediately be swept into a house of ill-repute, drugged, and then raped. Presenting the girl virgin both as absolutely innocent and absolutely vulnerable, the "Maiden Tribute" simultaneously confirms her absolute desirability.[23]

When the logic of Stead's campaign became enshrined in legislation in August 1885 and the age of consent was raised from thirteen to sixteen years of age, all girls were insistently sexualized at the very moment that it was declared that they were officially innocent. Refusing to admit that the problem of prostitution was confined to a relatively small, economically underprivileged section of society, the Criminal Law Amendment Act delivered a blanket ruling on sexual activity that implicated girls from every social stratum. Cast in this light, girls could no longer play their former role. For the nostalgic older man, the little girl no longer appeared to be the ideal representative of his lost childhood.

. . . . .

Oh, Mr. ——— is a gentleman who has a great penchant for little girls. I do not know how many I have had to repair after him. He goes down to the East-end and the City, and watches when the girls come out of shops and factories for lunch or at the end of the day. He sees his fancy, and marks her down. It takes a little time, but he wins the child's confidence. One day he proposes a little excursion to the West. She consents. Next day I have another subject, and Mr.——— is off with another girl.

If John Ruskin had opened up his *Pall Mall Gazette* on July 6, 1885, and read this paragraph, what might he have thought? All those afternoon tea parties at Coniston that he had organized for the little village girls, all the games on the lawn with the Winnington maidens, all those coins disbursed to dark-eyed urchins in Venice or tousled-haired waifs in Bethnal Green, how might they appear to him now? When Lewis Carroll unfolded his copy (and in this instance, we know that he actually did read the series), how must he have felt? To the man who apparently carried safety pins in his pockets so that he might help little girls to hitch up their frocks to paddle untrammeled, the description of Mr. ———'s pursuits must have seemed like a demonic parody of his own modus operandi. If Carroll did not go up to town to stake out the girls of the East End and the City, then he was constantly leaving Oxford to visit the West End, where he would sit enthralled in the theater, hoping that the child actress on the stage would enjoy his gift of the *Alice* books, because that might lead to a degree of intimacy that would allow him to propose an excursion, if not to the West, then to the South coast, and then that girl might join the succession of other girls who had stayed with him in his holiday apartments in Lushington Road, or accompanied him on other theater visits, where the whole process would begin again. How could Carroll fail to see lines of similarity between the Satanic Mr. ——— and the Reverend Charles Dodgson?

Far from identifying hard and fast lines, Carroll's written response to the "Maiden Tribute" refuses to focus on the central issue of the series altogether; indeed, in a paradoxical move, the nineteenth century's champion of photographical hard focus urges the people of England to avert their eyes, or, if it is absolutely necessary to look, to keep their vision blurred. Of Ruskin's reaction, however, we can say very little. It is a matter of record that the *Pall Mall Gazette* was one of the few newspapers delivered to the writer's home in Brantwood (and moreover was the sole periodical to which Ruskin sent review copies of his own publications at this time), but neither his journal nor his correspondence makes any mention of the newspaper articles or the subsequent parliamentary activity. Whether or not Ruskin read the "Maiden Tribute" that July, however, he was most certainly denied peace of mind for the rest of the year. In the same month that saw the publication of the first installments of his autobiography *Praeterita*, Ruskin was laid low by his most serious attack of mania to date, a period of insanity that effectively silenced him from July 20 until the end of December.[24] A single sentence in his diary stands in for the lost segment of time: "Between this entry and that on page 9 came my terrible fourth delirious illness? [*sic*] I am to-day only—Dec 22nd—remembering a wonderful vision in it of helm-like stone."[25]

Although Ruskin continued to work on *Praeterita* for four more years before his final collapse, the experiences of 1885 left him, in his own estimation, a permanently damaged man with a "distinct injury—a feeling not of the pleasant weakness of new life which means true recovery,—but of persistent illness,—feebleness of thought—and feverish disturbances of the nerves."[26] Henceforward, affairs of the moment occasionally had the power to disturb ("Politics so fearful now in the papers that I'm like a dog on a chain—like the dog in the woodyard that can't get at Mr Quilp"),[27] but Ruskin's writing life now took place at a remove from the present day. In *Praeterita* the author allows his creative imagination to explore only the pellucid memories of a distant past: the desperate currents of the social commentary in *Fors Clavigera* are resolutely avoided. It is perhaps symptomatic that the only traceable connection between Ruskin and the "Maiden Tribute of Modern Babylon" is formed by an enigmatic quotation from this earlier work, submitted by one Ernest Rickman of Balham in a letter to the *Pall Mall Gazette* that was printed on July 9 under the general heading "Public Feeling on the Subject: Extracts from Correspondence":

Your timely exposure of the festering evil which has for so long been undermining our national purity will be welcomed by every true philanthropist. With a few exceptions our modern preachers are apparently ignorant of the existence of this terrible social evil, or else if they are cognizant of it a false delicacy seals their lips, and, from the fear of shocking the refined and pure-minded members of their fashionable congregations, they refrain from lifting up their voices in faithful denunciation and solemn warning. Elijahs and John the Baptists are scarce just now. I earnestly hope that you will reprint your articles in pamphlet form, and I for one will gladly take one hundred copies and post one to every minister of my acquaintance. Ruskin's burning words may appropriately be reprinted as bearing on this great and important question:—

Venice, Feb. 8, 1877

My Dear ———

This is a nobly done piece of work of yours—a fireman's duty in fire of hell, and I would fain help you in all I could.

Venice, Feb. 10

Hence if from any place on earth I ought to be able to send you some words of warning to English youths, for the ruin of this mighty city was all in one word—fornication. Fools who think they can write history will tell you it was "the discovery of the Cape of Good Hope," and the like! Alas! it was indeed the covering of every hope she had in God and His law.

J. RUSKIN

But if Ruskin had fiery words to say on the subject of fornication in 1877, he was more than burned-out eight years later: it is impossible to know whether Stead's fervid scenarios of Minotaur lust for prepubescent girls, the most beloved objects in Ruskin's world, played any role in extinguishing either this particular Elijah's denunciatory voice, or his sanity.

Had Ernest Rickman followed through with his plan to send the ministers of England copies of the "Maiden Tribute," at least one reverend gentleman, Charles Lutwidge Dodgson, would have been more than ordinarily displeased. Three letters written by Lewis Carroll in response to the scandal reveal that the author entirely disagreed with Rickman's sentiments, feeling instead that Stead's act of "exposure of the festering evil" was itself just as likely to "undermin[e] our national purity" as the existence of the offenses themselves. Addressing himself twice to the prime minister, Carroll effectively, if unsuccessfully, called for censorship—first on July 7, when he asked for an injunction against any further publication of the series by the

Pall Mall Gazette, and then again on August 31, when he urged Lord Salisbury to consider legislation to control the spread of pornography.[28]

More interesting, however, is Carroll's letter of July 22 to the *St. James's Gazette*, which he entitled "Whoso Shall Offend One of These Little Ones . . . ," taking his text from St. Luke's Gospel.[29] Signing himself "Lewis Carroll" (an extremely rare—and perhaps calculated?—move for a man who usually took strenuous measures to keep his literary persona separate from all other activities in his life), the author is adamant that "[t]he question at issue is not whether great evils exist," and thus makes no mention whatsoever of the appalling lives, or even the existence, of child prostitutes, let alone the physical rape of innocent girls. Because he refuses to consider the central horrors of Stead's revelations, Carroll consequently has nothing to say about Stead's "solution" to the problem: the topic of age of consent legislation is thus conspicuous in its absence. From Carroll's idiosyncratic perspective, the "offen[se]" offered to the "little ones" in his title is the potential harm occasioned by the broadcasting of the particulars of sexual sin. Although Carroll, in ministerial mode, halfheartedly insists that publicizing the "most contaminating subjects" in the "sacred name of Religion" constitutes "the worst of the danger," we are not entirely convinced: in his account, the danger to Christianity pales in relation to the threat posed to little girls. In his nostalgic evocation of the customs of yesteryear, when "impure scandal[s]" were investigated *in camera*, the possibility that young girls might have needed protection does not arise: "[W]omen and boys were turned out of court" if "sickening details" had to be revealed, but Carroll does not even imagine that the most precious category of human beings would have been there in the first place. In stark contrast, Carroll now feels he must "plead for our pure maidens, whose souls are being saddened, if not defiled, by the nauseous literature that is thus thrust upon them."

Carroll's response is no doubt driven by very particular personal attitudes toward the intertwined concepts of childhood, innocence, and sexuality, but it also shows a broader historical awareness of the changing tenor of his times. To this writer at least, it is clear that the furor alters all little girls: although the well-to-do darlings of Carroll's world are in no danger of being violated in brothels, he is all too painfully conscious that the widespread sexualization of public debate has the power to transform the very concept of girlhood.

After Carroll makes his already belated plea for the preservation of girlish innocence, the focus of his letter shifts abruptly from those whose minds are being exposed for the first time to "highly-coloured pictures of vice" by the public excitement around the "Maiden Tribute" furor, to a rather different kind of consciousness. Up to now, Carroll has been considering individuals who are in different categories from himself (young men and boys, womankind, pure maidens), but, paradoxically enough, his introduction of a lengthy quotation from the "Sermons by the Rev. E. Monro" seems to signal the beginning of a more personal meditation. Whereas Carroll had been pleading for the protection of others, now, ventriloquizing through Monro (whose "words [are] better and more eloquent than any that I could devise") he sets forward strategies for the protection of a figure who seems rather similar to Carroll himself—an older person, imagined in relation to a much longer life span, who, unlike those "pure maidens," may be "regretting the past," and must be advised to take refuge in "an imperfect memory" or a "recollection of something past." As already noted, the metaphorical structure of Monro's advice would hardly seem calculated to earn the respect of a devotee of photographical hard focus, yet Carroll not only quotes the clergyman's counsel of astigmatism, but emphatically repeats his condemnation of those "who are doing their best to 'centre in a focus' the soul-destroying picture."

As an off-center and curiously diffuse response to the "Maiden Tribute" scandal and the age-of-consent debate, Carroll's letter as a whole perhaps stands as a fair enactment of the suggested stance. By refusing to countenance Stead's fundamental point—that grown men are having sex with young virgins, and that therefore legislation is required—Carroll does not have to reevaluate the nature of his own feelings for little girls. But, as we have seen, he is well aware that exposure to the general atmosphere created by the scandal may ultimately be as damaging as direct confrontation with its central revelations. Lindsay Smith has speculated that Carroll should have been in favor of the raising of the age of consent, because the legislation effectively "created" more little girls for his delectation by saying that girlhood officially ended at sixteen, rather than thirteen, years of age.[30] This rather cheerful assumption must, however, be challenged: the dismay evinced in the *St. James's Gazette* letter about the sexualization of the cultural climate caused by the campaign suggests a very different response. More little girls may have been created by the events of July and August 1885, but if *all* girls had then to be seen through a sexualized lens, then it is probably fair to say that Carroll would have considered the prize not worth the winning.

Carroll's reluctance—or inability—to talk about the central question of consent in his response to the "Maiden Tribute" is entirely unsurprising when considered in connection with his habitual modes of conduct toward little girls. As Smith argues in the same essay, Carroll's ways of behaving with his "child friends," most particularly in his stage-managing of photographic sessions, are entirely governed by his fantasy that he is realizing his models' own wishes.[31] The question of the girl's consenting to his desires, then, is neatly evaded: the photographer does not have to ask for her permission to mount a particular scene in a particular way because in effect he is not the director, but the technician, merely operating under his diminutive mistress's orders. In sharp distinction to Stead's tableau of the voracious male and the unconsenting, nonconsenting, or consenting-because-foolish girl, in Carroll's world it is the child who exhibits desire while he, the adult, simply consents.

More light is shed on Carroll's attitude to the consent issue by his response in 1889 to a further act that sought to regulate minors, this time in their capacity as stage children.[32] From the time that he saw the six-year-old Ellen Terry playing Mamillius in *The Winter's Tale*, Carroll had been fascinated by child actresses and was frequently to be found both in the audience and backstage in West End theaters. His connection with, and enthusiasm for, the stage was perhaps at its height in the 1880s: a dramatic version of *Alice in Wonderland* starring Phoebe Carlo opened in London in 1886 and then was revived in 1888, this time with Isa Bowman playing the lead. Both girls became particularly "dear friends," spending holidays with Carroll in Eastbourne and accompanying him on numerous theater trips.[33] The act that was proposed at the end of this decade sought to prohibit the employment of children under seven on the stage in any capacity and on any terms, and to make the engagement of children between seven and ten subject to special license. Salaries for child actors and actresses were also to be strictly controlled.

Carroll's involvement of himself in the debate around this issue (once again he wrote to the *St. James's Gazette*) is markedly different from his contribution to the controversy of 1885. While the schematics of the "Maiden Tribute" and, indeed, of popular morality, demanded that girls be seen under the constraint of male desire, rather than as desiring subjects themselves, the topic of child actresses gave Carroll full rein to talk about the "passions" of the little girl. Just as importantly, any question of his own desire to continue to see very young children performing on stage could be unobtrusively ignored. Diving straight into the heart of the matter (in this context the "focus" holds no terrors for him), Carroll considers in minute detail the proposed act's technical divisions according to age and then turns to anecdotal evidence to prove his thesis. As the following extract reveals, the ebullient child workers who are running on the pier, if not quite sporting on a Wordsworthian shore, in this celebration of the juvenile thespian bear no relation to the abject, imbecilic, or pathetically dependent specimens of girlhood who were perpetually at risk in the rapacious underworld of "Maiden Tribute":

> I spent yesterday afternoon at Brighton, where for five hours I enjoyed the society of three exceedingly happy and healthy little girls, aged twelve, ten and seven. I think that any one who could have seen the vigour of life in those three children—the intensity with which they enjoyed everything, great or small, that came in their way—who could have watched the younger two running races on the Pier, or have heard the fervent exclamation of the eldest at the end of the afternoon, "We *have* enjoyed ourselves!" would have agreed with me that here, at least, there was no excessive "physical strain," nor any imminent danger of "fatal results"! A drama, written by Mr. Savile Clarke, is now being played at Brighton, and in this (it is called "Alice in Wonderland") all three children have been engaged. They had been acting every night this week, and *twice* on the day before I met them, the second performance lasting till half-past ten at night, after which they got up at seven next morning to bathe! That such (apparently) severe work should co-exist with blooming health and buoyant spirits seems at first a paradox: but I appeal to any one who has ever worked *con amore* at any subject whatsoever to support me in the assertion that, when you really love the subject you are working at, the "physical strain" is absolutely *nil*; it is only when working "against the grain" that any strain is felt, and I believe that the apparent paradox is to be explained by the fact that a taste for *acting* is one of the strongest passions of human nature, that stage children show it nearly from infancy, and that, instead of being miserable drudges who ought to be celebrated in a new "Cry of the Children," they simply *rejoice* in their work "even as a giant rejoiceth to run his course."[34]

Drawing on his reader's memory of Elizabeth Barrett's poem just for the pleasure of rejecting its doleful associations, Carroll simultaneously spurns the definition of voiceless girlhood that was implicit in the raising of the age of consent four years earlier. Whereas Stead's girls' dubious ability to mean what they said was formalized into official incapacity by the legislation, Carroll's girls can both say what they mean ("We *have* enjoyed ourselves!"), and, thanks to the stage child's innate acting ability, say what they don't mean. Casting around for a comparison to capture his sense of the girls' power, Carroll transforms them, just as he had transformed his celebrated Alice, from childish figures into towering colossi. Exuberantly experiencing their working lives "even as a giant rejoiceth to run his course," these "three exceedingly happy and healthy little girls" are represented as self-willed and self-determining beings.

If Carroll preferred to focus solely on the little actress's pleasures, another contemporary commentator was quite happy to put forward a more self-interested argument for the preservation of junior performers. Taking shelter, admittedly, behind the bulwarks of aesthetics and the royal pronoun, Ernest Dowson declared in *The Critic* on August 17, 1889, that "artistically we find the child actress an enormous boon to the modern stage."[35] Written, like Carroll's letter, in response to the proposed new act, Dowson's article "The Cult of the Child" is liberally sprinkled with similarly audience-centered, or perhaps more accurately, self-centered, remarks. "There are an ever increasing number of people who receive from the beauty of childhood, in art as in life, an exquisite pleasure," the writer maintains, adding that it "is not surprising that an age which is, after all, chiefly pessimist, an age which is so deeply disillusioned, should turn with an immense delight to the constant charm of childhood." This is not to say that Dowson is insensitive to the feelings of the child actresses themselves: going even further than Carroll, he argues that "in childhood we are all spontaneously dramatic," and that because it is the most natural thing in the world for children to "cultivate their playful instinct," acting "is a pleasure to them; we believe that they delight in it."

This idyll of reciprocal delight enjoyed between performer and spectator, however, is no common thing: Dowson is careful to distinguish between mere "pantomime children" ("the fairy business," as *Nicholas Nickleby*'s Mr. Crummles would define it) and "the case of 'star' children." As the closing sentence of the article reveals, it is clear that Dowson is thinking throughout of his favorite player, the descriptively named "Minnie" Terry, niece of the very actress who had captivated Carroll's attention some forty years earlier. Nothing less than a hard-core fan, hanging about her residence, and racing to purchase her latest photographs ("My collection now comprises 3 cabinets 2 cartes de v. & 1 plaque," he notes excitedly at one point),[36] Dowson usually preferred to call his idol "Mignon," the name of the character she had played to considerable acclaim in a sentimental crowd-pleaser entitled *Bootle's Baby* in 1888.[37]

Dowson's obsession with Minnie Terry was by no means an isolated incidence of little-girl worship in his life. Chiefly remembered for his association with the Rhymers' Club and fin de siècle decadence, Dowson enjoyed a brief and consumptive existence, producing a small collection of poems and stories, and numerous translations of Flaubert, Zola, and other French authors, before he died in 1900 at the age of thirty-three. It is however in his capacity of girl lover that I include him in the final pages of this project, for the structure of Dowson's desires offers a vision of a very different model of adoration from those that we have considered at earlier points in the century. In certain ways, Dowson seems remarkably similar to other figures we have scrutinized: if Carroll is remembered in connection to Alice Liddell, and Ruskin with Rose La Touche, then for Dowson the beloved object was one Adelaide Foltinowicz, the daughter of the proprietor of a small Polish restaurant just off Piccadilly Circus. Dowson first fell in love with Adelaide—he called her "Missie"—when she was eleven years of age and he was twenty-two. He waited to propose until just before her fifteenth birthday, but the tentative engagement never came to any firm resolution, and the relationship as a whole seemingly brought little happiness to either party. The theme of doomed love and childhood innocence predominates in Dowson's oeuvre, which, although truncated, provides considerable opportunities for us to examine the distinctive features of this poet's attitude to little girls.

While Dowson's particular brand of adoration partakes of the overtly sexualized cultural climate that was the inevitable result of the events of the summer of 1885, it is obviously significant that the fascination is here harbored by a much younger writer—one who never gets the chance to be an old, or even a middle-aged, man. Yet this fact does not invalidate comparisons between Dowson and, for instance, Ruskin and Carroll: rather it is important to recognize that the older man's nostalgia for youth is no longer a necessary component of the girl-worshipping paradigm. The love that Dowson displays is apparently unconnected with a desire to see the little girl as a figure of his own lost childhood; furthermore, although the innocence of the little girl continues to be her defining and most beloved characteristic, this very quality is insistently sexualized by virtue of the fact that it is continually placed in relation to mature female sexuality (and often a sexuality that can be purchased by the hour, at that). The terms in which the little girl is described in Dowson's poetry reveal that the impenetrable stones and crystals of Ruskin's fantasies no longer have relevance to this new model of girl loving. It is overstating the case to say that Dowson's little girl is penetrable, the imaginary constructs of her interiority that appear in his verse demonstrate that the child has become a receptacle for emotion, rather than the guarantor of the sealed perfection of the man's lost girlhood.

Although both Dowson's artistic compositions and his correspondence are filled with eulogies to delicate sylphs like Minnie and Adelaide, a different sort of female also makes a fairly regular appearance therein. In an especially revealing letter of November 1889, Dowson chatters away to his best friend and most frequent correspondent Arthur Moore about a thwarted attempt to see his favorite actress, before switching to a (self-) thwarted sexual attempt on a girl called Bertha Van Raalte. Dowson had first told Moore of this potential conquest about two weeks earlier:

> By the by I have une *petite affaire* on hand which promises some amusement at any rate. The tart is aged $15\frac{3}{4}$ & belongeth to a tobacconist of Piccadilly who apparently views his parental responsibilities lightly. . . . She hath the *torso* of seventeen, at least, and wonderfully fine eyes.[38]

The later letter moves effortlessly from one girl to the other:

> How did *you* like the Haymarket? *We* were badly spoofé as for Miss Minnie Terry the play bill contained the name of Miss Dorothy Harwood. The latter is a very clever little girl but she is not pretty & she is not *mignonne* & my mater & I were both extremely bored by the play in consequence. I am glad you were not too depressed by the flat. Perchance we shall meet there again? re Van Raalte—I fancy that it has begun to pall. We spent a somewhat monotonous evening on Thursday & after I had sat for some two hours & a half on the sofa with my arm round the waist of the demoiselle & Lefroy ditto with his—we agreed that in view of the new act le jeu ne valait etc. And as we neither of us kept an appointment which we had made on Sunday evening with them & haven't written to explain since I guess the thing is off.[39]

Thus Dowson decides that the game is not worth the candle because "Miss Cigarettovitch," as he dubs her elsewhere, is below the age of consent, according to the legislation that had now been in effect for nearly four years. Consequently the potential sexual partner, the fifteen-year-old with the body of a seventeen-year-old, is placed not only in the same paragraph, but also in the same category, as the seven-year-old who is beloved for her *mignonne* charms. Equally off-limits, both girls are equally sexualized.

In his poetry Dowson juxtaposes the two categories of females in a far more self-conscious fashion. Although his aim seems to be to contrast the innocent girl with the experienced wanton in order to celebrate the former, this repeated device actually ends up collapsing the nonsexual and the sexual together. "[S]weet children's voices" threaten to merge with "harsh-laughing harlots' / Lascivious song" in one four-line stanza of "Transit Gloria," while "Rondeau" asks:

Why wine-stained lip and languid eye,
    And most unsaintly Maenad air,
Should move us more than all the rare
    White roses of virginity?[40]

In Dowson's most famous (certainly his most anthologized) poem, "Cynara," the speaker is visited by the memory of his virtuous lost love even as he enjoys "the kisses of [the] bought red mouth" of his bed companion:

Last night, ah, yesternight, betwixt her lips and mine
There fell thy shadow, Cynara! thy breath was shed
Upon my soul between the kisses and the wine.[41]

"I have been faithful to thee, Cynara! in my fashion" runs the refrain at the close of each of the four stanzas: from the rich red depths of his debauchery, the lover is still haunted by Cynara and her "pale, lost lilies." Although the speaker appears to be marveling at the paradoxical survival of the innocent passion of his youth, it is indubitably true that the poem places the girl in an explicitly erotic position—suspended between the desirous mouths of client and prostitute, Cynara's isolation from, and connection to, sexuality are simultaneously confirmed.

The same year that "Cynara" was composed, Dowson had been forced to consider how the much-vaunted purity of his love for Adelaide might appear when placed in the context of stories of the molestation of young girls by older men. Late in the summer of 1891, the newspapers were full of lurid details from the testimony of Lucy Pearson, a sixteen-year-old girl who had been abducted and sexually abused by a man named Newton. As his letter on the subject to Moore reveals, Dowson was not slow to see that the circulation of such stories had the power to affect the perception of his girl love, both in his own mind, and in the minds of others:

I have had a moral shock since yesterday, which has racked me ever since with an infinite horror that I may be misunderstood in the only thing that I really care about, by the only people to whom it matters. As ill luck would have it I came across the Star yesterday and read a most disgusting story of a disgusting person, which I suppose is a notorious scandal that one has escaped by being in Brittany. The worst of it was, that it read like a sort of foul and abominable travesty of—pah, what is the good of hunting for phrases. You must know what I mean, and how I am writhing. I imagine all the comments and analogies which one's kind friends will draw, and unfortunately I can't help feeling that even her people—and mine, as far as that goes—might take alarm & suspect my motives. And yet I swear there

never was a man more fanatically opposed to the corruption of innocence—
even where women are concerned—than I am. Unfortunately the excellence
of my conscience doesn't make any difference. This beastly thing has left a
sort of slimy trail over my holy places.[42]

While we may jib at some of the notes of would-be swaggering machismo
that show themselves here, as they frequently do in Dowson's letters to
Moore (that "even where women are concerned," for instance), the clear-
sighted candidness of the young man's response contrasts well with Carroll's deliberately tangential take on the "Maiden Tribute" furor. And
although Dowson is certainly not considering any wider application of
his words in this extremely personal lament, his diagnosis of the damage
done to sacred concepts by the spreading ooze of sexual discourse could
serve as a metaphorical representation of this chapter's basic argument
about the dissolution of the concept of the ideal girl. In the last fifteen
years of the nineteenth century, one of the male Victorian psyche's most
cherished "holy places" was indeed smeared with "a sort of slimy trail."

Can we identify traces of this contamination in Dowson's most sustained artistic celebration of the idea of the little girl? The eight component parts of the sonnet sequence "Of a Little Girl" were composed over
a ten-year period between 1886 and 1896, but only two of them were
published in the poet's lifetime.[43] Seen through the sexualizing lens of
the late nineteenth century, certain details seem to shimmer with dubious
associations. When Sonnet 2 tells us that "one passed the dark'ning road
along / And lit it with her childhood," are we wrong to glimpse the evanescent presence of the streetwalker?[44] Sonnet 1 eulogizes "a child's tender
love" in the following fashion:

> This love alone is stingless and can calm
> Life's fitful fever with its healing balm.[45]

Bearing a theme that is also picked up in the poem "Rondel" ("Ah, dear
child, in whose kiss / Is healing of my pain / . . . I shall not miss / Old
loves that did but stain"), the lines partake of the same queasy-making
metaphors that informed the hoary superstition that sex with a virgin was
a cure for venereal disease.[46]

More worthy of examination than these momentarily unsettling reso-
nances, however, is the pattern of concave images that pervades the landscape of the sonnet sequence. The cavern, the room with the opened window, even the "Hollow Lands" by name—all conspire to form a world

of receptacles that can both comfort and terrify. Sonnet 4 provides particularly rich material for our investigation of the sea change that befalls the image of the little girl in the last years of the century:

Even as a child whose eager fingers snatch
An ocean shell and hold it to his ear,
With wondering, awe-struck eyes is hushed to catch
The murmurous music of its coiled sphere;
Whispers of wind and wave, soul-stirring songs
Of storm-tossed ships and all the mystery
That to the illimitable sea belongs,
Stream to him from its tiny cavity.
As such an one with reverent awe I hold
Thy tender hand, and in those pure grey eyes,
That sweet child face, those tumbled curls of gold,
And in thy smiles and loving, soft replies
I find the whole of love—hear full and low
Its mystic ocean's tremulous ebb and flow.[47]

Thanks to the structure of the epic simile, the adult male speaker stands in relation to the little girl as the boy stands to the shell. Given the paucity of depictions of male childhood in the works of girl lovers that we have studied up to now, the appearance of this lad, all "snatch[ing] "eager fingers" until tranquilized by the shell's music, is striking in itself, and strongly suggests that we are no longer in Ruskin's and Carroll's particular corner of the girl-loving universe. Certainly the poem's arrangement of its terms makes it easier to imagine that the boy, not the girl, represents an earlier stage of the speaker's existence. But it is the parallelism of the girl and the shell that demands especial attention. Far from being a satisfyingly solid and sealed jewel or rock, the little girl is both open (that worrying "tiny cavity") and internally immense. Deceptively small on the outside, her capacious interiority encompasses "all the mystery / That to the illimitable sea belongs." Furthermore, the whispers of "storm-tossed ships" that reach the male ear hint at turbulence and danger—here there are no guarantees of calm or serenity. The ocean setting of the poem inevitably returns us to the nineteenth century's definitive *Ode* on childhood, but its Wordsworthian elements have been rearranged: whereas "the Children sport[ing] upon the shore" were, although part of the same vision, *separate* from "the mighty waters rolling evermore," "that immortal sea," a "mystic ocean" of love for Dowson, is now imagined as being *inside*

191

the child herself. Possessing a mysterious, illimitable interiority within her diminutive frame, the girl is a paradox, and like all of Dowson's pure children, both innocent and sexual at the same time.

Dowson and Ruskin died within days of each other in the opening months of the twentieth century; Carroll had passed away two years earlier in January of 1898. With them died the nineteenth-century phenomenon of girl worship: even though Dowson's ways of loving were vastly different from his forebears, his adoration, I would argue, represents the final, troubled phase of a peculiarly Victorian obsession.[48] But if the little girl had gone into a decline, then a new star was on the rise. In the early and mid-Victorian period, the boy had almost always been excluded from cultural fantasies about childhood, or, if included, he had been relentlessly feminized. Up until the 1880s, his stock was still low: although Stead had discovered evidence of widespread male juvenile prostitution in his researches into the underworld, the journalist barely mentions boys in the "Maiden Tribute" and chooses instead to stake his all on the appeal of violated femininity.[49] Excessive focus on the innocence of the little girl could not help but destroy her and left the way clear for the boy to embody a new image of childhood for a new age.[50]

Even before the nineteenth century came to an end, signs of the boy's elevation to preeminence had begun to appear. In 1893 a new monumental fountain was unveiled in the center of Piccadilly Circus, the very heart of London. Intended to represent Anteros, the angel of charity, of selfless love, the figure that balanced on one foot above the waters was a boy, dressed only in wings, a fluttering drapery and a whimsical feathered helmet.[51] Alfred Gilbert, the designer and sculptor of the piece, had modeled the figure on his fifteen-year-old studio assistant, Angelo Colorossi. The monument was erected as memorial to Anthony Ashley-Cooper, the earl of Shaftesbury, who had devoted over half a century of his life to improving the lot of the English child. Having played a significant role in almost every movement of Victorian reform that affected children's lives from the Factory Act of 1844 to the Criminal Law Amendment Act of 1885, Shaftesbury died two months after the passage of this latter bill. Although Eros, as he is commonly called, is now a much-loved symbol of London, the monument was not an initial success: the overflowing fountains (symbolizing Shaftesbury's love for humanity, but long since turned off) splattered passers-by, the seven ornamental drinking cups (representing the seven acts of mercy) were swiftly stolen or vandalized, and, more to the point, the statue was thought to be indecent on account of its nudity. Misrecognized as Cupid, rather than Anteros or Eros, the figure was furthermore deemed to be a highly dubious god to preside over what had become the capital's most notorious haunt of prostitutes. All in all, the work was hailed as "a dripping, sickening mess."[52] For my purposes, though, Gilbert's statue forms a fitting conclusion to this project. After prolonged scrutiny of the Victorian gentleman's obsession with the little girl, I place before you the figure of the boy, quite literally Erotic and intimately connected both with the nineteenth century's history of child-centered legislation and its evolving discourses of child sexuality.[53] In different ways, and for figures as diverse as J. M. Barrie, Rudyard Kipling, Baden Powell, and Sigmund Freud, the boy returned from his long obscurity to be childhood's supreme representative for the twentieth century.

APPENDIX

Lewis Carroll's Letter to the *St. James's Gazette*, July 22, 1885

"Whoso Shall Offend One of These Little Ones . . ."

I know that any writer who ventures to protest against what happens to be a popular cry has little chance even of respectful attention. The rapid inter-communication of our age had brought us one evil from which our forefathers were free: the mass is moved too suddenly and too violently: each tide of popular feeling runs headlong in one direction, sweeping all before it, and back again with an equally dangerous reflux, leaving ravage and ruin behind it. Only a few years ago, if any impure scandal arose, its investigation and punishment were left to those whose painful duty it was to know the sickening details: women and boys were turned out of court: no particulars were given in any respectable journal—nothing but the words "the evidence was unfit for publication." But a horrible fashion seems to be setting in, of making all things public, and of forcing the most contaminating subjects on the attention even of those who can get nothing from them but the deadliest injury. Against this I desire to raise a warning voice.

The question at issue is not whether great evils exist—nor again whether the rousing of public opinion is a remedy for those evils—on these two points we are agreed. The real question is, whether this mode of rousing public opinion is, or is not, doing more harm than good.

And the worst of the danger is that all this is being done in the sacred name of Religion. If we had no other evidence for the existence of a devil, we might find it, I think, in the Argument from Design—in the terrible superhuman ingenuity with which temptation is adapted to the taste of the age. Not so many years ago, Vice was fashionable, and the literature of the day was *openly* profligate: no pretext of piety was offered to readers who would only have despised it. But in our day, to be popular, one must profess the very highest and purest motives. Straightway Satan is transformed into an angel of light, and with an air "devout and pure, sober, steadfast, and demure," offers us his old wares, furbished up in new colours.

May I not plead with those, who have not yet lost their heads in the whirl and din of this popular Maelstrom, to consider whither the stream is really carrying us?

I plead for our young men and boys, whose imaginations are being excited by highly-coloured pictures of vice, and whose natural thirst for knowledge is being used for unholy purposes by the seducing whisper "read this, and your eyes shall be opened, and ye shall be as gods, knowing good *and evil!*" I plead for our womankind, who are being enticed to attend meetings where the speakers, inverting the sober language of the apostle, "it is a shame even to speak of those things which are done of them in secret," proclaim that it is a shame not to speak of them: who are being taught to believe that they are still within the bounds of true womanliness and modesty, while openly discussing the vilest of topics: and who all too soon prove, by the eagerness with which they turn to what so lately was loathsome to them, that there is but one step from prudishness to pruriency. Above all, I plead for our pure maidens, whose souls are being saddened, if not defiled, by the nauseous literature that is thus thrust upon them—I plead for them in the name of Him who said "Whoso shall offend one of these little ones which believe in me, it were better for him that a millstone were hanged about his neck, and that he were drowned in the depth of the sea." For all these I plead, with whosoever has the power to interfere, to stay, before it is too late, the flood of abomination with which we are threatened.

Let me add some words, bearing on this matter, better and more eloquent than any that I could devise. I quote from "Sermons by the Rev. E. Monro," published in 1850, p. 136:

By all means, and on all occasions, avoid dwelling on the object of impure sensation; we are told, by holy men of old, that on this point alone we may be cowards; we must fly from it. The mere dwelling on its forbidden pollutions, even to combat them, forms evil habits, and withers holiness. We are often led to bring the object of sinful desires before us, and that with the best intentions, when we pray against it, when we would examine ourselves on it, when we are regretting the past, when we would unfold our grief to another, when we compare ourselves with ourselves. But on all these occasions as far as possible shun the image; do not let the coloured lights fall into a shape or outline, nor suffer, if you can help it, your vision to centre them in a focus; if they are dimmed, leave them so, and do not restore the view; repress even the slightest image, lest it should strengthen and invigorate evil desire; you are too weak to bear it. If you have to pray against it, to examine yourselves on it, let the object be an imperfect memory, a recollection of something past, rather than of the object itself; mean it without expressing it, intend without defining it. Let no excuse avail to dwell on it.

The contrast between these wise words and the conduct of those who are doing their best to "centre in a focus" the soul-destroying picture, and to add yet some more "coloured lights" than the devil has already supplied needs no words of mine to emphasize it.

A beautiful fiend is abroad in the midst of us: let the wise know her and shun her while yet there is time. On her fair brow she wears the title of "Religion"; pacing with downward eyelids pure she passes, unsuspected, among our youths and maidens, and whispers to them the dark secrets of Hell. Like Arthur's profligate queen,

> being by our cowardice allow'd
> Her station, taken everywhere for pure,
> She like a new disease, unknown to men,
> Creeps, no precaution used, among the crowd,
> Makes wicked lightnings of her eyes, and saps
> The fealty of our friends, and stirs the pulse
> With devil's leaps, and poisons half the young.

LEWIS CARROLL

Notes

INTRODUCTION

1. See J. Laplanche and J. B. Pontalis, *The Language of Psycho-Analysis*, trans. Donald Nicholson Smith (London: Hogarth Press, 1973), 309–11.

2. See Leonore Davidoff and Catherine Hall, *Family Fortunes: Men and Women of the English Middle Class, 1780–1850* (Chicago: University of Chicago Press, 1987), 344, 413; John Tosh, *A Man's Place: Masculinity and the Middle-Class Home in Victorian England* (New Haven: Yale University Press, 1999), 103.

3. See Davidoff and Hall, *Family Fortunes*, 235, on the age at which education in the home generally ceased for boys; and Deborah Gorham, *The Victorian Girl and the Feminine Ideal* (Bloomington: Indiana University Press, 1982), 68, on the minimizing of differences between the sexes in early childhood.

4. See Philippe Ariès, *Centuries of Childhood: A Social History of Family Life*, trans. Robert Baldick (New York: Knopf, 1962).

5. Part 1 of Neil Postman's *The Disappearance of Childhood* (New York: Delacorte, 1982) contains an overview of these accounts (4–64).

6. Of particular interest are Ivy Pinchbeck and Margaret Hewitt's *Children in English Society*, 2 vols., *From the Eighteenth Century to the Children Act, 1948* (London: Routledge, 1969–73); Thomas Laqueur's *Religion and Respectability: Sunday Schools and Working Class Culture, 1780–1850* (New Haven: Yale University Press, 1976); and Peter Coveney's *The Image of Childhood: The Individual and Society: A Study of the Theme in English Literature* (Harmondsworth: Penguin, 1967).

7. See Hugh Cunningham, *The Children of the Poor: Representations of Childhood since the Seventeenth Century* (Blackwell: Oxford, 1991).

8. See the two collections of essays edited by Martha Vicinus, *A Widening Sphere: Changing Roles of Victorian Women* (Bloomington: Indiana University Press, 1977), and *Suffer and Be Still: Women in the Victorian Age* (Bloomington: Indiana University Press, 1972); Erna Olafson Hellerstein, Leslie Parker Hume, and Karen M. Offen, eds., *Victorian Women: A Documentary Account of Women's Lives in Nineteenth-Century England, France, and the United States* (Stanford, Calif.: Stanford University Press, 1981); and most importantly, Davidoff and Hall, *Family Fortunes*.

9. See Laura C. Berry's "Best Regulated Families: Victorian Social Welfare and the Novel," Ph.D. diss., University of California, Berkeley, 1992.

10. The information about *Cherry Ripe* is taken from Marion H. Spielmann's *Millais and His Works* (Edinburgh: Blackwood, 1898).

11. See Jacqueline Rose, *The Case of Peter Pan; or, The Impossibility of Children's Fiction* (London: Macmillan, 1984), 8.

12. See Tosh, *A Man's Place*, 42.

13. The publication in 1987 of *Family Fortunes*, Leonore Davidoff and Catherine Hall's highly influential study of the profoundly religious idiom of early- to mid-nineteenth-century middle-class life, marks an important turning point. In the following discussion of the spiritual culture of middle-class Victorian Britain and its effects on perceptions of childhood, I draw particularly on their work and on Tosh's *A Man's Place*; Claudia Nelson's *Boys Will Be Girls: The Feminine Ethic and British Children's Fiction, 1857–1917* (New Brunswick, N.J.: Rutgers University Press, 1991); and John Gillis's "Birth of the Virtual Child: A Victorian Progeny," typescript, 1998.

14. Nelson, *Boys Will Be Girls*, 11.

15. Gillis, "Birth of Virtual Child," 7.

16. Deborah Gorham's *Victorian Girl and the Feminine Ideal* is a particularly useful study of the relationship between the constructs of domestic ideology and the life experience of girls of the middle classes in nineteenth-century England.

17. See note 8.

18. Tosh, *A Man's Place*, 2.

19. I consequently side-step the contentious definitions of this problematic term that troubled the Victorians and continue to occupy scholars in fascinating ways today. See, for instance, James Eli Adams's *Dandies and Desert Saints: Styles of Victorian Manhood* (Ithaca, N.Y.: Cornell University Press, 1995). For other discussions of Victorian constructions of masculinity, see David D. Gilmore, *Manhood in the Making: Cultural Concepts of Masculinity* (New Haven: Yale University Press, 1990); Michael Roper and John Tosh, *Manful Assertions: Masculinities in Britain since 1800* (London: Routledge, 1991); Karen Volland Waters, *The Perfect Gentleman: Masculine Control in Victorian Men's Fiction, 1870–1901* (New York: Peter Lang, 1997); Trev Lynn Broughton, *Men of Letters, Writing Lives: Masculinity and Literary Auto/Biography in the Late Victorian Period* (London: Routledge, 1999).

20. Jeffrey Weeks provides a full description of this narrative in his *Sex, Politics, and Society: The Regulation of Sexuality since 1800* (London: Longman, 1981).

21. See Michel Foucault, *The History of Sexuality*, vol. 1, *An Introduction*, trans. Robert Hurley (New York: Pantheon, 1978).

22. My allegiance to the Foucauldian approach should make it clear that I am not endeavoring to produce psychobiographies of my different authors. Although it is of course impossible to separate oneself from the modes of thought that have devolved from psychoanalysis into everyday consciousness, I do not apply this body of theory as a methodological or explanatory tool. The paradigms produced in the late nineteenth and twentieth centuries by such figures as Freud and Lacan are fascinating to me not insofar as they illuminate the psychic patterns exhibited in earlier historical moments, but because they themselves are part of the continuing mythology of the creation of interiorized selves, a mythology to which this book aims to contribute one particular narrative.

23. James R. Kincaid, *Child Loving: The Erotic Child and Victorian Culture* (London: Routledge, 1992).

24. Although my study is to a large degree an exploration of self-love and its ramifications, I do not use the psychoanalytic concept of narcissism herein. In most accounts (not least Freud's in *Three Essays on the Theory of Sexuality*), narcissism has some relation to a temporal split between past and present selves (see Laplanche and Pontalis, *The Language of Psycho-Analysis*, 255), but the theory does not generally accommodate the gender crossing that is key to this investigation.

25. Carolyn Steedman, *Strange Dislocations: Childhood and the Idea of Human Interiority, 1780–1930* (Cambridge: Harvard University Press, 1995), 8–9.

26. I also wish to acknowledge the importance of Jacqueline Rose's work to my thinking. In the introduction to *The Case of Peter Pan* Rose defines the parameters of her project in a manner that has been extremely useful for this study: "What is at stake in *Peter Pan* is the adult's desire for the child. I am not using desire here in the sense of an act which is sought after or which must actually take place. It is not relevant, therefore, to insist that nothing ever happened, or that Barrie was innocent of any interest in sex (a point which is often made). I am using desire to refer to a form of investment by the adult in the child, and to the demand made by the adult on the child as the effect of that investment, a demand which fixes the child and then holds it in place" (3).

27. I have not engaged children's literature here primarily because of the compelling achievement of Claudia Nelson's *Boys Will Be Girls*. As is signaled by the gender crossing in her title, and by her repeated insistence that "the Victorian stereotype of childhood had much in common with the feminine ideal" (2), Nelson's work clearly anticipates some of my general claims and covers ground not reexplored here. Despite her title, however, Nelson concentrates much of her energy on examining a transition I also identify, but which I only gesture toward in my closing pages: *Boys Will Be Girls* seems most interested in examining late-Victorian and Edwardian texts in order to show that the feminized boy of the earlier nineteenth century is gradually ousted by a rough-and-tumble lad who could "never be mistaken for a girl in breeches" (30).

CHAPTER ONE

OF PRISONS AND UNGROWN GIRLS: WORDSWORTH, DE QUINCEY, AND CONSTRUCTIONS OF THE LOST SELF OF CHILDHOOD

1. For readings of the woodcock-snaring episode, see Timothy Bahti, "Wordsworth's Rhetorical Theft," in *Romanticism and Language*, ed. Arden Reed (Ithaca, N.Y.: Cornell University Press, 1984); and David Collings, *Wordsworthian Errancies: The Poetics of Cultural Dismemberment* (Baltimore: Johns Hopkins University Press, 1994), chap. 5.

2. I draw upon J. Chitty, Esq.'s *Treatise on the Game Laws and on Fisheries* (London: W. Clarke and J. Reed, 1812), 75–76. While it is clear that the young Wordsworth did not fulfill the property qualification of this law, and that "en-

gines" covers the "springes" or "toils" that he was setting, it is hard to determine exactly whether woodcocks would have been considered game in 1778 in Westmorland. As Chitty points out, referring to Johnson's *Dictionary* and Blackstone's *Commentaries*, the term *game* has designated different groups of beasts and fowls at different times. Although Justice Ashhurst felt in 1787 that the distinction was clear to all but urban fools ("an ignorant witness in the country might fancy that a woodcock or a rabbit was game," quoted in Chitty, 1225), it is not until 1808 that the issue is clarified in law, when 48 George 3 c55 specifically exempts those taking "woodcocks and snipes with nets and springes" from requiring a game license.

3. Pennant's *A Tour in Scotland, and Voyage to the Hebrides, 1772* (Chester: John Monk, 1774) records the following: "Saw on the plain part of these hills numbers of springes for woodcocks, laid between tufts of heath, with avenues of small stones on each side, to direct these foolish birds into snares, for they will not hop over the pebbles. Multitudes are taken in this manner in the open weather; and sold on the spot for sixteen pence or twenty pence a couple . . . and sent to the all-devouring capital by the Kendal stage."

4. Later in the chapter, I will explain more carefully the legal position on the age of criminal responsibility in England during this period, but this seems an appropriate juncture to mention that some seventy years after Wordsworth was prowling the heath in search of woodcocks, small children *were* being convicted of game offenses in parts of the British Isles. When Mary Carpenter was giving evidence to the Select Committee on Criminal and Destitute Juveniles in 1852, her starkest example of the inconsistencies inherent in the legal system was provided by the conviction of two Scottish children, aged two and six years old. I give below *Punch*'s report of the same case, on February 28, 1852, which appears under the heading "Infancy of Crime in Scotland":

> The *Edinburgh News* narrates as follows:
> "A strange but absurd case was brought before WILLIAM L. COLQUHOUN, ESQ., of Clathick, as Justice of the Peace for the county of Perth, at Crieff, on 10th instant [ult.], at the instance of LORD and LADY WILLOUGHBY DE ERESBY and LOUIS KENNEDY, their factor, as their mandatory, against two children of MR. MIDDLEMISS, labourer, Muthill, of the respective ages of *two and six years*. The youngest child attended the learned Justice carried in its mother's arms. The charge brought against them was that they had been found in the act of laying snares for the purpose of catching game in an adjoining field to the village of Muthill."
>
> The crime was proved, at least to the satisfaction of the magistrate, for the evil-doers, aged six years and two, were fined each £1 6s. 10d., including expenses; or, failing payment, thirty days' imprisonment.

5. The reference text for Wordsworth's poetry, with the exception of *The Prelude*, is *The Poetical Works of William Wordsworth*, ed. Ernest de Selincourt and Helen Darbishire, 5 vols. (Oxford: Clarendon Press, 1940–49). Further references appear in the text. Because of Wordsworth's express desire that the *Ode* should

always stand alone in its own section in any collected volume of his works, I give it the status of a longer work, and italicize its title.

6. The reference text here is William Wordsworth, *The Prelude, 1799, 1805, 1850*, ed. Jonathan Wordsworth, M. H. Abrams, and Stephen Gill (New York: W. W. Norton, 1979). I quote from the 1805 version unless otherwise noted. Further references appear in the text.

7. These events appear in *The Prelude* 1.310–32, 333–50, 372–426, 2.99–144.

8. For a more complex reading of the relationship between past and present selves, see David Simpson, *Irony and Authority in Romantic Poetry* (Totowa, N.J.: Rowman and Littlefield, 1979), chap. 2.

9. There are passages of book 5 that are very like the *Ode* in sentiment, and that were indeed composed at much the same time.

10. This is one of the instances in which Wordsworth makes repeated changes to his manuscript—I give here the 1799, pre-1805, and final versions.

11. The child is Coleridge's oldest son, Hartley, by all accounts.

12. See Daniel W. Ross, "The Uncanny in Wordsworth's 'Immortality Ode,' " *Studies in English Literature, 1500–1900* 32, no. 4 (1992): 625–43, for a useful bibliographical summary of critical readings of the *Ode* in the second half of the twentieth century.

13. See Samuel Taylor Coleridge, *Biographia Literaria* (London: Dent, 1965), 258–62.

14. Barbara Garlitz, "The Immortality Ode: Its Cultural Progeny," *Studies in English Literature, 1500–1900* 6, no. 3 (1966): 639–49. Her quotations are drawn from John Keble, *Lectures on Poetry*, 1832–41, trans. E. K. Francis (Oxford: Clarendon Press, 1912), 2:453; Ralph Waldo Emerson, *English Traits* (1856), in *The Complete Works*, ed. E. W. Emerson (Boston: Houghton and Mifflin, 1903–4), 5:298; Margaret Oliphant, *The Literary History of England* (London: Macmillan, 1882), 1:328. Carl Woodring's "Wordsworth and the Victorians" appears in *The Age of William Wordsworth: Critical Essays on the Romantic Tradition*, ed. Kenneth R. Johnston and Gene W. Ruoff (New Brunswick, N.J.: Rutgers University Press, 1987); U. C. Knoepflmacher's "Mutations of the Wordsworthian Child" is in *Nature and the Victorian Imagination*, ed. U. C. Knoepflmacher and G. B. Tennyson (Berkeley and Los Angeles: University of California Press, 1977).

15. Garlitz, "The Immortality Ode," 647.

16. A. B. M., "Wordsworth the Christian Poet," *Christian Examiner* 49 (1850): 104.

17. *The Prelude, Eclectic Review* 28 (1850): 550–62.

18. *Tait's Edinburgh Magazine* 17 (1850): 521–27.

19. *Graham's Magazine* (Philadelphia), 37 (1850): 322–23.

20. Mary Carpenter, *Juvenile Delinquents, Their Condition and Treatment* (London: W. and F. G. Cash, 1853), 15.

21. Select Committee on Criminal and Destitute Juveniles, 1852, in *British Parliamentary Papers, Crime and Punishment: Juvenile Offenders*, ed. P. Ford and

G. Ford (Shannon: Irish University Press, 1968–70), 2:8. All subsequent references to parliamentary papers will be to this series.

22. Michel Foucault, *Discipline and Punish: The Birth of the Prison*, trans. Alan Sheridan (New York: Pantheon Books, 1977); Michael Ignatieff, *A Just Measure of Pain: The Penitentiary in the Industrial Revolution, 1750–1850* (New York: Pantheon Books, 1978); Margaret E. DeLacy, "Grinding Men Good? Lancashire's Prisons at Mid-Century," in *Policing and Punishment in Nineteenth-Century Britain*, ed. Victor Bailey (London: Croom Helm, 1981).

23. William Blackstone, *Commentaries* (Oxford: Clarendon Press, 1765–9), IV, sec. 22. All further references will appear in the text.

24. See Leon Radzinowicz, *History of the English Criminal Law* (New York: Macmillan, 1948–56), 1:163.

25. J. M. Beattie, *Crime and the Courts in England, 1660–1800* (Princeton: Princeton University Press, 1986), 246–47.

26. John Howard, *State of the Prisons of England and Wales* (Warrington: W. Eyres, 1777).

27. See Pinchbeck and Hewitt, *Children in English Society*, 1:110–16.

28. For the early history of the Philanthropic Society, see Julius Carlebach's *Caring for Children in Trouble* (London: Routledge and Kegan Paul, 1970).

29. See in particular Margaret May, "Innocence and Experience: The Evolution of the Concept of Juvenile Delinquency in the Mid-Nineteenth Century," *Victorian Studies* 17 (September 1973): 7–29; and Susan Magarey, "The Invention of Juvenile Delinquency in Early Nineteenth-Century England," *Labour History* 34 (1978): 11–25.

30. Magarey, "Invention of Juvenile Delinquency," 16.

31. W. R. Cornish and G. de N. Clark, *Law and Society in England, 1750–1950* (London: Sweet and Maxwell, 1989), 585.

32. Pinchbeck and Hewitt, *Children in English Society*, 2:454.

33. Robert Hughes, *The Fatal Shore* (New York: Vintage Books, Random House, 1986), 408.

34. Pinchbeck and Hewitt give a good account of Mary Carpenter's unfair attack on Parkhurst (*Children in English Society*, 2:470–76).

35. Select Committee on the Execution of the Criminal Law, 1847 (*British Parliamentary Papers*, 1:212).

36. R. and F. Davenport Hill, *The Recorder of Birmingham: A Memoir of Matthew Davenport Hill* (London: Macmillan, 1878), 168–69, quoted in Pinchbeck and Hewitt, *Children in English Society*, 2:477.

37. As Cunningham argues, the cherished story of the process of nineteenth-century reform that improved the lot of English children functions as a romance of the nation (*Children of the Poor*, 8–17, 218–33).

38. Magarey, "Invention of Juvenile Delinquency," 24.

39. Select Committee on Criminal and Destitute Juveniles, 1852 (*British Parliamentary Papers*, 2:118–40).

40. Thus reformers who, in theory, oppose the Calvinistic position on the nature of children sometimes resemble hard-line adherents of the doctrine of original sin in their approach to discipline and punishment. See the introduction.

41. M. Hill and C. F. Cornwallis, *Two Prize Essays on Juvenile Delinquency* (London: Smith, Elder, 1853), and M. Carpenter, *Juvenile Delinquents*, both quoted in May, "Innocence and Experience," 19–20, 22.

42. M. D. Hill, "Practical Suggestions to the Founders of Reformatory Schools," in J. C. Symons, *On the Reformation of Young Offenders* (London: Routledge, 1855), quoted in May, "Innocence and Experience," 7.

43. S. Robins, *A Letter to the Right Honourable Lord John Russell on the Necessity and Mode of State Assistance in the Education of the People* (London: Ridgway, 1851), quoted in May, "Innocence and Experience," 21.

44. See Magarey, "Invention of Juvenile Delinquency."

45. On the general topic of Wordsworth's treatment of the feminine, see Margaret Homans, "Eliot, Wordsworth, and the Scenes of the Sisters' Instruction," *Critical Inquiry* 8, no. 2 (winter 1981): 223–41, and *Women Writers and Poetic Identity* (Princeton: Princeton University Press, 1980); Mary Jacobus, "The Law of/and Gender: Genre Theory and *The Prelude*," *Diacritics* 14 (1984): 47–57, and *Romanticism, Writing, and Sexual Difference* (Oxford: Clarendon Press, 1989); Marlon B. Ross, "Naturalizing Gender: Woman's Place in Wordsworth's Ideological Landscape," *ELH* 53 (1986): 391–410; Susan J. Wolfson, "Lyrical Ballads and the Language of (Men) Feeling: Wordsworth Writing Women's Voices," in *Men Writing the Feminine: Literature, Theory, and the Question of Genders*, ed. Thaïs E. Morgan (Albany: State University of New York Press, 1994); Judith W. Page, *Wordsworth and the Cultivation of Women* (Berkeley and Los Angeles: University of California Press, 1994).

46. Wordsworth, *Poetical Works*, 360.

47. See Wordsworth and Coleridge, *Lyrical Ballads*, ed. R. L. Brett and A. R. Jones (London: Methuen, 1963). Coleridge's speculation about the origin of this poem, which he first wrote in a letter to T. Poole in 1799, appears as a note on 300–301.

48. See *The Norton Anthology of English Literature*, 5th ed., ed. M. H. Abrams et al., vol. 2 (New York: W. W. Norton, 1962), 208.

49. Wordsworth, *Poetical Works*. "She dwelt among th' untrodden ways," l. 5; "Three years she grew in sun and shower," ll. 17–18.

50. Ibid, "She dwelt" l. 12; "A slumber" ll. 6–8.

51. Legitimacy, apparently, is all: Moorman discounts Caroline, Wordsworth's daughter by Annette Vallon. Interestingly enough for my purposes, Judith W. Page's analysis of the sonnet "It Is a Beauteous Evening" about this daughter comes to the conclusion that to describe Caroline as in "Abraham's bosom" is to imagine her dead. See " 'The Weight of Too Much Liberty': Genre and Gender in Wordsworth's Calais Sonnets," *Criticism* 30 (1988): 189–203.

52. See Mary Moorman, "Wordsworth and His Children," in *Bicentenary Wordsworth Studies in Memory of J. A. Finch*, ed. Jonathan Wordsworth (Ithaca, N.Y.: Cornell University Press, 1970).

53. E. Michael Thron discusses the two men's responses in "The Significance of Catharine Wordsworth's Death to Thomas De Quincey and William Wordsworth," *Studies in English Literature, 1500–1900* 28 (1988): 559–67.

54. For a much more extended treatment of De Quincey's narrative repetitions of what he calls "the myth of his own childhood," see John Barrell's fascinating *The Infection of Thomas De Quincey: A Psychopathology of Imperialism* (New Haven: Yale University Press, 1991).

55. See John E. Jordan, *De Quincey to Wordsworth: A Biography of a Relationship* (Berkeley and Los Angeles: University of California Press, 1962), 266.

56. Henry Crabb Robinson's opinions are quoted in Grevel Lindop's *The Opium-Eater: A Life of Thomas de Quincey* (London: J. M. Dent, 1981), 197–98.

57. *The Collected Writings of Thomas De Quincey*, ed. David Masson, 14 vols. (Edinburgh: A. and C. Black, 1889–90), 2:443. Unless otherwise indicated, all references will be to this edition and will appear in the text.

58. See Lindop, *Opium-Eater*, 207–8; Thomas McFarland, *Romantic Cruxes: The English Essayists and the Spirit of the Age* (Oxford: Clarendon Press, 1987); and Margaret Leighton, "De Quincey and Women," in *Beyond Romanticism: New Approaches to Texts and Contexts, 1780–1832*, ed. Stephen Copley and John Whale (New York: Routledge, 1992).

59. These references come from an alternate version of "The Affliction of Childhood," which appears in *Confessions of an English Opium Eater and Other Writings*, ed. Aileen Ward (New York: Signet Classics, New American Library, 1966), 131.

60. For important analyses of the representation of the death of De Quincey's sister, see Robert M. Maniquis, "Lonely Empires: Personal and Public Visions of Thomas De Quincey," in *Literary Monographs*, vol. 8, ed. Eric Rothstein and Joseph Anthony Wittreich Jr. (Madison: University of Wisconsin Press, 1976); and J. Hillis Miller, *The Disappearance of God: Five Nineteenth-Century Writers* (Cambridge: Harvard University Press, 1975).

61. See Grevel Lindop, "Pursuing the Throne of God: De Quincey and the Evangelical Revival," *Charles Lamb Bulletin* 52 (1985): 97–111.

62. As Barrell notes, De Quincey plays fast and loose with chronology: the ages he ascribes to himself and his siblings at various junctures, and the age gaps between individual members of his family, are often wrong (*Infection*, 25–26).

63. Barrell touches briefly on De Quincey's "identity as sister" (*Infection*, 58), but this is not a major theme in his approach.

64. De Quincey uses this phrase, in Greek, to describe his sister Mary at a later stage in his life (3:320).

65. To the best of my knowledge, the naughtiest thing the boy De Quincey ever did was to subscribe to the part-issue of a general history of navigation, without knowing to how many volumes he had committed either himself, or his guardian's wallet. The uncertainty into which this arrangement threw him produced "dim terrors" in his mind about the stationers' company: "I had often observed them in popular works threatening unknown men with unknown chastisements for offenses equally unknown, nay, to myself absolutely inconceivable. Could I be the mysterious criminal so long pointed out, as it were, in prophecy?" ("The Affliction of Childhood," 159).

66. Lindop, *Opium-Eater*, 302, explains how the process worked:

This curious ritual arose from the fact that imprisonment for debt was technically not sanctioned by Scottish law. Attitudes to debtors being no more friendly in Scotland than elsewhere, a procedure had evolved whereby a debtor could be imprisoned under the legal fiction that he was guilty of a different offense. The creditor would apply to a court which had power to issue a letter commanding the debtor in the name of the monarch to pay his debt. If he still "refused" to pay he was held to be disobeying a royal command, and an officer of the court would go to the market-place at Edinburgh and, with three blasts of the horn, publicly proclaim him a rebel. He then could be imprisoned.

67. Lindop, *Opium-Eater*, 322.
68. Ibid.

CHAPTER TWO
THE IDEAL GIRL IN INDUSTRIAL ENGLAND

1. See John Gillis, *A World of Their Own Making: Myth, Ritual, and the Quest for Family Values* (New York: Basic Books, 1996), 165–71, on the new importance of the child's birthday in the Victorian era. John Tosh's *A Man's Place* features *Many Happy Returns of the Day* on its cover and conducts a brief reading of the painting in the chapter "Father and Child." For Tosh, the painting's primary significance is its depiction of "the distant father," and it thus "exemplifies the ambivalence with which so many men viewed their paternal role" (97).

2. John Ruskin, *Royal Academy Notes* (London: Smith and Elder and Co., 1856), 46–47.

3. These paintings of Millais's are linked most obviously by the appearance of Isabella Nicol, the little blonde girl, in all three. *The Blind Girl* is a picture of two working-class girls, one blind, the other not, in an idyllic rural landscape. Although the blind girl cannot see the vibrant double rainbow that is enthralling her companion, her expression reveals that her other senses are fully alive to the beauties of the countryside. (For an illuminating discussion of the problems of establish-

ing contemporary responses to this painting, see Kate Flint's "Blindness and Insight: Millais's *The Blind Girl* and the limits of representation," *Journal of Victorian Culture* 1, no. 1 [1996]: 1–15.) *L'Enfant du Regiment* is perhaps even more relevant to the particular themes of this chapter: the little girl, removed from the battle scene where she has been wounded in the arm by a stray shot, sleeps on a marble tomb in an old church. Almost completely covered by the grenadier's jacket that has been draped over her, the child is lying directly (and, one would think, very uncomfortably) upon the supine statue of a medieval knight.

4. See *The Pre-Raphaelites* (London: Tate Gallery/Penguin, 1984), 141.

5. I am tempted to believe that this painting—and particularly the little girl with the apple and the somber expression—was a direct influence upon Gerard Manley Hopkins's poem "Spring and Fall," which begins with the lines "Margaret, are you grieving / Over Goldengrove unleaving?" If the religious connotations are underplayed in Millais's picture, however, Hopkins's version is much more in line with Catholic doctrine.

6. Circulation figures for *The Old Curiosity Shop* exceeded one hundred thousand, making this novel Dickens's most popular success. I will refer to the Penguin Classics edition, ed. Malcolm Andrews (Harmondsworth: Penguin, 1972). All page references will appear in the text.

7. Sarah Stickney Ellis, *The Daughters of England, their Position in Society, Character and Responsibilities* (London: Fischer, Son & Co. [1843]). Page references to this edition will appear in the text.

8. The many books that use Ellis include the two works edited by Martha Vicinus, *A Widening Sphere* and *Suffer and Be Still*; Patricia Branca, *Silent Sisterhood: Middle-Class Women in the Victorian Home* (London: Croom Helm, 1975); Catherine Gallagher, *The Industrial Reformation of English Fiction, 1832–1867* (Chicago: University of Chicago Press, 1985); Davidoff and Hall, *Family Fortunes*. For particular attention to *The Daughters of England*, see Gorham, *Victorian Girl*, 101, 103, 112; and Nelson, *Boys Will Be Girls*, 9–10.

9. Cf. Gorham, *Victorian Girl*, 6–7; and Davidoff and Hall, *Family Fortunes*, 346.

10. Cf. Gorham, *Victorian Girl*, 38, 44; and Davidoff and Hall, *Family Fortunes*, 331.

11. Cf. the hair-combing scene from A. S. Roe's *The Star and the Cloud: Or a Daughter's Love* (London, 1857), quoted by Gorham, *Victorian Girl*, 41.

12. On the broader topic of the tension between the evangelical belief that all souls are equal, and the conservative view that social hierarchies are inevitable, see Davidoff and Hall, *Family Fortunes*, 83, 92.

13. Anna Jameson, review of the *Report and Appendices of the Children's Employment Commission*, *Athenaeum*, March 4, 11, 18, 1843.

14. Ibid., 257.

15. Daniel Defoe, *A Tour through the whole Island of Great Britain, 1724–26* (New York: Garland, 1975), 42.

16. Neil J. Smelser has argued that the move into factories did not break up the family working unit as much as had been previously thought; see his *Social Change in the Industrial Revolution* (Chicago: University of Chicago Press, 1959) and Clark Nardinelli, *Child Labor and the Industrial Revolution* (Bloomington: Indiana University Press, 1990), 1–36, for a summary of the different positions in this discussion.

17. The 1802 act sought primarily to limit hours for apprentices and to regulate their employers' sanitary practices.

18. Select Committee on Children, Mills and Factories, 1816, *British Parliamentary Papers*, 1:170–71.

19. Ibid., 199.

20. Quoted in Gallagher, *Industrial Reformation*, 24.

21. Much has been written about whether the movement's appropriation of the image of the abused child constituted a cynical and self-interested ploy on the part of some adherents. E. P. Thompson's comments represent a useful summary of the debate: "Heavy weather has been made of this, [in this instance, the fact that handloom weavers supported the 10 Hours agitation] from the 1830s to the present day, with the men coming under the accusation of 'sheltering behind the skirts of the women' or of using the plight of the children as a stalking-horse in their own demand for shorter hours. But, in fact, the aim was openly declared by factory operatives and weavers. It was intrinsic to their alternative model of political economy that shorter hours in the factory should at one and the same time lighten the labour of children, give a shorter working day to the adult operatives, and spread the available work more widely among the hand-workers and unemployed." *The Making of the English Working Class* (New York: Vintage, 1963), 305.

22. William Cobbett, speech in the House of Commons, July 18, 1833, *Hansard's Parliamentary Debates*, 356 vols. (London: T. C. Hansard, 1831–91), 19:912.

23. Select Committee on Children, Mills and Factories, 1831–32, *British Parliamentary Papers*, 2:99.

24. Ibid., 88–89.

25. Ibid., 99.

26. In addition it was laid down that children between nine and twelve were required to attend school, and could not work more than nine hours a day, and that the older group and women could not work more than twelve hours a day.

27. R. H. Horne, ed., *A New Spirit of the Age*, 2 vols. (London: Smith, Elder and Co., 1844), 1:97.

28. R. Ferguson, "Colliers and collieries," *Quarterly Review* 70 (1842): 159; *The Spectator*, May 14, 1842, 462.

29. Royal Commission on Children's Employment, 1842–43, evidence collected by S. S. Scriven, *British Parliamentary Papers*, 8:103.

30. Horne changed his middle name after meeting a man called "Hengist" in the outback of Australia during his sojourn there from 1852 to 1869.

31. The commissioners were a very mixed bunch—although there were at least four doctors, their numbers also included an economist, a geologist and educational reformer, a scientific writer and antiquarian, and other occasional writers. Horne is thus not so much an oddball as might at first appear.

32. The *Dictionary* also sees fit to tell us that Horne was a "marvellous whistler" (1253).

33. Royal Commission on Children's Employment, 1842–43, report by R. H. Horne, *British Parliamentary Papers*, vol. 11, Q 19, par. 216. The sentence that immediately precedes the lines I have quoted above provides an useful illustration of the expectations Horne brings to his examination of boys: "[Y]ou will find boys who have never heard of such a place as London, nor of Willenhall (which is only three miles distant, and in constant communication with Wolverhampton), who have never heard the name of the Queen,—or who have believed that her Majesty's name was Prince Albert, who have never heard such names as Wellington, Nelson, Bunoparte, King George, & c. ."

34. Horne's implicit belief that underprivileged urban children would be saved if only their true and natural relationship to the rural landscape could be restored does of course continue to hold sway in contemporary twentieth-century thought (witness the *New York Times'* "Fresh Air Fund").

35. Horne presents all of his witnesses' responses in the third person, but other commissioners tend to use the first person.

36. Royal Commission on Children's Employment, 1842–43, evidence collected by R. H. Horne, *British Parliamentary Papers*, vol. 11, Q 8, no. 31

37. The stock characters of commedia dell'arte were appropriated by touring pantomime players in England from the sixteenth century onwards. Horne's question, then, is not about a foreign art form, but, in line with his other inquiries, springs out of his conception of England's rural heritage. Little Nell's connection with this tradition is made explicit by her association with the Punch-and-Judy men (Punch being an anglicized descendent of the Italian Punchinello). See Edwin M. Eigner, *The Dickens Pantomime* (Berkeley and Los Angeles: University of California Press, 1989). Punch is also one of the figures considered in Horne's *New Spirit of the Age* (see n. 58 below).

38. Royal Commission on Children's Employment, 1842–43, evidence collected by R. H. Franks, *British Parliamentary Papers*, 8:458.

39. Royal Commission on Children's Employment, 1842–43, report by R. H. Horne, *British Parliamentary Papers*, vol. 11, q 9, par. 101.

40. It should, however, be pointed out that unlike Mrs. Ellis, Horne presses lightly on the theme of dutiful service (after all, if his little girls know anything at all, they know about this). When the issue of domestic labor *is* addressed, the commissioners clearly tailor their questions or their remarks to a working-class

setting. Horne asks his interviewees if they could cook "a poor man's dinner," while other writers lament that the girls of the coalfields are incapable of cutting out or sewing a dress.

41. *Letters of Elizabeth Barrett Browning addressed to Richard Hengist Horne*, ed. S. R. Townshend, 2 vols. (London: R. Bentley, 1877), 1:80.

42. Elizabeth Barrett Browning, *Complete Works*, ed. Charlotte Porter and Helen Clarke, 6 vols. (New York: Crowell, 1900), 3:53–58. Further references appear in the text.

43. *League*, December 7, 1844, 171–72.

44. "Three years she grew in sun and shower" here joins the web of Wordsworthian allusions in this poem.

45. I am not suggesting that Barrett is doing anything original here—*Oliver Twist* (1837) is perhaps the most famous example of a child's speaking with a middle-class voice and sensibility, despite the extreme deprivation of his early years.

46. For a fascinating reading of Marx's treatment of the worker's body, see "Marx's *Capital* and the Mystery of the Commodity," in Ann Cvetkovich's *Mixed Feelings: Feminism, Mass Culture, and Victorian Sensationalism* (New Brunswick, N.J.: Rutgers University Press, 1992), 165–97.

47. Royal Commission on Children's Employment, 1842–43, report by R. H. Horne, *British Parliamentary Papers*, vol. 11, Q 15, par. 176.

48. Ibid., report by S. S. Scriven, *British Parliamentary Papers*, 8:65.

49. Ibid., 97.

50. Ibid., report by J. C. Symons, *British Parliamentary Papers*, vol. 8, Q 227, 196.

51. Ibid., evidence collected by S. S. Scriven, *British Parliamentary Papers*, nos. 7, 103.

52. Ibid., nos. 10, 103–4; evidence collected by J. C. Symons, nos. 284, 295; evidence collected by S. S. Scriven, no. 103.

53. W. R. Greg, "Protection of children in mines and collieries," *Westminster Review* 38 (July 1842): 123.

54. Royal Commission on Children's Employment, 1842–43, report by J. C. Symons, *British Parliamentary Papers*, vol. 8, Q 116, 181, Q 229, 196.

55. The 1844 Factory Act also *lowered* the minimum age of textile workers to eight and established a half-time system for eight- to ten-year-olds—half work, half school. This act remained in force until 1874, when the minimum age moved up to ten, and ten- to thirteen-year-olds were covered by the half-time system.

56. Horne, *New Spirit*, 1:125–26.

57. Because I am here concentrating primarily upon girls, and only incidentally upon women, my argument stresses the legislators' desire to *protect*. I am thus neglecting the other important strand in this discourse, which insisted that women employees had too much freedom and too much money, and thus had to be *con-*

trolled. See Gallagher, *Industrial Reformation*, 123–25, on Ashley's fears about "unnatural" mannish women; and Mary Poovey, *Uneven Developments: The Ideological Work of Gender in Mid-Victorian England* (Chicago: University of Chicago Press, 1988), 128–29, on the working-class male worry about female workers in the competitive labor market of the "hungry forties."

58. Horne cast his net wide, aiming to catch "opposite classes of intellect and endeavour—from the Actual to the Ideal; from Dickens to Wordsworth; from Southwood Smith to Carlyle; from the etherial wand of Tennyson to the 'touching' baton of Punch; from the unpopular Greek-souled Landor to the popular sea-king Marryatt; from fine poets little known, to old and high reputations; from Dr. Pusey to William Howitt" (x). Horne's friend Barrett is present, sharing a chapter with Caroline Norton (the latter, surprisingly enough, getting the credit for poetic skill in representing "hard and painful scenes of juvenile labours," presumably because "The Cry of the Children" had yet to be composed when Horne was writing the essay). Absent, however, is Mrs. Ellis, although Barrett did all she could to persuade Horne to include her: "Sarah Stickney is the actual Mrs. Ellis (or I am mistaken) who gives twelve editions of instructions to the 'Women'; 'Wives'; 'Daughters'; (and 'Grandmothers' says *Punch*) of our common England. Now, albeit you may opine, in your secret soul, that the race of Mrs. Ellis' disciples runs the risk of being model-women of the most abominable virtue, you can't help, I think, in the meantime, without exposing your work to a charge of imperfection, making mention of a voluminous female writer who has carried books through a dozen or more editions" (*Letters*, 2:154). Barrett's opinion is interesting on a number of counts, not least because it shows both her respect for the marketplace, and the kind of amused distaste for domestic ideology that we might be tempted to think of as our own privileged reaction. See Davidoff and Hall, *Family Fortunes*, for other contemporary responses to Ellis (182).

59. Horne, *New Spirit*, 1:64.

60. Ibid., 1:66.

61. Ibid., 1:65, 68.

62. Supporters of Little Eva's claim for this title should at least concede that Little Nell comes first.

63. " 'We were once so happy . . . I used to read to him by the fireside . . . we often walked in the fields and among the green trees" (97), a weeping Nell tells Mrs. Quilp, but this happy segment of her childhood, complete with domestic felicity and excursions to the countryside, is resolutely confined to memory, and distant from the action of the novel. As John Bowen has argued in "Performing Business, Training Ghosts: Transcoding *Nickleby*," *ELH* 63 (1996): 153–75, despite the popular image of Dickens as the champion of the home and hearth, family life in his novels is fraught by the kind of tensions that ought by rights to be excluded from the domestic sphere. Indeed, the very fact that Nell's first home is a shop, albeit a highly unsuccessful one, makes clear to us the uneasy relation between private and public, between fantasized ideal and actual reality, in this novel.

64. See Penguin edition, appendix, 678.

65. Ibid., 674.

66. Cf. Alexander Welsh, *The City of Dickens* (Oxford: Clarendon Press, 1971), 157, on this particular passage and "the timelessness of the female principle."

67. "Who should feel its force so much as I, in whom your little scholar lives again" (504), asks Nell of the schoolmaster, while the wild figure in the industrial city tells her that "when I saw you in the street to-night, you put me in mind of myself as I was after [Father] died, and made me wish to bring you to the old fire. I thought of those old times again when I saw you sleeping by it" (420).

68. I give only one of many possible examples: "[S]he soothed him with gentle and tender words, smiled at his thinking they could ever part, and rallied him cheerfully upon the jest. He was soon calmed and fell asleep, singing to himself in a low voice, like a little child" (176).

69. If we are being literal-minded, we can note that while the novel begins in the reign of Queen Victoria, it cannot go any further back than 1824, the year of Byron's death—Mrs. Jarley presents an image of the poet (actually "Mary Queen of Scots in a dark wig, white shirt-collar, and male attire" [288]) that generates responses that make it clear that his Lordship is no longer alive. If we are not being literal-minded, we can recognize that the Shropshire village is to all intents and purposes in the Middle Ages.

70. Although, like many things in the novel, the village is not given a proper name, popular tradition identifies Tong as its model.

71. It is worth mentioning that Nell's time on the road brings her into relation with a wide variety of landscapes, and with individuals drawn from all manner of class positions—to name but a few, the working-class bargemen; the educated but impoverished schoolmaster; the entrepreneurial Mrs. Jarley. As the lines describing Nell's relief on reaching the Shropshire village reveal, however, it is, paradoxically, her experience in the land of the *unemployed* industrial poor that haunts her most profoundly as the place of "labour."

72. Hannah More's late-eighteenth-century tracts see no difficulty in equating the girl's service in the factory with the domestic ideal (Gallagher, *Industrial Reformation*, 37–41). The fact that Miss Monflathers's formulations are clearly meant to be ridiculous reflects both a shift in attitudes toward child labor and technological and economic changes in the industries that had traditionally employed children.

73. Anticipating the work of Lewis Carroll, Miss Monflathers is here freely adapting "Against Idleness and Mischief," better known as "How Doth the Little Busy Bee," from Dr. Isaac Watts's *Divine Songs for Children*.

74. Dickens wrote of this section of the novel to his friend John Forster: "You will recognize a description of the road we travelled between Birmingham and Wolverhampton" (*The Letters of Charles Dickens*, ed. M. House and G. Storey [Oxford: Pilgrim Press, 1965], 2:131–32).

75. Charles Dickens, *Hard Times*, ed. David Craig (Harmondsworth: Penguin, 1969).

76. Ibid., 107, 146.

77. The novelist's two distinct approaches to manufacturing England in *The Old Curiosity Shop* and *Hard Times* may be exaggerated, but they are not arbitrary. Regional industries developed in divergent fashions in the first half of the nineteenth century, creating sharply idiosyncratic landscapes that lent themselves to different symbolic treatments. The monumental mills erected by Yorkshire and Lancashire's weaving industries, for example, have no complement in the West Midlands, where small and scattered machine shops tell the story of the haphazard growth of the metalworking trades.

78. The connection is made explicit by the fact that at the end of the story, Dick is heard "to remark at divers subsequent periods that there had been a young lady saving up for him after all" (668), an expression that relates back to his earlier part in Fred Trent's plan to marry him to his sister. As Dick tells Miss Sophy Wackles at the time, "It's a gratifying circumstance which you'll be glad to hear, that a young and lovely girl is growing into a woman expressly on my account, and is now saving up for me" (118).

79. The marked generic differences within the novel explain responses like Thackeray's, who said that he had "never read the Nelly part of *The Old Curiosity Shop* more than once; whereas I have Dick Swiveller and the Marchioness by heart" ("Jerome Paturot," *Fraser's Magazine*, September 1843, 351).

80. True to the *Märchen* that begins her name, the marchioness loses one of her ill-fitting shoes in her successful dash for justice for Kit Nubbles. Nursed back to health by his devoted protégée, Dick uses the proceeds of a recent inheritance to sweep the Marchioness out of the cinders and, by way of a finishing school, off to the altar, whereupon she is newly ennobled by the name of Sophronia Sphynx Swiveller. See Ella Westland, "Little Nell and the Marchioness: Some Functions of Fairy Tale in *The Old Curiosity Shop*," *Dickens Quarterly* 8 (1991): 68–75.

81. Thomas Hood, review of *Master Humphrey's Clock*, *Athenaeum*, November 7, 1840, 887–88.

82. To continue the (anachronistic) analogy between the mining children and the Marchioness, we could also see Quilp's catechizing of the slavey as akin to the commissioners' interviews:

> "Where do you come from?" he said after a long pause, stroking his chin.
> "I don't know"
> "What's your name?"
> "Nothing."
> "Nonsense!" retorted Quilp. "What does your mistress call you when she wants you?"
> "A little devil," said the child. (474)

In the published work, the identity of the Marchioness's parents remains a mystery. The manuscript reveals that Dickens had originally intended to reveal that Sally Brass was the child's mother, with Quilp as the likeliest suspect for the father. Residual traces of these intentions remain in the text.

83. Those interested in the phenomenon of foot fetishism may feel that this statement gives short shrift to the idea of the foot as erotic object. William A. Cohen's examination of the play of hands in *Great Expectations* provides a fine reading of the displacement of sexual energies in a Dickensian text ("Manual Conduct in *Great Expectations*," *ELH* 60 [1993]: 217–59).

84. Gissing also feels compelled to contemplate those feet: "Heaven forbid that I should attribute to Dickens a deliberate allegory; but, having in mind those hapless children who were then being tortured in England's mines and factories, I like to see in Little Nell a type of their sufferings; she, the victim of avarice, dragged with bleeding feet along the hard roads, ever pursued by heartless self-interest and finding her one safe refuge in the grave" (George Gissing, *Charles Dickens: A Critical Study* [London: Blackie, 1898] 177).

85. The following articles are of particular note: Mark Spilka, "Little Nell—Revisited," *Papers of the Michigan Academy of Science, Arts, and Letters* 45 (1960): 427–37; Michael Steig, "The Central Action of *The Old Curiosity Shop*; or, Little Nell Revisited Again," *Literature and Psychology* 15, no. 3 (summer 1965): 163–70; and Leonard Manheim, "Floras and Doras: The Women in Dickens' Novels," *Texas Studies in Language and Literature* 7 (1965): 181–200. In *Child-Loving* Kincaid argues that our culture has constructed the demonized figure of the pedophile in order to avoid the necessity of scrutinizing its own erotic desires for the child. In the reading he gives to *The Old Curiosity Shop* in this text, Kincaid is more interested in examining the eroticization of death, but his general formulation clearly has much to tell us about twentieth-century reactions to Quilp.

86. See the Penguin edition, 682 n. 3.

87. See Robert M. Polhemus, "Comic and Erotic Faith Meet Faith in the Child: Charles Dickens's *The Old Curiosity Shop* ('The Old Cupiosity Shape')," in *Critical Reconstructions: The Relationship of Fiction and Life*, ed. Robert M. Polhemus and Roger B. Henkle (Stanford, Calif.: Stanford University Press, 1994).

88. Nell sits on gravestones so often that I have lost count of exactly how many cemeteries she visits. One quotation must suffice: "[S]he felt a curious kind of pleasure in lingering among these houses of the dead, and read the inscription on the tombs of the good people (a great number of good people were buried there), passing on from one to another with increasing interest" (186). Cf. Robert Pattison's comment in *The Child Figure in English Literature* (Athens: University of Georgia Press, 1978): "Possessed of every virtue, pure beyond the sympathies of modern audiences, [Nell] can no more pass a graveyard than an alcoholic can a bar" (80). As so much of *The Old Curiosity Shop* presents us with the combina-

tion of young children and graveyards, it should come as no surprise that Dickens is unable to deny himself a "We are Seven" moment: "Some young children sported among the tombs, and hid from each other, with laughing faces. They had an infant with them, and had laid it down asleep upon a child's grave, in a little bed of leaves. It was a new grave—the resting place, perhaps of some little creature, who, meek and patient in its illness, had often sat and watched them, and now seemed to their minds scarcely changed" (490).

89. On sexualized relationships between old men and young women or girls, see Davidoff and Hall, *Family Fortunes*, 347–48; and John Kucich, *Excess and Restraint in the Novels of Charles Dickens* (Athens: University of Georgia Press, 1981), 180. Pattison considers Dickens's pairing of the old man and the child to be a figuration of the relationship between the Old and New Testaments (80–87).

90. On the topic of the eroticization of dead (or sleeping) females in the later part of the century, see Bram Dijkstra's *Idols of Perversity: Fantasies of Feminine Evil in Fin-de-Siècle Culture* (Oxford: Oxford University Press, 1986), particularly chap. 2.

91. On this particular scene, see also John A. Stoler, "Affection and Lust in *The Old Curiosity Shop*: Dickens and Mary—Again," *McNeese Review* 35 (1997): 90–102.

92. William Powell Frith, *My Autobiography* (London: Richard Bentley and Son, 1887–88), 3:5.

CHAPTER THREE
THE STONES OF CHILDHOOD: RUSKIN'S "LOST JEWELS"

1. John Ruskin, *Works,* ed. E. T. Cook and Alexander Wedderburn, 39 vols. (London: George Allen, 1903–12), 35:505. Unless otherwise indicated, subsequent citations of Ruskin's works refer to this edition and appear in the text.

2. The reference comes from the Mock Turtle's description of his education in chapter 9 of *Alice in Wonderland*. See Lewis Carroll, *The Complete Works* (London: Nonesuch Press, 1939), 95. All subsequent citations of Carroll's works refer to this edition and will appear in the text.

3. John Ruskin, *Praeterita* (Oxford: Oxford University Press, 1949), xiii–xiv.

4. Important work on Ruskin and the feminine includes Paul L. Sawyer's marvelous study *Ruskin's Poetic Argument: The Design of the Major Works* (Ithaca, N.J.: Cornell University Press, 1985), and his essay "Ruskin and the Matriarchal Logos," in *Victorian Sages and Cultural Discourse: Renegotiating Gender and Power*, ed. Thaïs E. Morgan (New Brunswick, N.J.: Rutgers University Press, 1990); Dinah Birch, "Ruskin's 'Womanly Mind,' " *Essays in Criticism* 38, no. 4 (1988): 308–24, and "*The Ethics of the Dust*: Ruskin's Authorities," *Prose Studies* 12 (1989): 147–58; Sheila Emerson, *Ruskin: The Genesis of Invention* (Cambridge: Cambridge University Press, 1993); and Cathy Shuman, "Different for

Girls: Gender and Professional Authority in Mill, Ruskin, and Dickens," Ph.D. diss., Yale University, 1995.

5. For discussions and analyses of *Praeterita*, see W. G. Collingwood, *The Life of John Ruskin* (London: Methuen, 1900); R. H. Wilenski, *John Ruskin: An Introduction to Further Study of His Life and Work* (London: Faber and Faber, 1933); Edward Alexander, "*Praeterita*: Ruskin's Remembrance of Things Past," *JEGP* 3 (1974): 351–62; Jay Fellows, *The Failing Distance: The Autobiographical Impulse in John Ruskin* (Baltimore: Johns Hopkins University Press, 1975); Gail Griffin, "The Autobiographer's Dilemma: Ruskin's *Praeterita*," in *Interspace and the Inward Sphere: Essays on the Romantic and Victorian Self*, ed. N. A. Anderson and M. E. Weiss (Macomb, Ill.: Western Illinois University Press, 1978); Linda M. Austin, "*Praeterita*: In the Act of Rebellion," *Modern Language Quarterly* 48 (1987): 42–58.

6. See John Dixon Hunt, *The Wider Sea: A Life of John Ruskin* (New York: Viking Press, 1982): "Though the title of his autobiography should accurately be translated as 'first things,' leading presumably to others, [Ruskin] told Kate Greenaway that 'Praeterita means merely Past things' " (394).

7. Paul Sawyer, one of the critics who has written at length about the myth of the garden in Ruskin's work, has pointed out how frequently "the compensatory fantasy of the child secluded in innocence" is invoked as an absolute good (*Ruskin's Poetic Argument*, 287).

8. Francis G. Townsend, "On Reading John Ruskin," in *The Victorian Experience: The Prose Writers*, ed. Richard A. Levine (Athens: Ohio University Press, 1982), 164.

9. Elizabeth Helsinger, "The Structure of Ruskin's *Praeterita*," in *Approaches to Victorian Autobiography*, ed. G. P. Landow (Athens: Ohio University Press, 1979), 88.

10. See Linda Peterson, *Victorian Autobiography: The Tradition of Self-Interpretation* (New Haven: Yale University Press, 1986).

11. See my comments in the introduction on boys' clothing in the nineteenth century.

12. Cf. Sawyer: "The three deaths that conclude Part 1—those of Miss Wardell and two other beautiful young women—symbolize the death of his own youth (as Jessie's death had at an earlier stage" (*Ruskin's Poetic Argument*, 320).

13. Helen Gill Viljoen investigated his background with painstaking care in *Ruskin's Scottish Heritage* (Urbana: University of Illinois Press, 1956).

14. Tim Hilton, *John Ruskin: The Early Years* (New Haven: Yale University Press, 1985); and Van Akin Burd, ed., *The Winnington Letters: John Ruskin's Correspondence with Margaret Alexis Bell and the Children at Winnington Hall* (Cambridge: Harvard University Press, 1969). Further citations of the latter work, abbreviated *WL*, will appear in the text.

15. During their son's childhood, the Ruskins did not adhere strictly to any one denomination: their choice of places of worship appears to have been determined by the Evangelical sympathies of particular clergymen and their own elevation in the English social scale (Hilton, *John Ruskin*, 20). John James and Margaret clearly had respect for their Scottish Presbyterian heritage: they had their son baptized in the Caledonian Chapel, Hatton Garden by a minister of the Church of Scotland and eighteen years later filed a record of his birth in the London Registry of Births for Protestant Dissenters. Hilton, however, remarks that "to place their son at the centre of the Anglican establishment, Christ Church, and to hope that he might become a bishop, was hardly to adhere to the Church of Scotland" (20). In Ruskin's early years the family worshipped at the Episcopal Chapel, Long Acre, and then at the Beresford Chapel, Walworth, where the minister, Edward Andrews, who was also one of Ruskin's first tutors, was an Evangelical Congregationalist. In time they decamped to the Church of England, taking pews first at St. Giles Church, Fleet Street, and then in Camden Chapel. The two principal clergymen at these places of worship, Thomas Dale and Henry Melvill, were both prominent Evangelicals within the established church; the former gentleman replaced Andrews as Ruskin's tutor.

16. See Davidoff and Hall, *Family Fortunes*, 114–16; and Tosh: "In Evangelical discourse the pivotal figure in a boy's upbringing was of course his mother. . . . She was considered better qualified to impart spiritual truths to him, notwithstanding her husband's formal role in family prayers. And her influence was supposed to hold him to a virtuous path even from beyond the grave" (*A Man's Place*, 113).

17. See, however, Gorham on Bible verse learning (*Victorian Girl*, 78), and Davidoff and Hall on the early Victorian middle-class mother's duties of inculcating religious faith in her children (*Family Fortunes*, 175).

18. See Davidoff and Hall, *Family Fortunes*, 234–40; and Tosh, *A Man's Place*, 104–5.

19. Of the featured writers, Ernest Dowson is also sisterless but had a younger brother (Rowland Corbet).

20. After Jane De Quincey died at the age of three, another daughter born later was given the same Christian name (Lindop, *Opium-Eater*, 3).

21. See Gorham, *Victorian Girl*, 22; Davidoff and Hall, *Family Fortunes*, 289–93; and Geoffrey Walford, *The Private Schooling of Girls: Past and Present* (London: Woburn Press, 1993).

22. Hunt, *The Wider Sea*, 261.

23. See Ruskin's letter to C. E. Norton (36:367).

24. The summary that follows is particularly indebted to *The Winnington Letters*, 64–75.

25. Cf. Sawyer: "Rose is in fact the vicarious object of his self-love, in particular of his childhood as a timeless moment before love and duty, and the child's will

and the parent's will were irremediably divided. Possessing her Ruskin could repossess the perfect past in his imperfect middle age" (*Ruskin's Poetic Argument*, 233).

26. See Ruskin's letter to C. E. Norton of March 10, 1863, 36:436.

27. J. A. Froude, *Thomas Carlyle: His Life in London*, 2 vols. (London: Longmans, Green, 1884), 2:298.

28. The words *rose* and *rosy* always carry a very particular charge in all of Ruskin's writings after he had fallen in love with Rose La Touche.

29. For an extremely useful summary of the development of geology as a discipline during the Victorian era, and for an explanation of the incrementalism versus catastrophism debate, see Dennis R. Dean, " 'Through Science to Despair': Geology and the Victorians," *Annals of New York Academy of Sciences*, vol. 360, *Victorian Science and Victorian Values: Literary Perspectives*, ed. James Paradis and Thomas Postlewait (New York: New York Academy of Sciences, 1981).

30. After rocks and gems, the second most prevalent system of representation is probably flower imagery: note the description of the girls in the "Roslyn Chapel" section of *Praeterita* that has already been quoted. *Sesame and Lilies* offers a significantly different system of representation: boys are (amongst other things) rocks that may be chiseled into shape, but "you cannot hammer a girl into anything. She grows as a flower does" (18:131). Acknowledgment must thus be made that Ruskin deploys a variety of metaphorical systems in different texts, but it is interesting to note that even when girls are blooms, they often display a tendency to transform themselves into the more permanent form of jewelry. See, for instance, the description of Emily La Touche later in this chapter. Ruskin's fondness for thinking of her as "a pretty piece of rose-quartz" (see Hunt, *The Wider Sea*, 330), also shows how easily his "wild Irish Rose" could be translated from the botanical to the mineralogical.

31. Here I depart from Sawyer, who maintains that "the device of describing girls in purely aesthetic terms no doubt serves to neutralize erotic emotion" (*Ruskin's Poetic Argument*, 243).

32. Perhaps the best illustration of this point is *Praeterita*'s extended description of the Rhone, which "flows like one lambent jewel . . . fifteen feet thick, of not flowing, but flying water; not water, neither,—melted glacier, rather, one should call it; the force of the ice is with it, and the wreathing of the clouds, the gladness of the sky, and the continuance of Time. . . . here was one mighty wave that was always itself, and every fluted swirl of it, constant as the wreathing of a shell. . . . the ever-answering glow of unearthly aquamarine, ultramarine, violet-blue, gentian-blue, peacock-blue, river-of-paradise blue, glass of a painted window melted in the sun blue and the witch of the Alps flinging the spun tresses of it for ever from her snow. . . . there were pools that shook the sunshine all through them, and were rippled in layers of overlaid ripples, like crystal sand; there were currents that twisted the light into golden braids, and inlaid the threads with tur-

quoise enamel . . . and in the midst of all . . . the dear old decrepit town as safe in the embracing sweep of it as if it were set in a brooch of sapphire" (35:296–97).

33. Letter to Joan Severn, July 29, 1869, Collection of the Ruskin Galleries, Bembridge School, Isle of Wight. On Ruskin's "inclination for baby-talk," see Hunt, *The Wider Sea*, 356. In later years, the Ruskin's family friend Mrs. Simon wrote to Joan Severn on the topic: "[T]he much more manly way of habitual speech & manner had been exchanged for the 'baby-talk' & 'small talk' & a 'talk-down-to-lower-intellects' style had begun [in the 1860s]. It could always be thrown off . . . but he ought never to have left the constant association with his equals, men of the time in their spheres, as he in his—Strength comes by intellectual wrestling—not by uncontradicted talks to a set of adorers & adorers who did not, moreover, understand the true divinity of the God they worshipped. Poor Rose . . . & that horrid Miss Bell etc have led on to this—I am sure" (letter of April 1, 1878, Collection of the Pierpont Morgan Library, New York City, 1771).

CHAPTER FOUR
LEWIS CARROLL AND THE LITTLE GIRL: THE ART OF SELF-EFFACEMENT

1. A notable exception is Carol Mavor, who in *Pleasures Taken: Performances of Sexuality and Loss in Victorian Photographs* (Durham, N.C.: Duke University Press, 1995) deplores this kind of slippage between imaginary and real girls (18).

2. Critics always have difficulties in deciding how they should refer to the Reverend Charles Lutwidge Dodgson/Lewis Carroll. Although he sometimes made exceptions for little girls (see my comments later in this chapter), Dodgson himself was usually insistent that his two selves be kept separate, even to the extent of refusing to accept letters addressed to Lewis Carroll if they were sent to his college in Oxford rather than to his publisher. Primarily for simplicity's sake, but also because I am interested in constructed identities, I shall mainly use the name Carroll in this chapter.

3. See the letter to Agnes Hull, December 10, 1877, in *The Letters of Lewis Carroll*, ed. Morton N. Cohen, with the assistance of Roger Lancelyn Green, 2 vols. (New York: Oxford University Press, 1979), 1:291.

4. Lindsay Smith, *The Politics of Focus: Women, Children, and Nineteenth-Century Photography* (Manchester: Manchester University Press, 1998); and the introduction to *Photography and Cultural Representation*, a special edition of *Textual Practice* 10, no. 1 (1996).

5. Roland Barthes, *Camera Lucida: Reflections on Photography*, trans. Richard Howard (New York: Hill and Wang, 1981).

6. According to Smith, these issues included, but were not limited to, discussion of photography's ontological status in relation to art and science; the relationship of the photographic process to concepts of temporality; the inherent abstraction of the medium evidenced by its inability to harness color; the status of the unitary versus the composite image; the question of "hard" versus "soft" focus; the impli-

cations of the relative ease with which multiple copies of an original could be made, and questions around the dissemination and ownership of such copies (*Textual Practice*, 1–3).

7. Mavor, *Pleasures Taken*, 3.

8. I draw my information on the history of photography primarily from Helmut Gernsheim's *Concise History of Photography*, 3d ed. (New York: Dover, 1986).

9. Quoted in Walter Benjamin, "A Small History of Photography," in *One Way Street and Other Writings*, trans. Edmund Jephcott and Kingsley Shorter (London: Verso, 1985), 255–56.

10. Review of the Photographic Exhibition, 1856–1857, *Photographic Journal*, February 21, 1857, quoted in Helmut Gernsheim's *Lewis Carroll, Photographer* (New York: Chanticleer Press, 1949), 5.

11. See notes 9 and 5. Mavor also makes this move in relation to Barthes (*Pleasures Taken*, 5), but not Benjamin.

12. Benjamin, "Small History of Photography," 247.

13. Barthes, *Camera Lucida*, 67.

14. Smith does not comment on it, but it is worth musing upon the eerie coincidence that both these Victorian children are posed in the liminal space of the conservatory, as if the photograph's act of conserving the child has already been prefigured by the placement of the delicate plant under glass.

15. See Christian Metz's essay "Photography and Fetish," *October* 34 (fall 1985): 81–90.

16. Barthes, *Camera Lucida*, 87.

17. Ibid, 92.

18. Smith, *Politics of Focus*, 6–7.

19. Mavor, *Pleasures Taken*, 6; J. M. Barrie, "A Dedication" to *Peter Pan, or the Boy Who Would Not Grow Up*, in *The Uniform Edition of the Plays of J. M. Barrie* (New York: Scribner's Sons, 1928), xxix.

20. As Susan Sontag remarks in *On Photography* (New York: Farrar, Straus and Giroux, 1977), the absolute reality of the photograph has nevertheless the uncanny effect of transforming it into unreality: "[P]hotographs are a way of imprisoning reality, understood as recalcitrant, inaccessible; of making it stand still. . . . But . . . to possess the world in the form of images is, precisely, to reexperience the unreality and remoteness of the real" (163–64).

21. Barthes, *Camera Lucida*, 85.

22. A revisionist biography of Lewis Carroll, which appeared after I wrote this chapter, has stirred up considerable debate in Carrollian and Victorianist circles, particularly the Victoria listserv. Karoline Leach's book *In the Shadow of the Dreamchild: A New Understanding of Lewis Carroll* (London: Peter Owen, 1999) claims that the image of the little-girl-loving don is a potent myth, created in the first instance by Carroll himself, and then perpetuated by his first biographer, nephew Stuart Collingwood (see *The Life and Letters of Lewis Carroll*, ed. Stuart

Dodgson Collingwood [London: T. F. Unwin, 1898]. Wishing to present a picture of his uncle that would bring no embarrassment to the family, Collingwood, Leach argues, deliberately avoided all mention of Carroll's relationships with women and instead placed particular stress on his special affinity with girls under what she claims was currently understood as the watershed of sexuality, the age of fourteen (see chap. 5 for my own opinion on this question). This face-saving measure, she demonstrates, was subsequently extended and propagated by a series of delicate memoirs and other biographies extolling "St. Lewis, patron of childhood." That such moves should then, in a twentieth century rabidly alert to the whiff of sexual deviancy, lay Carroll wide open to the charge of latent or manifest pedophilia is for Leach a delicious irony: "[T]he lovingly constructed defences of a sacred reputation had become the snares of a worse infamy than [Collingwood et al.] could ever have envisaged" (36). Leach certainly does not wish to deny that Carroll "worshipped the girl image," that he "relished girl beauty, photographed girl nakedness," but maintains that "when he did these things he was not, as in the diagnosis of most biographers, simply expressing sexual and emotional deviancy; he was being a man and an artist of his time, refracting through his own complex personality the social and sexual mores of the age" (62). While I am clearly in sympathy with Leach's desire to see Carroll's girl loving not as individual pathology, but as part of a general cultural tendency, I find that her zeal to reconstruct the don as a red-blooded Casanova encourages her to imagine scenarios (most prominently an adulterous liaision with Alice Liddell's mother) that are just as problematic as the pedophilic myths she criticizes. My own study of Carroll does not really engage with Leach's biographical arguments: it has no stake in discovering the "truth" about the nature or extent of his sexual activities and instead is explicitly concerned with the roles played by little girls in Carroll's literary and photographic art, and the relationship between these constructs and a nineteenth-century fantasy of original femininity. Nevertheless, Leach's account of the complex and frustrating history of missing, obscured, or falsified documentary evidence within Carrollian biography will henceforward make any writer on Carroll wary of making hard-and-fast distinctions between fact and fiction in his life story.

23. Most notable amongst Carroll's defenders are Helmut Gernsheim and Morton N. Cohen. See particularly Gernsheim's preface to the revised edition of *Lewis Carroll, Photographer* (New York: Dover, 1969); and Edward Guiliano's "Lewis Carroll in a Changing World: An Interview with Morten N. Cohen," *English Language Notes* 20 (1982): 97–108.

24. See Rupert Croft-Cooke, *Feasting with Panthers: A New Consideration of Some Late-Victorian Writers* (New York: Holt, Rinehart and Winston, 1967), 156.

25. This statement applies just as much to Leach's speculations as to the more familiar hypotheses about Carroll's predilections (see note 22.)

26. Carroll has been a very popular subject for biographers. The following list includes a number of the works which rehearse, with minor variations, the familiar Carroll story first presented by Collingwood: Langford Reed, *The Life of Lewis Carroll* (London: W. and G. Foyle, 1932); Florence Becker Lennon, *Lewis Carroll* (London: Cassell, 1947); Derek Hudson, *Lewis Carroll: An Illustrated Biography* (London: Constable, 1954); Anne Clark, *Lewis Carroll* (London: Dent, 1979); Morton N. Cohen, *Lewis Carroll: A Biography* (London: Macmillan, 1995); Michael Bakewell, *Lewis Carroll: A Biography* (London: Heinemann, 1996).

27. See the entry for March 18, 1857, in *The Diaries of Lewis Carroll*, ed. Roger Lancelyn Green, 2 vols. (Oxford: Oxford University Press, 1954), 107.

28. Carroll's enthusiasm for croquet, just like his passion for photography, shows him engaging in a thoroughly Victorian phenomenon: the sport was introduced to the British by a Mr. Jaques in 1851.

29. It is interesting to compare this stanza with lines from *The Hunting of the Snark* (1876)—"he thought of his childhood, left far behind / That blissful and innocent state" (691)—and "Puck Found" (1891)—"All too soon will childhood gay / Realize Life's sober sadness" (878).

30. *A Selection from the Letters of Lewis Carroll to His Child-Friends,* ed. Evelyn M. Hatch (London: Macmillan, 1933), 177.

31. Here are a few more examples of Carroll's sentiments on the subject: "with little boys I'm out of my element altogether"; "I am fond of children (except boys)"; "to your small, fat, impertinent, ignorant brother, my hatred" (*Life and Letters*, 393, 416, 424); "whenever you wish to punish your brothers, you will find it very convenient to do so by running the knife into their hands and faces (particularly the end of the nose); you will find it gives a good deal of pain if you run it in hard enough," "I confess I do not admire naked boys in pictures. They always seem to me need clothes" (*Letters*, 642, 947).

32. *Letters*, 455; *Selection of Letters*, 177.

33. This is the same little boy who is given "a violent shake at the end of every line" of the following tender lullaby:

Speak roughly to your little boy,
    And beat him when he sneezes:
He only does it to annoy,
    Because he knows it teases. (62)

34. I am aware of only one photograph composed by Carroll that depicts the photographer himself in the presence of little girls. Carroll appears with Mrs. George MacDonald and her son Greville and three daughters, Mary, Irene, and Grace in a photograph from 1863. Mother and son appear on the far left of the group; Carroll, significantly enough, is allied with neither the adult nor the male but has placed himself in the midst of the little girls, positioning Irene and Grace

so that they obscure the full length of his body. Carroll's handful of studies of men and girls are, predictably enough, father-and-daughter portraits: examples include the photographs of George and Lily MacDonald, Arthur and Agnes Hughes, and the Reverend C. Barker and his daughter May. Carroll recorded in his diary that he thought these last two studies "splendid" and "first rate" (*Diaries*, 206, 216), but others have not shared his opinion. "Less happy," comments Gernsheim, "are the few pictures in which a young girl has been posed with her father." He then speculates that "it must be remembered that such groups were taken for the sake of the daughter—papa is quite obviously only an appendage with which Lewis Carroll would much rather have dispensed" (*Lewis Carroll, Photographer*, 4). Whether or not we share Gernsheim's feelings, it is fair to say that the easy atmosphere of Carroll's best photographs of girls is certainly absent from at least the Barker and MacDonald double portraits: all the parties involved appear remarkably tense.

35. I discuss the issue of Carroll's fantasies about the little girl's power more fully in chapter 5.

36. See in particular discussions in Smith, *The Politics of Focus*; Mavor, *Pleasures Taken*; Gernsheim's *Lewis Carroll, Photographer*; and Nina Auerbach, "Falling Alice, Fallen Women, and Victorian Dream Children," in *Romantic Imprisonment: Women and Other Glorified Outcasts* (New York: Columbia University Press, 1986). See also Kincaid, *Child-Loving*, on Carroll and photography, 290, 303, and more broadly on the connections between the medium and pedophilia, 227–28.

37. See the series of letters to Mr. A. L. and Mrs. Mayhew in May and June 1879 (*Letters*, 337–41, 342–43), and further comments in chapter 5.

38. Mavor, *Pleasures Taken*, 29.

39. See for instance Anne Higonnet, *Pictures of Innocence: The History and Crisis of Ideal Childhood* (London: Thames and Hudson, 1998), 123–25.

40. Morton N. Cohen, *Lewis Carroll, Photographer of Children: Four Nude Studies* (New York: Potter, 1978).

41. See Auerbach, "Falling Alice," 168; and Mavor, *Pleasures Taken*, 11–14.

42. See U. C. Knoepflmacher, "The Balancing of Child and Adult: An Approach to Victorian Fantasies for Children," *Nineteenth-Century Literature* 37, no. 4 (1983): 497–530, for a broader consideration of this general topic.

43. An additional prefatory poem, "Christmas Greetings [From a Fairy to a Child]" was added to the 1867 edition of *Alice in Wonderland*.

44. Numerous biographers have pointed out that metereological records give the lie to the myth of that sunny day: the afternoon in question was apparently wet and miserable.

45. For readings of the closing moments of *Alice in Wonderland*, see for example Lionel Morton, "Memory in the Alice Books," *Nineteenth-Century Fiction* 33 (1978): 285–308; George Dimock, "Childhood's End: Lewis Carroll and the Image of the Rat," *Word and Image* 8, no. 3 (1992): 183–205; and Susan Sherer,

"Secrecy and Autonomy in Lewis Carroll," *Philosophy and Literature* 20 (1996): 1–19. Dimock's essay pays close attention to Carroll's original handwritten and drawn version of *Alice's Adventures under Ground*, and its conclusion, a photograph of the seven-year-old Alice Liddell, under which lies Carroll's drawing of the same photograph (193–96). As he remarks, because five years had passed between the taking of the photograph and Carroll's presentation of the manuscript to his muse, "the twelve-year-old Alice, poised on the verge of adolescence and adult sexuality, will be looking at herself as she was at seven" (194). This act of imagined looking, then, repeats, albeit in less polarized form, the split between the child Alice and the older Alice that appears in the work's final paragraph.

46. For analyses of this scene, see for example Morton, "Memory in Alice Books"; U. C. Knoepflmacher, "Revisiting Wordsworth: Lewis Carroll's 'The White Knight's Song,' " *Victorians Institute Journal* 14 (1986): 1–20; Donald Rackin, "Love and Death in Carroll's Alice," in *Modern Critical Views: Lewis Carroll*, ed. Harold Bloom (New York: Chelsea House, 1987); and Sherer, "Secrecy and Autonomy."

47. Calling *Sylvie and Bruno* the later work belies the complexity of its composition history. Chapters 14 and 15, "Fairy Sylvie" and "Bruno's Revenge," began life as a fairy tale that Carroll wrote in 1867 for Mrs. Gatty's publication, *Aunt Judy's Magazine*. The origin of the work, which was to grow to over four hundred pages and to be published in two halves, thus falls squarely between the celebrated first telling of Alice's adventures to Alice Liddell and her sisters in 1862, and the appearance of *Through the Looking-Glass* in 1872. Only in 1874, Carroll tells us in the preface to *Sylvie and Bruno*, did he think of making the little fairy-tale "the nucleus of a longer story" (255). He then "jotted down, at odd moments, all sorts of odd ideas, and fragments of dialogue," eventually amassing "a huge unwieldy mass of litterature—if the reader will kindly excuse the spelling—which only needed stringing together, upon the thread of a consecutive story, to constitute the book" (256). Because "the story had to grow out of the incidents, not the incidents out of the story" (256), the task of organization, Carroll declares, was formidable and took more than ten years to complete. *Sylvie and Bruno*, then, has claims to represent both a midway stage between *Wonderland* and *Looking-Glass*, and the endpoint of Carroll's writing career.

48. For valuable analyses of *Sylvie and Bruno*, see for example Jan B. Gordon, "Lewis Carroll, the *Sylvie and Bruno* Books, and the Nineties: The Tyranny of Textuality," in *Lewis Carroll: A Celebration*, ed. Edward Guiliano (New York: Potter, 1982); Jean Gattegno, "*Sylvie and Bruno*, or the Inside and the Outside," in Guiliano, *Celebration*; and Edmund Miller, "The *Sylvie and Bruno* Books as Victorian Novel," in Bloom, *Modern Critical Views*. Leach is one of the few Carroll biographers interested in the work: she trawls it for evidence to support her hypothesis that Carroll was obsessed with Mrs. Lorina Liddell.

49. This is also the case in *The Ethics of the Dust*, which has even less interest in paternal metaphors.

CHAPTER FIVE
A "NEW 'CRY OF THE CHILDREN' ": LEGISLATING INNOCENCE IN THE 1880S

1. *The Letters of Ernest Dowson*, ed. Desmond Flower and Henry Maas (London: Cassell, 1967), 162, 221.

2. Robert Louis Stevenson, *Dr Jekyll and Mr Hyde and Other Stories*, ed. Jenni Calder (Harmondsworth: Penguin, 1979), 31. All further citations are to this edition and appear in the text.

3. Stevenson thanks W. E. Henley for sending him the "wonderful" *Pall Mall Gazette* series on July 10, 1885 (see *The Letters of Robert Louis Stevenson*, ed. Bradford A. Booth and Ernest Mehew, 8 vols. [New Haven: Yale University Press, 1994–95], 5:119); he wrote the novella in the September and October 1885 (see Martin A. Danahay's introduction to *The Strange Case of Dr. Jekyll and Mr. Hyde* [Ontario: Broadview Press, 1999], 15.)

4. See Eve Kosofsky Sedgwick's *Between Men: English Literature and Male Homosocial Desire* (New York: Columbia University Press, 1985). *Dr. Jekyll and Mr. Hyde* is now frequently referred to in gay and gender studies criticism as a parallel text not only to *Dorian Gray* but also to Henry James's "The Beast in the Jungle" (1903): see for instance Richard Dellamora, *Masculine Desire: The Sexual Politics of Victorian Aestheticism* (Chapel Hill: University of North Carolina Press, 1990), 196. For studies of *Dr. Jekyll and Mr. Hyde* that are attentive to issues of sexuality, see Stephen Heath, "Psychopathia Sexualis: Stevenson's *Strange Case*," *Critical Quarterly* 28, nos. 1–2 (spring–summer 1986): 93–108; and Elaine Showalter's discussion of Stevenson in *Sexual Anarchy: Gender and Culture at the Fin de Siecle* (Harmondsworth: Penguin, 1990).

5. See Jerry Phillips's "The Mem Sahib, the Worthy, the Rajah, and His Minions: Some Reflections on the Class Politics of *The Secret Garden*," *The Lion and the Unicorn* 17 (1993): 168–94, for an illuminating discussion of the justification for, and the potential benefits of, what he calls "the allegorical inference" in contemporary literary criticism.

6. See Edward J. Bristow, *Vice and Vigilance: Purity Movements in Britain since 1700* (Dublin: Gill and Macmillan, 1977), 61. Glen Petrie's *A Singular Iniquity: The Campaigns of Josephine Butler* (New York: Viking, 1971) is also an useful source of information about the social purity movement and connected legislation.

7. This act reaffirmed that it was a felony for a man to have sex with a girl under ten, and a misdemeanor if she were between ten and twelve years of age. For a summary of the act's other provisions, which primarily benefited well-to-do families whose daughters were enticed away by fortune-hunters, see Deborah Gorham's essay "The 'Maiden Tribute of Modern Babylon' Re-examined: Child Prostitution and the Idea of Childhood in Late-Victorian England, *Victorian Studies* 21 (spring 1978): 353–79. I also draw on Gorham's essay in my later discussion of the "Maiden Tribute."

8. See Petrie, *A Singular Iniquity*, 113.

9. Ibid., 116.

10. See Bristow, *Vice and Vigilance*, 91.

11. See Petrie, *A Singular Iniquity*, 224.

12. "The Maiden Tribute of Modern Babylon," *Pall Mall Gazette*, July 6, 1885. All further references will appear in the text, cited by date.

13. Judith R. Walkowitz, *City of Dreadful Delight: Narratives of Sexual Danger in Late-Victorian London* (London: Virago, 1992), 83.

14. Walkowitz devotes a considerable portion of her chapter on the "Maiden Tribute" in *City of Dreadful Delight* to the examination of these very issues.

15. See Samuel Richardson, *Clarissa; or, The History of a Young Lady*, ed. Angus Ross (Harmondsworth: Penguin, 1985), 1008.

16. Frances Ferguson, "Rape and the Rise of the Novel," *Representations* 20 (1987): 88–112.

17. See Carolyn Steedman's discussions of the avatars of Mignon, both in *Childhood, Culture, and Class in Britain: Margaret McMillan, 1860–1931* (New Brunswick, N.J.: Rutgers University Press, 1990), 76–80, and *Strange Dislocations*. Steedman does not discuss Emily and her fondness for "mignonette," but her general formulations provide an important context for a full understanding of the story.

18. Here, as elsewhere, Stead's narrative uncritically reinforces the idea of the singular *attractiveness* of innocence.

19. The words are borrowed by Wordsworth from Horatio's description of the ghost of Hamlet's father.

20. See, for instance, Josephine Butler's "Letter to my Countrywomen, Dwelling in the Farmsteads and Cottages of England" (1871) and Elizabeth Blackwell's chapter "On the physiological laws which influence the physical and mental growth of sex; and on the social results of neglecting these laws" from *The Moral Education of the Young in Relation to Sex* (1879), both of which are reprinted in *The Sexuality Debates*, ed. Sheila Jeffreys (London: Routledge and Kegan Paul, 1987).

21. Jeffreys, *The Sexuality Debates*, 359. See also Gorham, *Victorian Girl*, 13 n. 20, for the relatively late introduction of the concept of adolescence in the nineteenth century's changing definitions of girlhood. John R. Gillis's *Youth and History: Tradition and Change in European Age Relations, 1770–Present* (New York: Academic Press, 1974) is the landmark study of changing perceptions of male youth in this period.

22. It is one of Stead's favorite themes to insist that the material he is uncovering will incite revolution, but significantly enough, he is always talking about a moral, not an economic, revolution.

23. My construction here owes a debt to one aspect of Kincaid's general paradigm in *Child-Loving*.

24. Only one diary entry, on October 18, appears between July 20 and December 21. Significantly enough, it makes no mention of current events but shows Ruskin in retrospective mode, as the following representative sentence reveals: "The entirely happy times at Thun, with green field at back. Drive to Stockhorn with my Father—when?" *The Diaries of John Ruskin*, ed. Joan Evans and John Howard Whitehouse, 3 vols. (Oxford: Oxford University Press, 1956), 3:1117.

25. The fact that this vision of rock should replace the experiences and recording of day-to-day life merits further examination. See the discussion of stone imagery and its connection with little girls in chapter 3.

26. John Ruskin, *Works*, 37:540.

27. In line with the thematics of this project and the topic of chapter 2, it is interesting that Ruskin should represent the foe he is unable to combat as *The Old Curiosity's Shop*'s Quilp, Dickens's demonized child-predator par excellence (*The Diaries of John Ruskin*, 3:1123).

28. See *Letters of Lewis Carroll*, 586–87, 599–600.

29. Because this article, although clearly referenced in Dodgson's diary, has never been reprinted, I provide its full text in an appendix.

30. See "'Take Back Your Mink': Lewis Carroll, Child Masquerade, and the Age of Consent," *Art History* 16, no. 3 (September 1993): 369–85 n. 3, reprinted in *The Politics of Focus*. Although Smith's essay considers some of the same materials that I am examining in this chapter, she does not refer to the *St. James's Gazette* letter.

31. See my discussion of the same dynamic in chapter 4.

32. See Steedman, *Strange Dislocations*, chap. 8, for a fuller consideration of "Children of the Stage."

33. The fact that Isa Bowman stayed at Carroll's holiday lodgings when she was between the ages of fifteen and nineteen is one of the pieces of evidence Leach uses to support her hypothesis that the clergyman was not primarily interested in "little" girls (see chap. 4, n. 22).

34. As quoted in *The Life and Letters of Lewis Carroll*, 180–81.

35. "The Cult of the Child" is reprinted in an appendix of Dowson's *Letters*, 433–35.

36. Dowson, *Letters*, 142.

37. Six years old at the time of this triumph, Minnie would thus have been unable to perform at all if the proposed ruling had been in effect a year earlier, and, even if she had been granted a special license for the production when she had attained the age of seven, would have discovered that her pay packet contained a maximum of two pounds a week, rather than the princely sum of ten pounds that she actually had received. (As an indicator of the contemporary theatrical climate, it is also interesting to note that this same play also featured the dramatic talents of a two-year-old, playing a younger version of Mignon who is mysteriously discovered one night in Sergeant-Major Bootle's bed. Fortunately this was a non-

speaking role.) Carroll, incidentally, found himself "a little disappointed with Minnie Terry" in *Bootle's Baby*. In his opinion, as he confided to his journal on July 2, 1888, "she recites her speeches, not very clearly, without looking at the person addressed" (*Diaries of Lewis Carroll*, 460). In *Strange Dislocations* Steedman discusses *Bootle's Baby* at some length and Minnie Terry briefly, but she does not comment on Dowson's passion for both play and performer.

38. Dowson, *Letters*, 116.

39. Ibid., 118.

40. *The Poetry of Ernest Dowson*, ed. Desmond Flower (Cranbury, N.J.: Associated University Presses, 1970), 167, 120.

41. Ibid., 52.

42. Dowson, *Letters*, 213.

43. Sonnet 4 appeared in the magazine *London Society*, November 1886; Sonnet 7 was published in Dowson's second and last book of verse, *Decorations* (London: Leonard Smithers, 1899).

44. *Poetry of Ernest Dowson*, 47. In chapter 4 of *City of Dreadful Delight*, Walkowitz demonstrates that the charged atmosphere of fin de siècle London made any female's appearance on certain streets a morally dubious—and in certain cases, a criminally liable—act.

45. *Poetry of Ernest Dowson*, 146.

46. *Poetry of Ernest Dowson*, 183. In the "Maiden Tribute" Stead provides numerous illustrations of the disturbing prevalence of this superstition.

47. *Poetry of Ernest Dowson*, 149.

48. This is not to deny that all the other phases of the phenomenon had been troubled in their own particular ways as well.

49. The very title of the series, of course, is ample evidence of the bias. Stead chooses not to expand on the fact that in the story of the Minotaur, a tribute of "*seven youths* and seven maidens" was demanded (emphasis added). But as I imply at the beginning of the chapter, in the twentieth century, historical, and indeed literary, discussion of the Criminal Law Amendment Act of 1885, in a way, redressed the gender imbalance: the Labouchère Amendment attracted more interest than the raising of the age of consent for girls.

50. Compare Nelson's arguments in *Boys Will Be Girls* about the rise of the masculine hero in boys' fiction in this period (see note 27 of the introduction) and Tosh's description of the demise of domesticated masculinity in the era of high imperialism after 1880 (*A Man's Place*, 7).

For considerations of the ways in which the cultural category of girlhood is redefined from the 1880s onwards, see especially Carol Dyhouse, *Girls Growing Up in Late Victorian and Edwardian England* (London: Routledge and Kegan Paul, 1981); and Sally Mitchell, *The New Girl: Girls' Culture in England, 1880–1915* (New York: Columbia University Press, 1995).

51. The helmet is not only whimsical, but nonsensical: its wings point the wrong way.

52. I draw my information about the Shaftesbury Memorial from Richard Dorment's *Alfred Gilbert: Sculptor and Goldsmith* (London: Royal Academy of Arts in association with Weidenfeld and Nicolson, 1986), 135–43.

53. For an illuminating discussion of the deployment of the figure of the adolescent boy by homosexual men and women writers at the end of the nineteenth century, see Martha Vicinus, "The Adolescent Boy: Fin-de-Siècle Femme Fatale?" in *Victorian Sexual Dissidence*, ed. Richard Dellamora (Chicago: University of Chicago Press, 1999). On the boy's adventure story and general cultural fascination with boyhood in this period, see Joseph Bristow's excellent *Empire Boys: Adventures in a Man's World* (London: HarperCollins, 1991).

Works Cited

PRIMARY SOURCES

Barrett Browning, Elizabeth. *Complete Works*. Ed. Charlotte Porter and Helen A. Clarke. 6 vols. New York: Crowell, 1900.

Letters of Elizabeth Barrett Browning addressed to Richard Hengist Horne. Ed. S. R. Townshend. 2 vols. London: R. Bentley, 1877.

Barrie, J. M. *Peter Pan; or, The Boy Who Would Not Grow Up*. In *The Uniform Edition of the Plays of J. M. Barrie*. New York: Scribner's Sons, 1928.

Blackstone, William. *Commentaries*. Oxford: Clarendon Press, 1765–69.

British Parliamentary Papers. Ed. P. Ford and G. Ford. Shannon: Irish University Press, 1968–70.

Carpenter, Mary. *Juvenile Delinquents, Their Condition and Treatment*. London: W. and F. G. Cash, 1853.

Carroll, Lewis. *The Complete Works*. London: Nonesuch Press, 1939.

———. *The Diaries of Lewis Carroll*. Ed. Roger Lancelyn Green. Oxford: Oxford University Press, 1954.

———. *The Letters of Lewis Carroll*. 2 vols. Ed. Morton N. Cohen. London: Macmillan, 1979.

———. *The Life and Letters of Lewis Carroll*. Ed. Stuart Dodgson Collingwood. London: T. F. Unwin, 1898.

———. *A Selection from the Letters of Lewis Carroll to His Child-Friends*. Ed. Evelyn M. Hatch. London: Macmillan, 1933.

———. "Whoso Shall Offend One of These Little Ones . . ." Letter to *St. James's Gazette*, July 22, 1885.

Chitty, J. *Treatise on the Game Laws and on Fisheries*. London: W. Clarke and J. Reed, 1812.

Cobbett, William. Speech in the House of Commons, July 18, 1833.

Coleridge, Samuel Taylor. *Biographia Literaria*. London: Dent, 1965.

De Quincey, Thomas. *The Collected Writings of Thomas De Quincey*. Ed. David Masson. 14 vols. Edinburgh: A. and C. Black, 1889–90.

———. *Confessions of an English Opium Eater and Other Writings*. Ed. Aileen Ward. New York: Signet Classics, 1966.

Defoe, Daniel. *A Tour through the Whole Island of Great Britain, 1724–26*. New York: Garland, 1975.

Dickens, Charles. *Hard Times*. Ed. David Craig. Harmondsworth: Penguin, 1969.

———. *The Letters of Charles Dickens*. Ed. M. House and G. Storey. Oxford: Pilgrim Press, 1965.

———. *The Old Curiosity Shop*. Ed. Malcolm Andrews. Harmondsworth: Penguin, 1972.

Dowson, Ernest. *Decorations*. London: Leonard Smithers, 1899.

————. *The Letters of Ernest Dowson*. Ed. Desmond Flower and Henry Maas. London: Cassell, 1967.

————. *The Poetry of Ernest Dowson*. Ed. Desmond Flower. Cranbury, N.J.: Associated University Presses, 1970.

Ellis, Havelock. *Studies in the Psychology of Sex*. 7 vols. Philadelphia: F. A. Davis, 1904–28.

Ellis, Sarah Stickney. *The Daughters of England, Their Position in Society, Character and Responsibilities*. London: Fischer, Son and Co., 1843.

Emerson, Ralph Waldo. *English Traits*. In *The Complete Works*. Ed. E. W. Emerson. Boston: Houghton and Mifflin, 1903–4.

Ferguson, R. "Colliers and Collieries." *Quarterly Review* 70 (1842): 159.

Frith, William Powell. *My Autobiography*. London: Richard Bentley and Son, 1887–88.

Froude, J. A. *Thomas Carlyle: His Life in London*. 2 vols. London: Longmans, Green, 1884.

Gissing, George. *Charles Dickens: A Critical Study*. London: Blackie, 1898.

Greg, W. R. "Protection of children in mines and collieries." *Westminster Review* 38 (July 1842).

Hansard's Parliamentary Debates. 356 vols. London: T. C. Hansard, 1831–91.

Hill, M., and C. F. Cornwallis. *Two Prize Essays on Juvenile Delinquency*. London: Smith, Elder, 1853.

Hill, M. D. "Practical Suggestions to the Founders of Reformatory Schools." In *On the Reformation of Young Offenders*, by J. C. Symons. London: Routledge, 1855.

Hill, R. Davenport, and F. Davenport Hill. *The Recorder of Birmingham: A Memoir of Matthew Davenport Hill*. London: Macmillan, 1878.

Hood, Thomas. Review of *Master Humphrey's Clock*. *Athenaeum*, November 7, 1840, 887–88.

Horne, R. H., ed. *A New Spirit of the Age*. 2 vols. London: Smith, Elder and Co., 1844.

Howard, John. *State of the Prisons of England and Wales*. Warrington: W. Eyres, 1777.

Jameson, Anna. Review of the *Report and Appendices of the Children's Employment Commission*. *Athenaeum*, March 4, 11, and 18, 1843.

Keble, John. *Lectures on Poetry, 1832–41*. Trans. E. K. Francis. Oxford: Clarendon Press, 1912.

League, December 7, 1844.

London Society, November 1886.

M., A. B. "Wordsworth the Christian Poet." *Christian Examiner* 49 (1850): 104.

Oliphant, Margaret. *The Literary History of England*. London: Macmillan and Co., 1882.

Pennant, Thomas. *A Tour in Scotland, and Voyage to the Hebrides, 1772*. Chester: John Monk, 1774.

Punch, February 28, 1852.

Review of *The Photographic Exhibition, 1856–1867*. *Photographic Journal*, February 21, 1867.

Review of *The Prelude*, by William Wordsworth. *Eclectic Review* 28 (1850): 550–62.

Review of *The Prelude*, by William Wordsworth. *Graham's Magazine* (Philadelphia), 37 (1850): 322–23.

Review of *The Prelude*, by William Wordsworth. *Tait's Edinburgh Magazine* 17 (1850): 521–27.

Roe, A. S. *The Star and the Cloud: Or a Daughter's Love*. New York: Derby and Jackson, 1857.

Richardson, Samuel. *Clarissa; or, The History of a Young Lady*. Ed. Angus Ross. Harmondsworth: Penguin, 1985.

Robins, S. *A Letter to the Right Honourable Lord John Russell on the Necessity and Mode of State Assistance in the Education of the People*. London: Ridgway, 1851.

Ruskin, John. *The Diaries of John Ruskin*. Ed. Joan Evans and John Howard Whitehouse. 3 vols. Oxford: Oxford University Press, 1956.

———. Letter to Joan Severn, July 29, 1869. Collection of the Ruskin Galleries. Bembridge School, Isle of Wight.

———. *Praeterita*. Intro. Kenneth Clark. Oxford: Oxford University Press, 1949.

———. *Royal Academy Notes*. London: Smith and Elder and Co., 1856.

———. *The Winnington Letters: John Ruskin's Correspondence with Margaret Alexis Bell and the Children at Winnington Hall*. Ed. Van Akin Burd. Cambridge: Harvard University Press, 1969.

———. *Works*. Ed. E. T. Cook and Alexander Wedderburn. 39 vols. London: George Allen, 1903–12.

Simon, Mrs. John. Letter to Joan Severn, April 1, 1878. Collection of the Pierpont Morgan Library, New York City, 1771.

Spectator, May 14, 1842.

Stead, W. T. "The Maiden Tribute of Modern Babylon." *Pall Mall Gazette*, July 6–9, 1885.

Stevenson, Robert Louis. *Dr. Jekyll and Mr. Hyde and Other Stories*. Ed. Jenni Calder. Harmondsworth: Penguin, 1979.

———. *The Letters of Robert Louis Stevenson*. Ed. Bradford A. Booth and Ernest Mehew. 8 vols. New Haven: Yale University Press, 1994–95.

———. *The Strange Case of Dr. Jekyll and Mr. Hyde*. Intro. Martin A. Danahay. Ontario: Broadview Press, 1999.

Wordsworth, William. *The Poetical Works of William Wordsworth*. Ed. Ernest de Selincourt and Helen Darbishire. 5 vols. Oxford: Clarendon Press, 1940–49.

———. *The Prelude, 1799, 1805, 1850*. Ed. Jonathan Wordsworth, M. H. Abrams, and Stephen Gill. New York: Norton, 1979.

Wordsworth, William, and Samuel Taylor Coleridge. *Lyrical Ballads.* Ed. R. L. Brett and A. R. Jones. London: Methuen, 1963.

SECONDARY SOURCES

Abrams, M. H., et al., eds. *The Norton Anthology of English Literature.* 5th ed. Vol. 2. New York: Norton, 1962.

Adams, James Eli. *Dandies and Desert Saints: Styles of Victorian Manhood.* Ithaca, N.Y.: Cornell University Press, 1995.

Alexander, Edward. "*Praeterita*: Ruskin's Remembrance of Things Past." *JEGP* 3 (1974): 351–62.

Ariès, Philippe. *Centuries of Childhood: A Social History of Family Life.* Trans. Robert Baldick. New York: Knopf, 1962.

Auerbach, Nina. "Falling Alice, Fallen Women, and Victorian Dream Children." In *Romantic Imprisonment: Women and Other Glorified Outcasts.* New York: Columbia University Press, 1986.

Austin, Linda M. "*Praeterita*: In the Act of Rebellion." *Modern Language Quarterly* 48 (1987): 42–58.

Bahti, Timothy. "Wordsworth's Rhetorical Theft." In *Romanticism and Language.* Ed. Arden Reed. Ithaca, N.Y.: Cornell University Press, 1984

Bakewell, Michael. *Lewis Carroll: A Biography.* London: Heinemann, 1996.

Barrell, John. *The Infection of Thomas De Quincey: A Psychopathology of Imperialism.* New Haven: Yale University Press, 1991.

Barthes, Roland. *Camera Lucida: Reflections on Photography.* Trans. Richard Howard. New York: Hill and Wang, 1981.

Beattie, J. M. *Crime and the Courts in England, 1660–1800.* Princeton: Princeton University Press, 1986.

Benjamin, Walter. "A Small History of Photography." In *One Way Street and Other Writings*, trans. Edmund Jephcott and Kingsley Shorter, 255–56. London: Verso, 1985.

Berry, Laura C. "Best Regulated Families: Victorian Social Welfare and the Novel." Ph.D. diss., University of California, Berkeley, 1992.

Birch, Dinah. "*The Ethics of the Dust*: Ruskin's Authorities." *Prose Studies* 12 (1989): 147–58.

———. "Ruskin's Womanly Mind." *Essays in Criticism* 38, no. 4 (1988): 308–24.

Bowen, John. "Performing Business, Training Ghosts: Transcoding *Nickleby*." *ELH* 63 (1996): 153–75.

Branca, Patricia. *Silent Sisterhood: Middle-Class Women in the Victorian Home.* London: Croom Helm, 1975.

Bristow, Edward J. *Vice and Vigilance: Purity Movements in Britain since 1700.* Dublin: Gill and Macmillan, 1977.

Bristow, Joseph. *Empire Boys: Adventures in a Man's World*. London: Harper Collins, 1991.

Broughton, Trev Lynn. *Men of Letters, Writing Lives: Masculinity and Literary Auto/Biography in the Late Victorian Period*. London: Routledge, 1999.

Carlebach, Julius. *Caring for Children in Trouble*. London: Routledge and Kegan Paul, 1970.

Clark, Anne. *Lewis Carroll*. London: Dent, 1979.

Cohen, Morton N. *Lewis Carroll: A Biography*. London: Macmillan, 1995.

———. *Lewis Carroll, Photographer of Children: Four Nude Studies*. New York: Potter, 1978.

Cohen, William A. "Manual Conduct in *Great Expectations*." *ELH* 60 (1993): 217–59.

Collings, David. "Characters of Danger and Desire: Deviant Authorship in the 1799 *Prelude*." In *Wordsworthian Errancies: The Poetics of Cultural Dismemberment*. Baltimore: Johns Hopkins University Press, 1994.

Collingwood, W. G. *The Life of John Ruskin*. London: Methuen, 1900.

Cornish W. R., and G. de N. Clark. *Law and Society in England, 1750–1950*. London: Sweet and Maxwell, 1989.

Coveney, Peter. *The Image of Childhood: The Individual and Society: A Study of the Theme in English Literature*. Harmondsworth: Penguin, 1967.

Croft-Cooke, Rupert. *Feasting with Panthers: A New Consideration of Some Late-Victorian Writers*. New York: Holt, Rinehart and Winston, 1967.

Cunningham, Hugh. *The Children of the Poor: Representations of Childhood since the Seventeenth Century*. Oxford: Blackwell, 1991.

Cvetkovich, Anne. "Marx's Capital and the Mystery of the Commodity." In *Mixed Feelings: Feminism, Mass Culture, and Victorian Sensationalism*. New Brunswick, N.J.: Rutgers University Press, 1992.

Danahay, Martin A. Intro. to *The Strange Case of Dr. Jekyll and Mr. Hyde*. Ontario: Broadview Press, 1999.

Davidoff, Leonore, and Catherine Hall. *Family Fortunes: Men and Women of the English Middle Class, 1780–1850*. Chicago: University of Chicago Press, 1987.

Dean, Dennis R. " 'Through Science to Despair': Geology and the Victorians." In *Annals of New York Academy of Sciences*. Vol. 360, *Victorian Science and Victorian Values: Literary Perspectives*. Ed. James Paradis and Thomas Postlewait. New York: New York Academy of Sciences, 1981.

DeLacy, Margaret E. "Grinding Men Good? Lancashire's Prisons at Mid-Century." In *Policing and Punishment in Nineteenth-Century Britain*. Ed. Victor Bailey. London: Croom Helm, 1981.

Dellamora, Richard. *Masculine Desire: The Sexual Politics of Victorian Aestheticism*. Chapel Hill, North Carolina: The University of North Carolina Press, 1990.

Dijkstra, Bram. *Idols of Perversity: Fantasies of Evil in Fin-de-Siecle Culture*. New York: Oxford University Press, 1986.

Dimock, George. "Childhood's End: Lewis Carroll and the Image of the Rat." *Word and Image* 8, no. 3 (1992): 183–205.

Dorment, Richard. *Alfred Gilbert: Sculptor and Goldsmith.* London: Royal Academy of Arts in Association with Weidenfeld and Nicolson, 1986.

Dyhouse, Carol. *Girls Growing Up in Late Victorian and Edwardian England.* London: Routledge and Kegan Paul, 1981.

Eigner, Edwin M. *The Dickens Pantomime.* Berkeley and Los Angeles: University of California Press, 1989.

Emerson, Sheila. *Ruskin : The Genesis of Invention.* Cambridge: Cambridge University Press, 1993.

Fellows, Jay. *The Failing Distance: The Autobiographical Impulse in John Ruskin.* Baltimore: Johns Hopkins University Press, 1975.

Ferguson, Frances. "Rape and the Rise of the Novel." *Representations* 20 (1987): 88–112.

Flint, Kate. "Blindness and Insight: Millais' *The Blind Girl* and the Limits of Representation." *Journal of Victorian Culture* 1, no. 1 (1996): 1–15.

Foucault, Michel. *Discipline and Punish: The Birth of the Prison.* Trans. Alan Sheridan. New York: Pantheon, 1977.

———. *The History of Sexuality.* Vol. 1: *An Introduction.* Trans. Robert Hurley. New York: Pantheon, 1978.

Gallagher, Catherine. *The Industrial Reformation of English Fiction, 1832–1867.* Chicago: University of Chicago Press, 1985.

Garlitz, Barbara. "The Immortality Ode: Its Cultural Progeny." *Studies in English Literature* 6 (autumn 1966): 639–49.

Gattegno, Jean. "*Sylvie and Bruno*, or the Inside and the Outside." In *Lewis Carroll: A Celebration.* Ed. Edward Guiliano. New York: Potter, 1982.

Gernsheim, Helmut. *Concise History of Photography.* 3d ed. New York: Dover, 1986.

———. *Lewis Carroll, Photographer.* Rev. ed. New York: Dover, 1969.

Gillis, John. "Birth of the Virtual Child: A Victorian Progeny." Typescript, 1998.

———. *A World of Their Own Making: Myth, Ritual, and the Quest for Family Values.* New York: Basic, 1996.

———. *Youth and History: Tradition and Change in European Age Relations, 1770–Present.* New York: Academic Press, 1974.

Gilmore, David D. *Manhood in the Making: Cultural Concepts of Masculinity.* New Haven: Yale University Press, 1990.

Gordon, Jan B. "Lewis Carroll, the *Sylvie and Bruno* Books, and the Nineties: The Tyranny of Textuality." In *Lewis Carroll: A Celebration.* Ed. Edward Guiliano. New York: Potter, 1982.

Gorham, Deborah. "The 'Maiden Tribute of Modern Babylon' Re-examined: Child Prostitution and the Idea of Childhood in Late Victorian England." *Victorian Studies* 21 (spring 1978): 353–79.

————. *The Victorian Girl and the Feminine Ideal*. Bloomington: Indiana University Press, 1982.

Griffin, Gail. "The Autobiographer's Dilemma: Ruskin's *Praeterita*." In *Interspace and the Inward Sphere: Essays on the Romantic and Victorian Self*. Ed. N. A. Anderson and M. E. Weiss. Macomb, Ill.: Western Illinois University Press, 1978.

Guiliano, Edward. "Lewis Carroll in a Changing World: An Interview with Morton N. Cohen." *English Language Notes* 20 (1982): 97–108.

Heath, Stephen. "Psychopathia Sexualis: Stevenson's *Strange Case*." *Critical Quarterly* 28, nos. 1–2 (spring–summer 1986): 93–108.

Hellerstein, Erna Olafson, Leslie Hume Parker, and Karen M. Offen, eds. *Victorian Women: A Documentary Account of Women's Lives in Nineteenth-Century England, France, and the United States*. Stanford, Calif.: Stanford University Press, 1981.

Helsinger, Elizabeth. "The Structure of Ruskin's *Praeterita*." In *Approaches to Victorian Autobiography*. Ed. G. P. Landow. Athens: Ohio University Press, 1979.

Higonnet, Anne. *Pictures of Innocence: The History and Crisis of Ideal Childhood*. London: Thames and Hudson, 1998.

Hilton, Tim. *John Ruskin: The Early Years*. New Haven: Yale University Press, 1985.

Homans, Margaret. "Eliot, Wordsworth, and the Scenes of the Sisters' Instruction." *Critical Inquiry* 8, no. 2 (winter 1981): 223–41.

————. *Women Writers and Poetic Identity*. Princeton: Princeton University Press, 1980.

Hudson, Derek. *Lewis Carroll: An Illustrated Biography*. London: Constable, 1954.

Hughes, Robert. *The Fatal Shore*. New York: Vintage, 1986.

Hunt, John Dixon. *The Wider Sea: A Life of John Ruskin*. New York: Viking Press, 1982.

Ignatieff, Michael. *A Just Measure of Pain: The Penitentiary in the Industrial Revolution, 1750–1850*. New York: Pantheon, 1978.

Jacobus, Mary. "The Law of/and Gender: Genre Theory and *The Prelude*." *Diacritics* 14 (1984): 47–57.

————. *Romanticism, Writing, and Sexual Difference*. Oxford: Clarendon Press, 1989.

Jeffreys, Sheila, ed. *The Sexuality Debates*. London: Routledge and Kegan Paul, 1987.

Jordan, John E. *De Quincey to Wordsworth: A Biography of a Relationship*. Berkeley and Los Angeles: University of California Press, 1962.

Kincaid, James R. *Child Loving: The Erotic Child and Victorian Culture*. London: Routledge, 1992.

Knoepflmacher, U. C. "The Balancing of Child and Adult: An Approach to Victorian Fantasies for Children." *Nineteenth-Century Literature* 37, no.4 (1983): 497–530.

———. "Mutations of the Wordsworthian Child." In *Nature and the Victorian Imagination.* Ed. U. C. Knoepflmacher and G. B. Tennyson. Berkeley and Los Angeles: University of California Press, 1977.

———. "Revisiting Wordsworth: Lewis Carroll's 'The White Knight's Song.' " *Victorians Institute Journal* 14 (1986): 1–20.

Kucich, John. *Excess and Restraint in the Novels of Charles Dickens.* Athens University of Georgia Press, 1981.

Laplanche, J., and J. B. Pontalis. *The Language of Psycho-Analysis.* Trans. Donald Nicholson Smith. London: Hogarth Press, 1973.

Laqueur, Thomas. *Religion and Respectability: Sunday Schools and Working Class Culture.* New Haven: Yale University Press, 1976.

Leach, Karoline. *In the Shadow of the Dreamchild: A New Understanding of Lewis Carroll.* London: Peter Owen, 1999.

Leighton, Margaret. "De Quincey and Women." In *Beyond Romanticism: New Approaches to Texts and Contexts 1780–1832.* Ed. Stephen Copley and John Whale. New York: Routledge, 1992.

Lennon, Florence Becker. *Lewis Carroll.* London: Cassell, 1947.

Lindop, Grevel. *The Opium Eater: A Life of Thomas de Quincey.* London: J. M. Dent, 1981.

———. "Pursuing the Throne of God: De Quincey and the Evangelical Revival." *Charles Lamb Bulletin* 52 (1985): 97–111.

McFarland, Thomas. *Romantic Cruxes: The English Essayists and the Spirit of the Age.* Oxford: Clarendon Press, 1987.

Magarey, Susan. "The Invention of Juvenile Delinquency in Early Nineteenth-Century England." *Labour History* 34 (1978): 11–25.

Manheim, Leonard. "Floras and Doras: The Women in Dickens' Novels." *Texas Studies in Language and Literature* 7 (1965): 181–200.

Maniquis, Robert M. "Lonely Empires: Personal and Public Visions of Thomas De Quincey." In *Literary Monographs.* Vol. 8. Ed. Eric Rothstein and Joseph Anthony Wittreich Jr. Madison: University of Wisconsin Press, 1976.

Mavor, Carol. *Pleasures Taken: Performances of Sexuality and Loss in Victorian Photographs.* Durham, N.C.: Duke University Press, 1995.

May, Margaret. "Innocence and Experience: The Evolution of the Concept of Juvenile Delinquency in the Mid–Nineteenth Century." *Victorian Studies* 17 (1973): 7–29.

Metz, Christian. "Photography and Fetish." *October* 34 (fall 1985): 81–90.

Miller, Edmund. "The *Sylvie and Bruno* Books as Victorian Novel." In *Modern Critical Views: Lewis Carroll.* Ed. Harold Bloom. New York: Chelsea, 1987.

Miller, J. Hillis. *The Disappearance of God: Five Nineteenth-Century Writers.* Cambridge: Harvard University Press, 1975.

Mitchell, Sally. *The New Girl: Girls' Culture in England, 1880–1915*. New York: Columbia University Press, 1995.

Moorman, Mary. "Wordsworth and His Children." In *Bicentenary Wordsworth Studies in Memorial of J. A. Finch*. Ed. Jonathan Wordsworth. Ithaca, N.Y.: Cornell University Press, 1970.

Morton, Lionel. "Memory in the Alice Books." *Nineteenth-Century Fiction* 33 (1978): 285–308.

Nardinelli, Clark. *Child Labor and the Industrial Revolution*. Bloomington: Indiana University Press, 1990.

Nelson, Claudia. *Boys Will Be Girls: The Feminine Ethic and British Children's Fiction, 1857–1917*. New Brunswick, N.J.: Rutgers University Press, 1991.

Page, Judith W. " 'The Weight of Too Much Liberty': Genre and Gender in Wordsworth's Calais Sonnets." *Criticism* 30 (1988): 189–203.

———. *Wordsworth and the Cultivation of Women*. Berkeley and Los Angeles: University of California Press, 1994.

Pattison, Robert. *The Child Figure in English Literature*. Athens: University of Georgia Press, 1978.

Peterson, Linda. *Victorian Autobiography: The Tradition of Self-Interpretation*. New Haven: Yale University Press, 1986.

Petrie, Glen. *A Singular Iniquity: The Campaigns of Josephine Butler*. New York: Viking, 1971.

Phillips, Jerry. "The Mem Sahib, the Worthy, the Rajah, and His Minions: Some Reflections on the Class Politics of *The Secret Garden*." *The Lion and the Unicorn* 17 (1993): 168–94.

Pinchbeck, Ivy, and Margaret Hewitt. *Children in English Society*. 2 vols. London: Routledge, 1969–73.

Polhemus, Robert M. "Comic and Erotic Faith Meet Faith in the Child: Charles Dickens's *The Old Curiosity Shop* ('The Old Cupiosity Shape')." In *Critical Reconstructions: The Relationship of Fiction and Life*. Ed. Robert M. Polhemus and Roger B. Henkle. Stanford, Calif.: Stanford University Press, 1994.

Poovey, Mary. *Uneven Developments: The Ideological Work of Gender in Mid-Victorian England*. Chicago: University of Chicago Press, 1988.

Postman, Neil. *The Disappearance of Childhood*. New York: Delacorte, 1982.

The Pre-Raphaelites. London: Tate Gallery/Penguin, 1984.

Rackin, Donald. "Love and Death in Carroll's Alice." In *Modern Critical Views: Lewis Carroll*. Ed. Harold Bloom. New York: Chelsea House, 1987.

Radzinowicz, Leon. *History of the English Criminal Law*. New York: Macmillan, 1948–56.

Reed, Langford. *The Life of Lewis Carroll*. London: W. and G. Foyle, 1932.

Roper, Michael, and John Tosh, eds. *Manful Assertions: Masculinities in Britain Since*. London: Routledge, 1991.

Rose, Jacqueline. *The Case of Peter Pan; or, The Impossibility of Children's Fiction*. London: Macmillan, 1984.

239

Ross, Daniel W. "The Uncanny in Wordsworth's 'Immortality Ode.' " *Studies in English Literature, 1500–1900* 32, no. 4 (1992): 625–43.

Ross, Marlon B. "Naturalizing Gender: Woman's Place in Wordsworth's Ideological Landscape." *ELH* 53 (1986): 391–410.

Sawyer, Paul L. "Ruskin and the Matriarchal Logos." In *Victorian Sages and Cultural Discourse: Renegotiating Gender and Power.* Ed. Thaïs E. Morgan. New Brunswick, N.J.: Rutgers University Press, 1990.

———. *Ruskin's Poetic Argument: The Design of the Major Works.* Ithaca, N.Y.: Cornell University Press, 1985.

Sedgwick, Eve. *Between Men: English Literature and Male Homosocial Desire.* New York: Columbia University Press, 1985.

Sherer, Susan. "Secrecy and Autonomy in Lewis Carroll." *Philosophy and Literature* 20 (1996): 1–19.

Showalter, Elaine. *Sexual Anarchy: Gender and Culture at the Fin de Siecle.* Harmondsworth: Penguin, 1990.

Shuman, Cathy. "Different for Girls: Gender and Professional Authority in Mill, Ruskin, and Dickens." Ph.D. diss., Yale University, 1995.

Simpson, David. "Kindling the Torch." In *Irony and Authority in Romantic Poetry.* Totowa, N.J.: Rowman and Littlefield, 1979.

Smelser, Neil J. *Social Change in the Industrial Revolution.* Chicago: University of Chicago Press, 1959.

Smith, Lindsay. Intro. to *Photography and Cultural Representation.* A special edition of *Textual Practice* 10, no. 1. (1996).

———. *The Politics of Focus: Women, Children, and Nineteenth-Century Photography.* Manchester: Manchester University Press, 1998.

———. " 'Take Back Your Mink': Lewis Carroll, Child Masquerade, and the Age of Consent." *Art History* 16, no. 3 (September 1993): 369–85.

Sontag, Susan. *On Photography.* New York: Farrar, Straus and Giroux, 1977.

Spielmann, Marion H. *Millais and His Works.* Edinburgh: Blackwood, 1898.

Spilka, Mark. "Little Nell—Revisited." *Papers of the Michigan Academy of Science, Arts, and Letters* 45 (1960): 427–37.

Steedman, Carolyn. *Childhood, Culture, and Class in Britain: Margaret McMillan, 1860–1931.* New Brunswick, N.J.: Rutgers University Press, 1990.

———. *Strange Dislocations: Childhood and the Idea of Human Interiority, 1780–1930.* Cambridge: Harvard University Press, 1995.

Steig, Michael. "The Central Action of *The Old Curiosity Shop*; or, Little Nell Revisited Again." *Literature and Psychology* 15, no. 3 (summer 1965): 163–70.

Stoler, John A. "Affection and Lust in *The Old Curiosity Shop*: Dickens and Mary—Again." *McNeese Review* 35 (1997): 90–102.

Thompson, E. P. *The Making of the English Working Class.* New York: Vintage, 1963.

Thron, E. Michael. "The Significance of Catharine Wordsworth's Death to Thomas De Quincey and William Wordsworth." *Studies in English Literature, 1500–1900* 28 (1988): 559–67.

Tosh, John. *A Man's Place: Masculinity and the Middle Class Home in Victorian England*. New Haven: Yale University Press, 1999.

Townsend, Francis G. "On Reading John Ruskin." In *The Victorian Experience: The Prose Writers*. Ed. Richard A. Levine. Athens: Ohio University Press, 1982.

Vicinus, Martha. "The Adolescent Boy: Fin-de-Siecle Femme Fatale?" In *Victorian Sexual Dissidence*. Ed. Richard Dellamora. Chicago: University of Chicago Press, 1999.

———, ed. *A Widening Sphere: Changing Roles of Victorian Women*. Bloomington: Indiana University Press, 1977.

———, ed. *Suffer and Be Still: Women in the Victorian Age*. Bloomington: Indiana University Press, 1972.

Viljoen, Helen Gill. *Ruskin's Scottish Heritage*. Urbana: University of Illinois Press, 1956.

Walford, Geoffrey, ed. *The Private Schooling of Girls: Past and Present*. London: Woburn Press, 1993.

Walkowitz, Judith R. *City of Dreadful Delight: Narratives of Sexual Danger in Late-Victorian London*. London: Virago, 1992.

Waters, Karen Volland. *The Perfect Gentleman: Masculine Control in Victorian Men's Fiction, 1870–1901*. New York: Peter Lang, 1997.

Weeks, Jeffrey. *Sex, Politics, and Society: The Regulation of Sexuality since 1800*. London, 1981.

Welsh, Alexander. *The City of Dickens*. Oxford: Clarendon Press, 1971.

Westland, Ella. "Little Nell and the Marchioness: Some Functions of Fairy Tale in *The Old Curiosity Shop*." *Dickens Quarterly* 8 (1991): 68–75.

Wilenski, R. H. *John Ruskin: An Introduction to Further Study of His Life and Work*. London: Faber and Faber, 1933.

Wolfson, Susan J. "Lyrical Ballads and the Language of (Men) Feeling: Wordsworth Writing Women's Voices." In *Men Writing the Feminine: Literature, Theory, and the Question of Genders*. Ed. Thaïs E. Morgan. Albany: State University of New York Press, 1994.

Woodring, Carl. "Wordsworth and the Victorians." In *The Age of William Wordsworth: Critical Essays on the Romantic Tradition*. Ed. Kenneth R. Johnston and Gene W. Ruoff. New Brunswick, N.J.: Rutgers University Press, 1987.

Index

Acts of Parliament: Chimney Sweepers Act of 1788, 58–59; Contagious Diseases Acts of 1864, 1866, and 1869, 158–60; Criminal Law Amendment Act of 1885, 14, 155–56, 160, 179, 192, 229n.49; Factories Regulation Act of 1833, 60, 62; Factory Act of 1819, 59, 192; Offences Against the Person Act of 1861, 158–59, 226n.7; Act to Protect Women under Twenty-One from Fraudulent Practices to Procure Their Defilement, 158; Summary Jurisdiction Act of 1847, 27; Youthful Offenders Act of 1854, 24–25, 28–29

adolescence: adolescent boy, icons of, 230n.53; Victorian definitions of girl-hood and, 172, 227n.21

adulthood, childhood as, in Carroll's work, 144–50

"Affliction of Childhood, The" (De Quincey), 41, 45

age-of-consent legislation, 14, 157–58, 160, 172–75, 178–79; Carroll's reaction to, 183–86

Agnes Grace Weld as Little Red Riding Hood (Carroll), 141–43

Alice in Wonderland (Carroll): adult viewpoint expressed in, 141, 144, 146–48; dramatization of, 184; public reception of, 139

Alice Liddell as a Beggar-Child (Carroll), 141–42, 145

archaeological metaphors, De Quincey's use of, 41

Archer, Frederick Scott, 132

Ariès, Philippe, 5, 9

Armstrong, Eliza, 163–64, 167–68

Arthur, Sir George, 28

arts: idealization of childhood in, 5–6; role of girls and, in *Daughters of England,* 54–55

Ashley (Lord), Anthony (later Earl of Shaftesbury), 73–74, 158, 192

"A Slumber Did My Spirit Seal," 33

Australia, children's penal colonies in, 28

Autobiographic Sketches (De Quincey), 38, 41, 45

Autumn Leaves (Millais), 48, 134–35, 208n.5

baby-talk, Ruskin's inclination for, 124–25, 220n.33

Baden-Powell, Lord, 193

Barrett Browning, Elizabeth, 12–13, 63–69, 73, 165–66, 185, 212n.58

Barrie, J. M., 135, 193

Barthes, Roland, 131, 133–34, 136–37

Beattie, J. M., 26

Bell, Margaret, 111, 114–15

Benjamin, Walter, 133

Blackstone's *Commentaries,* 24–25

Blackwell, Elizabeth, 172

Blake, William, 5

Blind Girl, The (Millais), 48, 207n.3

body imagery: of laboring child, 68–74, 211n.46; in *Old Curiosity Shop,* 86–93; in Ruskin's work, 123–24

Bootle's Baby (Winter), 186, 228n.37

Bowman, Isa, 184, 228n.33

British Labourer's Protector, 60

Broad Church movement, 115

Burd, Van Akin, 107–8

Butler, Josephine, 159, 172

Cameron, Julia Margaret, 132

Carlo, Phoebe, 184

Carlyle, Thomas, 111, 114–15

Carpenter, Mary: on juvenile delinquency, 24, 28–30; Kingswood established by, 27

Carroll, Lewis, 213n.73; age-of-consent legislation, views on, 183–86; alleged pedophilia of, 9, 12, 14; biographical information on, 138–39; boy abuse in work of,